Globalisation and Japanese Organisational Culture

T0311878

Globalisation – the global movement, and control, of products, capital, technologies, persons and images – increasingly takes place through the work of organisations, perhaps the most powerful of which are multinational corporations. Based in an ethnographic analysis of cross-cultural social interactions in everyday workplace practices at a subsidiary of an elite, Japanese consumer electronics multinational in France, this book intimately examines, and theorises, contemporary global dynamics. Japanese corporate 'know-how' is described not simply as the combination of technological innovation riding on financial 'clout' but as a reflection of Japanese social relations, powerfully expressed in Japanese organisational dynamics. The book details how Japanese organisational power does and does not adapt in overseas settings: how Japanese managers and engineers negotiate conflicts between their understanding of appropriate practices with those of local, non-Japanese staff – in this case, French managers and engineers – who hold their own distinctive cultural and organisational inclinations in the workplace. The book argues that the insights provided by the intimate study of persons interacting within and across organisations is crucial to a fulsome understanding of globalisation. This is assisted, further, by a grounded examination of how 'networks'– as social constructions – are both expanded *and* bounded, a move which assists in collapsing the common reliance on micro and macro levels of analysis in considering global phenomena. The book poses important theoretical and methodological challenges for organisational studies as well as for analysis of the forces of globalisation by anthropologists and other social scientists.

Mitchell W. Sedgwick is Senior Lecturer in Anthropology, and Director of the Europe Japan Research Centre at Oxford Brookes University, UK. He was formerly Associate Director of the Program on US–Japan Relations, Harvard University, and Yasuda Fellow at the Faculty of Oriental Studies, and affiliated with King's College, University of Cambridge. During the 1980s, Dr Sedgwick was a consulting organisational anthropologist in South East Asia and West Africa for the World Bank, and later worked in Cambodia on its first postwar election for the United Nations.

Japan Anthropology Workshop Series

A Japanese View of Nature
The World of Living Things by
Kinji Imanishi
Translated by Pamela J. Asquith,
Heita Kawakatsu, Shusuke Yagi and
Hiroyuki Takasaki
Edited and introduced by Pamela J.
Asquith

Japan's Changing Generations
Are Young People Creating a New
Society?
Edited by Gordon Mathews and
Bruce White

The Care of the Elderly in Japan
Yongmei Wu

Community Volunteers in Japan
Everyday Stories of Social Change
Lynne Y. Nakano

Nature, Ritual and Society in
Japan's Ryukyu Islands
Arne Rokkum

Psychotherapy and Religion in Japan
The Japanese Introspection
Practice of Naikan
Chikako Ozawa-de Silva

Dismantling the East-West
Dichotomy
Essays in Honour of Jan van Bremen
Edited by Joy Hendry and Heung
Wah Wong

Pilgrimages and Spiritual Quests in
Japan
Edited by Maria Rodriguez del
Alisal, Peter Ackermann and
Dolores Martinez

The Culture of Copying in Japan
Critical and Historical Perspectives
Edited by Rupert Cox

Primary School in Japan
Self, Individuality and Learning in
Elementary Education
Peter Cave

Globalisation and Japanese
Organisational Culture
An Ethnography of a Japanese
Corporation in France
Mitchell W. Sedgwick

Globalisation and Japanese Organisational Culture

An ethnography of a Japanese corporation in France

Mitchell W. Sedgwick

 Routledge
Taylor & Francis Group

LONDON AND NEW YORK

First published 2007
by Routledge
2 Park Square, Milton Park, Abingdon, Oxon, OX14 4RN

Simultaneously published in the USA and Canada
by Routledge
605 Third Avenue, New York, NY 10017

Routledge is an imprint of the Taylor & Francis Group, an informa business

Typeset in Times New Roman by
Taylor & Francis Books

British Library Cataloguing in Publication Data
A catalogue record for this book is available from the British Library

Library of Congress Cataloging in Publication Data
Sedgwick, Mitchell W., 1955–
    Globalization and Japanese organisational culture: an ethnography
of a Japanese corporation in France/Mitchell W. Sedgwick.
        p. cm. – (Japan anthropology workshop series)
    Includes bibliographical references and index.
    ISBN 978-0-415-44678-5 (hardback: alk. paper) 1. Corporations,
Japanese–France–Sociological aspects. 2. Corporate culture–Japan.
3. Organizational sociology. 4. Business anthropology–Japan. I. Title.

HD2907.S4125 2007
306.3′40952–dc22

                                         2007026822

ISBN13: 978-0-415-44678-5 (hbk)
ISBN13: 978-0-415-49216-4 (pbk)
ISBN13: 978-0-203-93344-2 (ebk)

Contents

Part II
Organising persons in places

Part III
Incorporating cultures: local reductions, global repercussions　　161

Acknowledgements

In spite of my own limitations I have found myself surrounded by considerable intellectual talent down the years. Among many others, I acknowledge in particular the influence of the following scholars, all of them, also, inspiring teachers: Bob Meagher; John Curtis Perry; Arpad von Lazar; Yamakage Susumu; Brian Moeran; Ishibashi Chiyoko, who was my first Japanese language teacher; Bradd Shore; Sally Falk Moore; Alan MacFarlane; Peter Case; and Marilyn Strathern, who implicitly obliged me to remain, and explain, at the edge of what I did not yet know. Meanwhile, just back from my first overextended journey to Japan, as a keen and thoroughly sophomoric 19-year-old I had the very good fortune of finding 'Anthropology of Japan' among my course choices at the University of California, Santa Cruz. Little did I know that I was about to walk into the classroom of one of the finest minds to have ever considered Japan from anthropological perspective. Tom Rohlen helped to organise my original enthusiasms for Japan, and has provided inspiration and a light hand for many years.

As befits the tradition, I am amazed by the generosity of those specifically un-nameable 'informants', with whom one hopes to have at least exchanged amusing company and, more often than not, friendship. Although I, therefore, use pseudonyms for the 'Yama' corporation and the very real people described in this book, in my naming I also honour the Marchalot, and the Nagata and Yama families, who have welcomed me, respectively, in France and Japan since the 1970s. Finally, I thank Caroline Harper, shoreline for both the smooth sailing and rough seas of this ongoing project.

Mitchell W. Sedgwick
London, 2007

Preface

Sedgwick's study leads the Japan Anthropology Workshop series into new realms – in not one, but two – important ways. First, he has taken our study of Japan and things Japanese out of the country itself and into an examination of Japan's highly significant contribution to the world at large. This is still detailed ethnography, the hallmark of our anthropological trade, but it has been carried out with a Japanese company, and with Japanese people, living and working in France. He is thus able to address some of the new issues that arise in the context of cross-cultural interaction; he is in a situation where the Japanese company and their Japanese managers and engineers are still carrying out their business, but with mostly non-Japanese employees, and in totally non-Japanese surroundings. As a long-time anthropologist of Japan, Sedgwick is at home in the Japanese company, but he has also had to make himself at home in France, and this he carries off with skill and aplomb.

Second, this is our first contribution to what has become known as organisational anthropology. We are still dealing with people on the ground, and Sedgwick brings the reader into contact with highly personal and individual situations, but these people are part of a huge organisation, and their behaviour and its cultural features can only be understood by looking at the organisation properly as well. And this is a multinational organisation, not one that can be neatly analysed within a single national framework, so the material needs to be seen in the whole global context. In fact, as the title would suggest, Sedgwick uses the rubric of globalisation as a main focus, but he sees globalisation as a process organised through social relations, and he uses his rich ethnography to challenge more general elements of organisation theory, actor–network theory, and even general anthropology's approach to globalisation.

The potential contributions of this volume are multiple, then, and it will move our series beyond the shelves of anthropology and Japanese Studies into the bigger pond of business and corporations. I hope it will also inspire more anthropologists to work in the hugely important areas that global Japan has to offer. It is high time that more people looked at the sources of this phenomenon called globalisation outside its often assumed centre in North America, and I am delighted that the Japan Anthropology Workshop series is taking a leading role in this direction.

Joy Hendry

Earthrise seen for the first time by human eyes; photographed by William Anders, Apollo 8, December 24, 1968; (c) 1999 from *Full Moon* by Michael Light.

Part I
Siting an organisation

1 Introduction

Opening

This book examines the implications of globalisation upon social relations. Although a widely used contemporary term, 'globalisation' remains largely undelimited and unspecified. As such, anxiety accompanies efforts to conceive its meaning. At a general level it may be agreed that globalisation is an outcome, or an artefact, of rapid change upon boundaries of social, technological, political and economic arena that seemed previously to be less permeable. That said, although an increasing number of scholars have sought to pin down globalisation by specification, in my view they have met with limited success. 'Globalisation' seems unwilling to be packaged. The more interesting analytical problem, rather, is 'globalisation's' ubiquitous yet hazy explanatory usage by actors within myriad contemporary contexts. Thus, while this study explores an unambiguously globalised site in considerable ethnographic detail, as a methodological strategy it purposefully allows 'globalisation' its evasive and open-ended quality. My ethnographic emphasis is not upon what scholars have said about 'globalisation', then, but how persons caught up in it, as we all are, make sense of their contemporary experience.

By any definition, multinational corporations are active vehicles of globalising processes, directly engaged in the movement of persons, images, capital, products and technologies across regional, national, urban, suburban, rural, ethnic, linguistic and other frames. Multinational corporations' activities, their public relations statements and their products affect – some would say they drive – our excited and often contradictory understandings of 'globalisation', and 'the globe'. For example, multinational corporations have placed tools into our hands, i.e. communications technology, that would seem to untether all sorts of spatial, temporal and social relations from the day to day human ground of tangible physical localities. Further afield, a coalition of corporate, governmental and scientific interests has made possible the travel of persons and things 'out of this world'. While not widely known, some corporations – for example, those seeking to make perfectly spherical ball-bearings – go so far as to take industrial production into the gravity-free environment of outer space. In 'bringing it back *home*' they perhaps inadvertently reinforce appreciation of our *globe* as a discrete and interconnected whole. Perhaps more directly meaningful to us, this work in outer space aligns with literal images of *the globe* that have only become available (as fully believable photographs) within the last thirty-five years. Multinational corporations assist, then, in giving 'the globe', as a unifying concept, more precision and tangibility than ever. Meanwhile they assist in the apparent displacement of the relevance of locality. A structuralist might claim that with the one understanding – an estranged spatiality – we have required the other – a unified globe.

In spite of their perhaps inadvertent contributions to such complex perceptual matters, multinational corporations also create specific, indeed tightly bounded, local places of considerable social *gravitas*. Among these are found an increasingly common feature of our social landscape: the cross-cultural organisation. In order to make sense of globalisation, this book examines globalisation's bearing upon social relations in one such location: a French subsidiary of a large, Japanese multinational corporation, which I call 'YamaMax'. Here the French and their Japanese colleagues, along with their accompanying technologies, make videotape-based products with materials – 'inputs' – from three continents. Their 'output' is subsequently sold and used in every corner of the globe. Members of YamaMax are participants in a network, headquartered in Tokyo, of a famous Japanese consumer electronics giant – called here the 'Yama Corporation' – which employs over 150,000 persons, more than half of them outside of Japan.

Members of YamaMax, in France, are thus engaged in processes immediately attributable to globalisation. I take day to day formal and informal practices of the Japanese and French in this setting to constitute an ongoing negotiation in cross-cultural relations. Separated by language, knowledge and power, the Japanese and their French colleagues at YamaMax accommodate and resist each other's understanding of appropriate organisational activity; creating an obviously 'hybrid' organisation.

There are specific and important differences between 'foreign' (or 'hybrid' or 'cross-cultural') corporations and 'domestic' corporations. It is understood – at what is commonly referred to as the 'macro'-level – that multinational corporations' decisions to make investments abroad, and their de facto authority over these investments, challenge state control over domestic economic affairs. Multinational corporations thus (perhaps inadvertently) contribute to destabilising the authority of local and national political actors. Meanwhile – at locations that are commonly described as 'micro' – day to day social relations in a 'foreign' subsidiary make 'work' quite unlike what it has meant, respectively, in well-analysed domestic organisations such as, say, a Toyota automobile factory in Japan, or a French-state bureaucracy.[1] Due to the organisation's Japanese–French constitution, action in and around YamaMax may be partially delinked from the French or Japanese sources of social identity and political discourse with which its members no doubt feel a more 'natural' affinity. That is, both Japanese and French members to some extent experience YamaMax as a 'foreign' locality. If that is the case, what are the effects of this foreign *feel* to working at an industrial firm or, in taking the same question at a slightly different angle, what are its effects on forms and practices of the organisation itself? This study seeks to make sense, then, of how members of 'hybrid' organisations, that are increasingly produced by processes attributed to globalisation, interpret and act on the delinkage of their organisational experience from the cultural frames with which they are more familiar, and, indeed, among my French informants, to which they literally return home daily.

I argue in this book that in-depth study of such complex organised contexts – in this case a 'hybrid' subsidiary of a multinational corporation – may assist in collapsing the analytic relevance of commonly deployed macro–micro distinctions. That is, the central problem encountered in such contexts is the day to day organising of socio-technical relations. If 'scale' is in play at all, it is as a flexibly deployed individual perspective brought to bear in any particular interaction. Within the contemporary context of modernity those socio-technical relations are increasingly exhibited within and across organisations: the core arena reproductive of that very modernity in which we live. The quality of social interaction in hybrid organisations thus alerts us that we may need to adjust the methodological and analytical parameters by which general organisational behaviour is interpreted.

Ethnographically, the book focuses most intimately on the Japanese manager/engineers at YamaMax, who experience the most radical displacement among all members of the Japanese–French subsidiary. Their day to day interactions together, and with their French colleagues, both at work and at leisure, are described. However, I also consider in detail an analysis of social relations and power within the firm that was co-produced through my interactions with a group of highly qualified French engineers. This discussion is revealing, I believe, with regard to how 'data', or information, are organised and communicated among engineers and, so, suggestive in relation to anthropological analysis of technology, and, of course, industrial organisation. Furthermore, given that their data set reached back several years before my fieldwork even began, it also encourages a review, from a fresh perspective, of questions regarding who is 'the ethnographer', who 'an informant' and what constitutes, and validates, data, interpretation and ethnographic time and place. That said, in this book I grant primary analytic weight to interpreting the interactions of Japanese and French engineers in overseeing mass production and, especially, the very stressful periods during which their work is redesigned, i.e. in order to more efficiently produce higher-quality goods, typically through the integration of new technology or know-how into day to day industrial activities. In this context, the cross-cultural and cross-linguistic experiences of members of YamaMax are treated as a platform for critiquing, among other things, traditional organisational studies' and actor–network theory's analytic dependence on the cultural continuities inferred by the prerogatives of single-language use, based implicitly or directly in language theory and its methods. The book also intimately examines how Japanese managers construct and reproduce for themselves the (large, Japanese) corporation as a 'seamless social whole' and how, in turn, they make sense of – through what appear to be forms of erasure – their own experiences of globalisation, i.e. through working at places like YamaMax. I argue, finally, that from an entirely different perspective, but through similarly totalising methods, anthropology's 'new ethnography' at times also entertains such powerful, and myopic, constructions.

If I might describe 'globalisation' as a metaphoric fluid, I take the socio-technical relations constituting YamaMax to be a cloth, tightly woven by the knowledge and experiences of its members, that filters and is, in part, shaped as processes of globalisation pass through it. It is my hope that through analysis of the social relations of a group of Japanese and French people attending seriously to the work of organising and reproducing globalisation's effects in the world, this study may help to untangle the significance of globalisation, and its attendant hybridity, without excessive anxiety.

Analytic perspectives on globalisation in anthropology

Analysis of globalisation is dominated by reference to data gathered at the 'macro' level and the decision-making required to cope with it. In academia, these arenas overlap with, and indeed are generated by, the theoretical, methodological and practical concerns of the closely linked disciplines of political science, government and international relations, as well as economics and business studies. I will return to a discussion of the uses and misuses of macro approaches at a later point. Here I wish simply to note that in pressing 'globalisation in a local context' in my own work I am pushing against the general analytic stream.

In spite of anthropology's supposed explicitly localised methodology, i.e. participant-observation, I am, surprisingly, also pushing against the bulk of anthropology's assessment of 'the global'. Anthropology has acknowledged that 'our' contemporary 'villages' – and their occupants – are substantively influenced by global phenomena. However, for the most part, our theoretical account of how problems of scale are to be engaged, and, more specifically, what a local analysis of the 'global' would consist in – assuming that is the sort of arena where anthropologists can make the most important contribution – remain naive. Not unlike other disciplines, and typical of an early stage of interest, anthropology has so far tended to name, rather than analyse, the effects of globalisation. The most widely circulated of such work is Appadurai's five 'scapes' of 'global cultural flow': 'ideo-scapes', 'ethno-scapes', 'finance-scapes', 'media-scapes' and 'techno-scapes' (1990). While I acknowledge that such grand categories may be helpful at the start for thinking through the boundaries of an analytic field, similar to macro-data gathering and analysis, the work of these categories is detached and externalised; they seem flat. In spite of the suggestiveness of the phrase 'global cultural flow' we gain no sense of how 'scapes' intersect with each other, as they obviously do, how persons move within and between them, nor a sense of what difference it might make to engage such categories at macro- or micro-levels of analysis. As Tsing puts it: 'flow is valorized but not the carving of the channel' (2000: 330).

Sharing the top-down approach characteristic of anthropology's rather insightful analyses of the effects of colonialism (Asad 1973) or development (Ferguson 1990; Escobar 1995; Mosse 2005), anthropology typically considers the impact of globalisation *upon* communities. There tends to be little, at the very least, theoretical consideration of the reciprocal effects of local and global actors, or activities, the one upon the other. This would assume, of course, that local–global categorisations are analytical relevant to unpacking the effects of globalisation. Indeed, albeit an atypical site of ethnographic fieldwork, analysis of activities *within* a global corporation would suggest problematising such analytic divisions altogether. My own perspective suggests, rather, that in our mundane day to day, local activities, we are all global actors.

Another anthropological strategy for coping with the 'global' is to describe extremely displaced communities or persons. Implicit in this approach is the claim that stories about people in unusual circumstances, generated by 'global' effects, provide more leverage on analysis of globalisation than do examinations of how average people live. It might be argued that I do just this: the obviously strong global effects on the people at my study site assist in focusing my analysis. However, care needs to be taken in acknowledging and expressing degrees of difference between subjects' (or our own) experience and that of others. (This would especially be the case when discussing 'global' phenomena, a word which, in commonsense terms, conjures universality.) Where this is not done, analysis may easily be read towards absolute difference and, so, uncommensurability, unapproach-ability, inaccessibility and so irrelevance to our own, more typical, experiences. Thus, Hannerz's work on the radically decentred lives of those working as foreign correspondents seems in its analysis, not choice of subject matter, to excessively stretch the qualities of communications under conditions of globalisation (1996: 112–24). If the case were extended to roving correspondents and photographers, some of whom seek out battle-field or other violent situations, their flirtations with 'danger' so literally pepper their lives that it may serve to undermine analytically the 'contingency' of all lived experience, and so weaken the potential theoretical expansions arising from our considerations of globalisation.

Meanwhile, Appadurai's work on persons in a globalised world is also, unfortunately, displaced and anecdotal, and under-localised. For instance, unless couched in a theory of change in forms of political mobilisation, the finding is unremarkable that, due to the 'net', activists on the political front lines in Third World nations now stay in near real-time contact with supporters in cosmopolitan centres (Appadurai 1996: 195–8). Nor is it significant to claim that 'globalisation' should create the circumstances whereby a visit to an Indian temple shared by an academic, his academic wife and their son should generate three quite different perspectives on the meaning of the temple to each of them (Appadurai 1996: 56–8). In the latter study, there is no particular perspectival gain thrown up by the distance travelled, literally, from 'home' by the key subjects: the case regarding varied perspectives could indeed be argued more persuasively on the basis of generational or gender distinctions between the persons involved. This self-conscious analysis also serves to isolate, as irrelevant, the perspectives on globalisation of the persons who actually live in that 'visited' 'local' context. What would these interlopers' visitation(s) mean to them?

It might be argued, then, that most anthropological analyses have, to date, largely missed out the reciprocal effects of 'our' 'villages' upon globalisation.[2] Rather than a listing of what 'globalisation' is or is not, analysis of exchanges between 'the local' and 'the global' needs to engage the meaning and uses of material objects, experiences and memories, ideas about distance and non-presence and, most importantly and directly, therefore, notions of relations between persons. Why, in spite of anthropology's explicit prioritisation of 'the local', or, in any case, the deployment and use of knowledge in a local context, have our analyses of 'globalisation' shared with other social science disciplines the tendency to focus, or feel, 'out there'? Is it somehow that the externalised and highly abstract resonances of 'the global' as 'macro' activity are rooted in the day to day activities and lay perceptions of persons? If so, why is this so?

Our displaced perceptions, and analyses, are the result of two interrelated phenomena. First, in daily discourse we grant macro-level discussions our attention because we think globalisation concerns something that unfolds beyond us and over which we have little control. We are aware that it occurs across wide physical or comparatively all-inclusive expanses, but is also accomplished through unexpectedly intimate, technologically enhanced time compressions, generating unorthodox communicative dependencies over which we seem to have little volition. Thus, because methodology in most social science disciplines is impersonal, as globalisation would seem to be, their perspectives, which are ordinarily macro, are suggestively global and all-encompassing. And, indeed, they encourage reflections on globalisation, even by anthropologists, that are detached, or seem disembodied, from the presences of quotidian experience, including day to day usage of notions linking social relations and distance. This is an excellent example of the proliferation into our academic discourse of 'ideologies of scale' with regard to globalisation: a slippage which we anthropologists would do better to use for reflection upon the practices of others with regard to globalisation than to mirror upon ourselves (cf. Tsing 2000: 347). Second, it is easier to make broad and apparently all-pervasive claims about 'global' phenomena when analytic tools are not in place to refine information gathering, and thereby further specify analysis, i.e. in political science. Meanwhile, what analytic approaches might anthropology use to understand better the association of social relations and 'the global'?

Hannerz claims that his 'macroanthropological [*sic*]' project addresses the by-now typical social arenas – that are increasingly the sites of field research – 'where diversity ... gets organized' (Hannerz 1989: 211).[3] As above, where focused on the floating world of foreign correspondents, his subject matter is superficial and, to my reading, analytically unhelpful. He is, however, far more successful in making sense of global effects upon the 'cultural mosaics' of the (African) urban spaces that he knows well (Hannerz 1989; see also 1969, 1979, 1980, 1985). While it is not the only strategy, these inquiries gain purchase through granting analytic density to 'place' for their subjects (for instance, see Hannerz 1996: 127–71). In any case, through the provocative phrase, 'organizing diversity', Hannerz possibly intuits another of anthropology's most promising methodological routes into analysis of, rather than description of, the global: an empirical focus on *organisations*. In citing 'the global' as personally experienced phenomena I am marking it as *produced* by local activities that may be persuasively examined *through* actors' own engagements with varied organisational contexts, broadly construed. Organisations are core contexts for organising our understandings of the global, then, and this study is an attempt to operationalise this perspective.

The history and disciplining of Japanese organisational studies

In asking the questions: what is particular about organising a 'Japanese' corporation in France? and how might this case elucidate globalisation?, let me first forward the character of interest in Japanese organisations by anthropologists and ethnographically-oriented sociologists, and the analytic underpinnings of their treatment of Japanese corporations in Japan. The many thorough studies of corporations by anthropologists and sociologists suggest that Japanese corporate 'know-how' is more than technological innovation riding on financial clout.[4] Developed in Japan's specific social and political economic context, the organisational practices of Japanese corporations have been understood as powerful reflectors of Japanese socio-cultural forms. As in other Japanese organisations, Japanese manufacturing firms in Japan, such as the Yama Corporation, weave generalised Japanese cultural practices and technical expertise into an organisational fabric that is conducive to information flows which assist the processes of design, production and marketing upon which these firms depend. Analysis of this theoretical point in a foreign context is the major ethnographic theme of the present work. That is, in overseas subsidiaries of 'Japanese' firms how are the communicative forms upon which such organisations evidently depend combined with those of local, non-Japanese staff, who hold their own distinctive organisational (cum cultural) inclinations, who speak no Japanese, and have diverse educational and technical backgrounds and varied work experiences before joining the Japanese firm?

Obviously, we must begin by asking on what basis we can make such elaborate claims about Japanese organisations in Japan. Dore's (1973) and Rohlen's (1974) work, in particular, generated sophisticated, non-economic-rewards driven, and perhaps 'culture'-based explanations of Japanese workgroup behaviour and the dynamics of, what came to be called, 'knowledge-creation' in Japanese corporations. These were analytic and methodological breakthroughs, and continue to be cited often. Dore's is known for its comparative rigour complemented by a thorough sense of the embeddedness of the Japanese and British factories he studied in their respective sociological and institutional contexts. Rohlen's, meanwhile, is the first long-term participant–observation ethnography of a white-collar orga-nisation: a Japanese bank. It has set a standard methodologically and in terms of clarity of writing.

Younger generations of anthropologists of Japan, studying such topics as education, sport, media, entertainment and religion, have nearly all been working on subject matter that 'takes place' within organisations, albeit some places more formally organised than others, i.e. the voluntary sector.[5] Unlike Dore and Rohlen, however, most have avoided making an explicit focus on organisational dynamics a central concern of their work. Perhaps they have seen in 'organisations' a dull subject matter residual to the accomplishments of education, sport, and so on; or the ghosts of an earlier generation of scholars who studied plodding white- and blue-collar workers driving the (somewhat problematised) 'Japanese economic miracle'; or a subject of unworthy theoretical merit, i.e. a reflection in Japan anthropology of the lack of attention, until quite recently, to organisations, or other 'modern' subject matter prevalent in 'advanced industrial societies' by gen-eral anthropology. Other Japan anthropologists, meanwhile, have become enamoured of Japan's prolific yield of 'media' output, i.e. popular culture.[6] While interesting and important, Japanese media images are, especially in the context of mass consumption, surface expressions of the productions of a complex industrial society that are driven by the inter-relations of members of Japanese organisations. This study is therefore in part an attempt to reclaim Japanese organisations as core sites for the anthropology of Japan. The fact that the organisation studied here is a multinational corporation and highly successful consumer electronics firm – which also produces an enormous number of media images – places it both at the cutting edge of a changing Japanese society and, I argue, as a subject of study, at the cutting edge of theoretical discourse on the general character of the contemporary modernity and, of course, discussion regarding 'globalisation'.

Despite my arguing that much anthropological analysis of Japanese organisations *per se* has been indirect, it is often of extremely high quality, and not simply as means for explaining other subjects. I note here in particular Ben-Ari's (1997) work on child care in Japan, and the strong sense of the networks organising the production of adult *manga* (comics) by Kinsella (2000). Even if arguably superseded by attention to more 'trendy' subject matter, based, as above, in either an appreciation of or as a response to early, classic studies of large, elite Japanese organisations, more recent work focusing explicitly on private corporations in Japan has broadened the range of business 'sectors' attracting scrutiny, including small and medium-size enterprises (SMEs). Most importantly its subtlety and complexity has expanded the exposure of day to day relations between employees and companies, or, effectively, understanding employees *as* companies, through direct examinations of the ethos and experience of work in Japan. Moeran's (1996) wide-ranging research on an advertising agency stands out here. He is especially successful in elaborating the centrality of interpersonal dynamics in 'the firm's' relations with their client firms, while the work provides an understanding of advertising as a medium between major producer firms and the world of media presentation that may or may not deliver sales, and so the success of their products. Meanwhile as do both Roberts' (1994) and Turner's (1995) in their focus on women, Roberson's (1998) study of men working at a medium-size factory is compelling with regard to the practically literal grind of day to day assembly line work, as well as in exposing the sensibilities of interpersonal relations within and across hierarchies in and outside of the workplace. Matsunaga (2000) and Wong (1999) focus on department stores; the former incisive with regard to the complex interactions of hierarchy and, often, exploitation of gender in organisational life in Japan, and the latter exposing the intense competition and politically cliquey nature of the relationship between Japanese managers overlaid with a local/foreign dynamic at a Japanese department store in Hong Kong. Sedgwick (1996, 1999, 2000a, 2000b, 2001) focuses on cross-cultural organisational dynamics in subsidiaries of large Japanese manufacturing firms abroad, including the present volume. Miyazaki (in press) explores knowledge and behaviour among traders in Tokyo's financial markets. Meanwhile, Kondo's (1990) work on a small, artisanal sweets maker unpacks the family-like relations of Japan's many intimate work settings where there are very few employees, and has been noted widely both for its exposure of the conundrums of identity in fieldwork and its theoretical strength with regard to the development of a feminist anthropology.

This list by no means exhausts a very large literature. It is presented simply to offer a feel for the breadth of work conducted, directly and indirectly, on Japanese organisations over the last thirty-five years. Meanwhile, it should be noted that, although it has not yet been tapped in this way, this body of work is sufficiently robust to support cross-sectoral analysis and longitudinal work. That is, in the context of a Japanese society evolving over time some of these scholars are in a position to track the career courses of individuals, and changes within particular firms, across decades. Further, this by-now substantial and unmatched body of work based on Japanese organisational forms and processes may cue more substantive theoretical analysis in the slowly expanding study of modern organisational settings in general anthropology. This Japan work is a valuable comparative resource that may act as a counterweight also to the overwhelming bulk of general organisational analysis, little of it in anthropology itself, based in studies of Western organisations that has, incidentally and usually inadvertently, often made use of the idea of 'organisational culture' as it was originally developed in generating understanding of Japanese organisational dynamics (Sedgwick, 2007). Indeed, what has occurred in the general study of organisations is exemplary of the analytic opportunities available to treatment of the 'case of Japan', and is a continuous source of interest for those engaged in its study. As the only non-Western society at a comparable level of economic development to the West, Japanese society provides an important comparative corrective to, and often a thorn in the side of understandings of complex industrial modernity that have traditionally, and presumptuously, been based upon observations of Western societies alone. This matter of audience regarding knowledge of Japan is something I will take up more substantively later in this chapter in an examination of management studies' interest in Japan as an economic threat to the West.

The analytic strength of anthropological work on Japanese organisations has made it abundantly clear that activity within formal organisations and relations across organisations are a pervasive feature of the experience of modernity in Japan, as elsewhere. Among Japanologists working in disciplines that had not previously considered such matters, the co-production of Japanese 'culture', social relations and the particularities of Japan's institutional contexts thus became available and convincing explanations for how Japan's forms of organising modernity worked, and how they might even exceed the successes of Western modernisation. Such so-called 'soft' explanations may have also been actively entertained by non-anthropologist specialists of Japan because they have tended to be marginal players in their academic disciplines. A possible explanation of why this may be the case follows. Training in Japanese, which by any measure is difficult, highly time-consuming and nearly always includes study in Japan itself, may have meant less rehearsal by graduate students of core disciplinary theories. As a result, relatively speaking, Japanologists have perhaps tended away from preoccupations with theory in their careers.[7] In addition, it might be argued by disciplinary 'gatekeepers' that Japan, an Asian case, and an enigmatic one at that,[8] could not be related to core theoretical problems of advanced (Western) countries, while Japan was far too advanced for comparison with most 'developing' country situations. Japan was, thus, made opaque and inaccessible to those who had not made the substantial personal investment involved in gaining specialist knowledge of it. It is probably the case, as well, that the community of Western-trained Japan scholars – through the late-1980s, close-knit and small in number – has tended to protect their turf from the passing interests of non-specialist interlocutors. In any case, on an intellectual plane the result was more positive. In order to reach a self-sustaining, intellectual 'critical mass', cross-disciplinary interactions inspired inclusive interdisciplinary approaches to analysis of Japan,[9] with many scholars perhaps considering themselves 'Japanologists' before representatives of particular disciplines.

Meanwhile, I would argue that until the 1990s general anthropology was by and large content to keep the ethnographic roots of its theorising based in apparently 'traditional', 'simple' societies rather than 'complex', 'modern' societies; or perhaps it was driven in this direction inadvertently as most of anthropology's major theorists had conducted fieldwork in relatively 'less-developed' contexts.[10] In terms of general reception, then, anthropology of Japan has suffered from its de facto status as analysis of a modern society. In spite of a large number of high-quality ethnographic studies, anthropologists of Japan have unfortunately not, until quite recently, pressed the tension between the study of 'traditional' (or 'simple') versus 'modern' (or 'complex') societies onto the theoretical agenda of general anthropology. Rather, they have been largely content to review the traditional/modern problem, or the use of 'tradition' in modern contexts, within the confines of the 'particularity' of Japan, which has no doubt also deflected attention to Japan from the potentially interested non-Japanese-speaking academic audience required for general theory.[11] More recently, however, categorical divisions such as traditional–modern, simple–complex, nomadic–agricultural–industrial, and so on, have come to feel problematic theoretically, perhaps due in part to the embedding among anthropologists of common lay assumptions regarding global economic–technological, and interpersonal, connectedness. That said, anthropologists unavoidably must still grapple with these category divisions because they are pervasive in the anthropology's intellectual history, they linger – and with some justification at that – in other, more practically oriented fields of study, and because integrated theoretical explanations have not transcended observation: grinding poverty, for instance, is pervasive in many less developed countries .

Coinciding with the revaluation of the Japanese yen, from the mid-1980s Japanese studies in the West, and, in turn, in other regions, benefited from substantial support from the Japanese government and private sector.[12] As was its intent, the healthy expansion in the number of scholars studying Japan-related topics led to a diffusion of the Japanese studies community as old programmes expanded, new ones were established and field research opportunities in Japan grew enormously.[13] However, while the number of persons studying Japanese and the diversity and quantity of scholarship on Japan has expanded, it seems to me that the study of Japan has become redisciplined. That is, studies of Japan have been increasingly captured theoretically by mainstream disciplinary trends.

In the case of the anthropology of Japan, this has generally proved an excellent advance, even if in some quarters, as related to my initial comments above regarding preoccupation with pop culture and material artefacts, there has been some excess. Perhaps led by the study of Japanese intellectual history in Japan anthropology, criticism of the roots and deployment of the idea of Japan's 'particularity' – especially as it has been deployed by Japanese scholars in the so-called *nihonjinron* movement – has been of a high calibre and especially impressive for the historicisation of analysis, a traditional point of weakness in anthropology.[14] This critique of Japanese scholarship has perhaps been implicitly self-referential to Western-trained anthropologists of Japan as well, for through it analyses of how 'tradition' operates within, or beside, contemporary, modern Japan has finally begun to be theorised beyond the context of Japan's 'particularity' in a way that fits amply into general anthropological discussion.[15]

Our central concern is with analysis of Japanese *organisations*, however, and, more generally, with how Japanese society organises its modernity, including Japan's organisational relations to globalising processes. Here, positions have unfortunately hardened in what appears as an unbridgeable gap between scholars favouring 'soft' (culturally related) explanations and the 'hard' (rationalist) explanations often forwarded by economists and political scientists. Unfortunately, the political economy of this debate – that is, as above, the policing of disciplinary boundaries – is a more significant explanation for this division than is the quality of its intellectual content. Does Japanese 'culture' influence the behaviour of the Japanese as 'rational actors' in neo-classical economic theory? Is culture primary or secondary to the deployment of power and political interest in Japan? Does Japanese culture or merely the prerogatives of mercantilism influence decision-making regarding Japan's foreign relations? Is culture necessary to explain activity in modern Japanese organisations? These questions require examination only insofar as to explain why the suggested contradictions, and so the analytic relevance of divisions between 'rationality' and 'culture', are ill-conceived. I am comfortable, as I expect would be Dore and Rohlen, who did much of the original work on modern Japanese organisations, with the power of notions such as the 'culture of rationality' to describe many general attributes of modern societies, including how Japan is organised. Meanwhile, in general anthropology Sahlins has described the 'rationality, utility [and] [t]he reasonableness of our [modern] institutions ... [as] the principled way we explain ourselves to ourselves. Rationality is our rationalization' (1976: 72). Nonetheless, in its most facile articulations, 'culture' has, with distressing and increasing tenacity, been deployed by some who study Japan as 'tradition', and other kindred (apparently) conservative and normalising notions.[16] As such 'culture' may be dismissed with ease as evidence mounts of societal change simply due to the passage of time: even if 'tradition' cum 'culture' had been important, it is receding further and further into the past.[17] Thus, it is in the context of academic debate over core concepts that some analysts of Japan have denied culture's relevance.[18] Meanwhile, anyone with knowledge of Japanese would recognise that the Japanese words translated into English as 'tradition', 'rational interest' and 'culture' are used in distinctive ways within Japanese social contexts by Japanese persons. That these terms may thereby be mobilised with different intent than that of trained academics in a competition of ideas perhaps demonstrates the relevance of context in conferring, or demeaning, meaning.

In any case, although I do not have the space to expand on this matter here, this 'local' debate regarding basic principles among academics who focus on Japanese organisations and institutional contexts now lags well behind more progressive discussions in general theoretical analysis of organisations (Smircich 1983a, 1983b; Pettigrew 1979). It is nonetheless a suggestive undercurrent in my examination below of the case of Japan organisations as considered in Western-based 'business studies'.

Japanese corporations, 'knowledge-creation' and the problem of cross-cultural relations

Management, or business, studies is a vast subject area, much like 'area studies', where analytic boundaries are often vaguely defined, for example, East Asian, South Asian, South East Asian studies, and so on. Similarly, it enjoys the possibilities and practice of borrowing from and recombining a tremendous range of approaches. In turn, and again often like 'area studies', the lack of accountability to the rigours of traditional academic disciplines is both its advantage, in that it makes available a breadth of analytic opportunities, and a disadvantage in that findings risk seeming comparatively thin, theoretically speaking, and lacking in generalisability to other 'areas'. In any case, business studies has a well-resourced practitioner audience that allows it to go its own way in the enterprise of academia (and consulting). Most scholars of Japanese business have tended, therefore, to be eclectic, open-minded and as creative as other Japan scholars. The best work, by Japanologists with long-term experience in Japan, or Japanese scholars themselves, appreciates Japanese business as a co-production of economic, political, technological and cultural activities, a perspective that would naturally align with approaches in anthropology today. Within the larger, general study of business, however, 'Japan' has been predictably dominated by perspectives derived from Western academia and analysis of Western business. Indeed this general literature is, if anything, even more self-servingly Western in orientation than consideration of the case of Japan in traditional social science disciplines.

I described above the 'case of Japan' as a thorn in the side of analytical treatment of modernised societies', read Western societies', social/ institutional forms. Work in 'business studies' is no exception here. In this literature Westney (1999) has succinctly delineated the organisational structures, processes and the comparative evolution of Japanese firms, and, by extension, their forms of multinationalisation. Indicative of delay in academic analysis (and publication) relative to perceived successes of business, through the 1970s Japanese firms were understood to lag behind Western firms (when they were noticed at all), while in the 1980s they were said to lead Western firms in terms of firm-level 'knowledge-generating processes'. In the last ten to fifteen years they have again been perceived as immature compared with the current, idealised 'transnational enterprise' model, based around pan-organisational, i.e. global-scale, information sharing and – thanks to the Japanese – intra-organisational 'knowledge-generation'.[19]

If I may elaborate this progression of analysis further, the study of multinational corporations[20] is a logical extension of preceding studies of (usually) large enterprises in any particular national context. Studies of Western, especially US, corporations have traditionally tended to be large-scale, comparative, statistics-driven exercises, based in the resources of economic analysis, accounting for the historic structural evolution of particular business sectors based on the rational economic/market choices of firms in each sector. By contrast, some of the most important work in even the early literature on Japanese firms was based on detailed analysis of internal organisational dynamics. Yoshino's (1968) study of Japanese managerial systems and Tsurumi's (1968) analysis of the style of technology transfer and foreign trade of Japanese firms stand out here (Westney 1999: 16.) This methodological emphasis corresponded empirically with the 'high knowledge–low resources' conditions of Japan's domestic environment, i.e. an extraordinary public sector commitment to pan-societal education and training, and the necessary importing of nearly all natural resources required of industrialisation. The trend was encouraged further by the extremely rich 'culture-based' analyses, noted previously – and focused on particular domestic Japanese corporations – by both Rohlen (1974) and Dore (1973), respectively an anthropologist and sociologist, conducted well before the West was worried about the success of Japanese business. All of this work was presented at book length, based in long-term ethnography or extremely sophisticated, multiple field research techniques, for example, by Dore. Each of these authors has been instrumental, then, in drawing the evolving discourse on Japanese corporations toward a focus on organisational style, processes and innovations *within* firms rather than on the preoccupations with external economic opportunities that had driven studies of Western/US firms.

When, from the late 1970s, Japan was acknowledged as an economic threat, Western business leaders needed an explanation of Japanese industrial success that could be accessibly packaged so that they could improve workgroup dynamics and knowledge-creation in their own companies, and so continue to compete. That package was delivered by business scholars and consultants in the 1980s through the ethos of 'organisational culture': something the Japanese apparently had, and something which Western firms needed. However, and typical of the watering-down of analysis as it is translated across fields, whereas the substantial studies of Japanese organisations by Japanologists had recognised Japanese culture at work in their dynamics, and had recognised organisations as reflections of the work of culture more broadly in the institutions of Japanese society, in the 1980s 'organisational culture' was conceptually wrapped up within the boundaries of particular organisations and, therefore, was something that could and should be developed under the control of and in order to fit the goals of management. A quasi-academic, popular and mainly consultant-based literature thus evolved along the following trajectory: what is the ethos of Japanese organisational culture that generates intensive employee commitment, and what can we do to develop something like it? What are Japanese work methods, and how can they be imported into non-Japanese contexts? Which of our (Western) companies (also) have strong organisational cultures, with committed and knowledge-creating employees, and what can we do to be more like them, i.e. how do we build strong cultures out of who we already are? (Ouchi 1981; Pascale and Athos 1982; Peters and Waterman 1982; Deal and Kennedy 1988). However intellectually watered-down in practice, it seems clear that empirical studies of Japanese corporations in large part provided the impetus for proliferation of the term 'organisational culture' in general organisational studies (Ouchi and Wilkins 1985).

Therefore, when highly successful, domestic Japanese corporations seriously threatened Western firms – most notably through exports from the 1970s to Western countries in the automotive and consumer electronics sectors – in the 1980s internal 'innovation' as a source of international competitiveness became an 'essential' concern of large corporations throughout the world; and one around which the Japanese were recognised masters. 'Knowledge creation' at Japanese firms – especially 'quality control circles' and related innovations on assembly lines – burst into the popular Western press, followed by the appearance of a veritable industry of quasi-academic Western experts in Japanese methods. This also created the opportunity for established scholars to entitle books along the lines of Dore's, *Taking Japan Seriously* (1987) and, if somewhat less significant academically, Vogel's remarkably popular *Japan as Number One* (1979). Person-centred reflections on the strengths of Japanese firms, often based on cultural explanations of working style, were sufficiently pervasive that it has allowed the Japanese *salaryman* to join *samurai* and *geisha* as enduring personages representing Japan in the general consciousness of Westerners.

Meanwhile, at the practical level of the international political economy the key response to the extensive success of Japanese consumer goods exports was an international agreement – the Plaza Accord (1985) – which doubled the value of the Japanese yen against the US dollar (and by extension nearly all foreign currencies). In so doubling the cost of Japanese exports (and labour), and halving the cost of foreign purchases (and labour), Japanese firms were well positioned to globalise in terms of the prerogatives of economics. That is, these firms were, in effect, obliged to become multinational corporations not only, as previously, in trade but in production as well. Of direct interest to us, they were obliged to move increasingly significant proportions of industrial production and, therefore, their *organisations* – the source of their domestic knowledge-creation successes – abroad. They created organisations such as YamaMax.

Japanese investment abroad spiked upwards from the mid-1980s, however the bulk of Japan's newly found, 'paper' wealth fuelled dramatic inflation of property valuations in Japan itself. In turn, an inevitable bursting of the Japanese economic 'bubble' occurred in the early 1990s.[21] These structural economic conditions, meanwhile, contributed to the bursting of the bubble of over-exalted general academic interest in Japanese corporations' organisational forms and processes. The convoluted logic at hand was, perhaps, the following: if the Japanese economy was in poor condition, its firms were surely no longer worthy subjects. (I presume that with the upturn in the Japanese economy from the middle of the first decade of the new millennium, we can expect another surge of positive reflection on Japanese forms of organising their firms, especially should Western firms seem to be losing ground.) In any case in the 1990s large, Japanese firms (by now, thoroughly 'multinational' in terms of locations of production) fell off the conceptual forefront of idealised (Western) modellings of multinational corporations. As previously mentioned, that ideal was, by-now, 'transnational enterprises'. Here, unlike knowledge generated from within an inward-oriented Japanese organisation which is highly centralised 'at home' in Japan itself, the 'transnational enterprise' model calls for knowledge-generation from a *global* network of cross-national, cooperating sub-organisations in an 'Integration–Responsiveness' (I–R) framework (Bartlett and Goshal 1989; Bartlett 1986). The prescriptive notion was that 'transnational enterprises' should 'respond' to local markets and information while they seek cross-border 'integration' of their extensive, global organisational capacities.[22, 23]

Whether or not one accepts the possibility of 'transnational' firms as anything more than a utopian model sold to managers as a 'mindset'[24] – and the internal contradictions of the model are striking – it nonetheless seems to be true that the generation of intensive organisational learning in Japanese firms is limited to Japanese persons themselves, operating within a bounded, 'Japanese' system. In the foreign environments with which they are increasingly in direct contact through their globalising processes this would seem, for instance, to restrict the capacity of Japanese firms to gain knowledge 'locally' and to include substantively that knowledge within their general knowledge-generating practices. A dense ethnographic elaboration of this point, set in a local French context, and thus 'foreign' to the Japanese, is, of course, the central ethnographic interest and contribution of this study. And this potential weakness of Japanese firms, if by-now articulated far more fully and with increasing evidence to hand, was recognised early on by both Tsurumi (1968) and Yoshino (1968, 1976).

Westney succinctly sums up the distinctive thrust of analyses of Japanese firms respectively in their domestic and overseas settings, suggesting that the differences are 'paradoxes' (1999: 20–1). I quote her at length:

> [A] voracious reader able to keep pace with the rapidly expanding academic literature on Japanese management in Japan and the smaller but still substantial literature on the strategy and organisation of Japanese MNCs [multinational corporations] would, if he or she tried to integrate the two literatures, have discovered some rather puzzling paradoxes:
>
> > 1. The Japanese management system has been a key source of Japan's competitive advantage, especially its decision-making processes, which acted to encourage extensive information sharing and knowledge creation, and its HRM [human resource management] system (see, for example Aoki, 1988; Nonaka 1988).
> >
> > The Japanese management system has been a key weakness of Japan's MNCs, especially its decision-making processes, which weakened information sharing across borders, and its HRM system (Bartlett and Yoshihara 1988; Lifson 1992).
> >
> > 2. Japanese firms have exhibited a remarkable capacity for learning from other countries (Cole 1989; Rosenberg and Steinmueller 1988).
> >
> > Japanese MNCs have exhibited a notable incapacity for learning from their subsidiaries in other countries (DeNero 1990; Okumura 1989)
> >
> > 3. Japanese firms have been models of effective linkage between strategy and organisation, in terms of developing dynamic core capabilities (Prahalad and Hamel 1990).
> >
> > Japanese MNCs are struggling to build organisational capabilities to match their international strategies (Bartlett and Goshal 1989).

Rather than 'paradoxes', as Westney would have it, the matter at hand is a straightforward recognition of differences, and problems, in the ways Japanese firms manage in foreign settings in contrast to within Japan itself. Since persons 'manage' corporations the problem is differences in the ways Japanese persons interact with and consider 'other' persons, even pro forma 'members' of their own firms, in contrast to how they interact among Japanese members, i.e. themselves. At various levels of sophistication, this problem has puzzled analysts of Japanese firms abroad for some years, i.e. in the work of Hamada (1992), Brannen (1993), Kleinberg (1994), Botti (1995), Sumihara (1996),

Sedgwick (1996, 1999, 2000a, 2000b), Fruin (1999), Wong (1999) and Sakai (2000), as well as in the naturally-related literature on non-Japanese persons working in Japanese firms in Japan itself (Hamada 1991; Grimshaw 1997; Clemons 1999; Reed 2005). The crux of the matter in the study of Japanese multinational corporations, which are organisations at the very core of Japan's inevitable engagement with globalisation, whether dressed up as evolutionary stages of multinationalism, responses to structural macro-economic conditions, market opportunities, and so on, comes down specifi-cally to the Japanese in cross-national, and so, cross-*cultural,* relations. In the following section I begin to unpack this problem in theoretical terms through the notion of organisational hybridity.

Bringing across cultures: an innocent constructing of hybridity, and an informed rejection of the analytic efficacy 'race' and 'ethnicity'

Since organisations in any particular society are artefacts of the practices of that society, an important problem arises within what I am calling 'cross-cultural' organisations. In the context of this study that is the following: as I have described earlier, in overseas subsidiaries of 'Japanese' firms how are the communicative forms upon which such organisations evidently depend combined with those of local, non-Japanese staff, who hold their own dis-tinctive organisational (cum cultural) inclinations, who speak no Japanese, and have diverse educational and technical backgrounds and varied work experiences before joining the Japanese firm?

The French and Japanese employees of the organisation I focus on are engaged in production of videotape twenty-four hours a day, 360 days a year, with the remaining five days in the year a general 'shut-down' for machinery maintenance. I take their day to day, formal and informal practices in this workplace to constitute an ongoing 'negotiation' of cross-cultural rela-tions.[25] As briefly suggested in the introduction to this chapter, separated by language, knowledge (including techniques specific to the product) and power (to mobilise resources within and beyond the subsidiary), the French and their Japanese colleagues variously *accommodate* and resist (cf. Scott 1985) each other's understanding of appropriate organisational activity.[26] They generate a corporation that may be understood, following Bahktin, as an 'intentional hybrid' (1981). Specifically, Bahktin contrasts 'organic' and 'intentional' hybridity. The former 'evolve[s] historically through unre-flective borrowings' (Werbner 1997: 4) that are 'mute and opaque ... unconscious', the latter 'a collision between different points of view on the world' (Bakhtin 1981: 360). Indeed Bahktin links the two in a far more refined manner than suggested by this bifurcation of the unconscious ('organic') and the intentional; arguing that 'organic' hybridity prepares the ground for more radical disruptions accompanying 'intentional' mixes of languages and images. In any case, it is clear that the literally constructed and cross-linguistic, cross-cultural qualities of YamaMax would site it squarely, in Bakhtin's scheme, as an 'intentional', formal, 'hybrid' corporation, perhaps informed by 'organic' features of contemporary processes of globalisation. Although 'hybridity' is deployed by Bakhtin in discussion of processes affecting the evolution of language, there is no reason why it should not be used for linguistic as well as other forms of communication in analysis of organisational dynamics. (This will, indeed, be a key point of discussion in Chapter 4.)

I understand the word 'hybrid' in the commonsense way that I first came to it; unadulterated by its ubiquitous usage in the social science literature. When using the term 'hybrid organisation' I take 'hybrid', as defined by the *Oxford Concise Dictionary*, as a metaphorical 'offspring of two ... plants of different species or varieties', and literally '(fig.) thing[s] composed of incongruous elements, esp. words with parts taken from different languages' and 'heterogeneous' (Sykes 1982: 488). To my reading there is no inconsistency between this idea of 'things' or 'parts' making up hybridity from that deployed by Bahktin. Below I argue that it is what is called 'different' and what happens when differences are brought together 'in' a hybrid context that matters to analysis.

'Hybridity' has become a troubling term in social science, and especially at the intersection of anthropology and 'cultural studies'.[27] 'Hybrids' seem to have proliferated as divisions inherent to analysis have been understood to generate hybrid conceptual packages. Refining processes – our 'breaking apart' for analysis – lead in turn to the creation of concepts 'built up' of their recombination. For instance, classically – and at a highly abstract level of analysis – anthropologists have forwarded contrasts such as nature–culture, raw–cooked, and currently, and of specific interest in this study, local–global, real–virtual, Fordist–flexible.[28] These need not necessarily be 'binary oppositions'; they may be triplicates, or a far more complex nexus (for example, see Wagner 1986). In any case, to initiate analysis, a recognition of separation, or difference, is required. The subsequent recombination, presumably offering a new perspective, brings about analytic closure, even if temporary, and so the generation of new boundaries that lies at the root of the production of hybrids. If possibly stripped thin in my description, the logic is straightforward and elegant; its very parsimony limits its use, however. There would seem to be no limit to hybridity's capacity to penetrate all boundaries and enter all categories. For instance, if analysis is understood as a viewing of – a removal from – reality (and/or a separate reality itself), the contrast with reality (or the new reality generated, which is also something 'held apart'), is hybrid. What is not hybrid, then, once we think about it?

Allow me to cut short this quasi-philosophical argument by suggesting that the more relevant problem surrounding the use of the word 'hybridity' concerns what is held apart or kept together; that is, what distinctions are drawn and what are their limits as categories. The question at hand is: what constitutes difference? The genesis of this problem may be examined, for instance, in anthropology's intellectual history. It might be expected that early efforts in anthropology to trace the diffusion of cultural artefacts (for recent examples, see Gamble 1993; Diamond 1998 [1997]) – typically through environmental change and exchanges of kin, trade, religion and warfare – would theoretically challenge the notion of independent societies or cultural groups as distinctive entities. Rather, in the interest of defining societies or groups, particular characteristics – language, physical proximity (and so circumscription of contact between groups), ethnicity, kinship patterns, economic bases of intra-societal relations, and so on – have traditionally been mobilised in anthropology to defend boundaries, divisions and distinctiveness. That is, to defend the specific organisation of characteristics required, methodologically, in order to have anthropologically studied 'a people' or 'a community'.[29]

By contrast, in the contemporary intellectual context, attention to the process of the *construction* of boundaries, difference and, so, categories – for instance, 'constructing' reality (Berger and Luckman 1967), 'keeping' time (Thompson 1967), 'inventing' tradition (Hobsbawm and Ranger 1983), 'imagining' the nation (Anderson 1983) – has stimulated engagement with *when* categorical difference is made important by subjects, and *how* this is, or is not, achieved. The question asked is: what are *the conditions in which* distinctions are drawn and their limits as categories *described?* As such, boundaries, and other structures, are treated as epiphenomena of the conditions of power that allow those boundaries to be defined and maintained in the various social relations that make up the human enterprise – including the analytic endeavours of anthropologists. Thus, I am making a specific analytic choice, that in the contemporary intellectual climate I feel compelled to explain, in calling the French and Japanese different in order to examine the processes involved in their co-organising, or 'construction', of YamaMax.

I understand this mediation – our exposure to *constructionism* in the production and analysis of social phenomena – as social science's response to the twentieth century's most significant paradigm shift (Kuhn 1970): the theoretical discovery of what I construe broadly as 'contingency', first recognised in the methodological impact of observation on the results of experimental physics as the Heisenberg principle. As a result most social 'scientists', or students of humanity, have, I believe and hope, theoretically and practically rejected both the claim and the possibility of conducting purely objective analysis modelled on truth claims attributed to 'nature' as defined traditionally by 'hard' science. In turn we have lost interest in attempting to do so.[30] That is, we now operate more vividly than ever through the sensibility that no socially generated 'fact', category or concept ever stands alone; each is contingent on contestable forms of relatedness, dependent on perspective; each constructed through our imaginations and requiring combination with other phenomena. As such, 'contingency' is a generator of 'hybrids', and it is no surprise that contingency and hybridity have arisen together in the intellectual and socio-technical context of contemporary constructionism.

I began my discussion of 'hybridity' with the suggestion that I would, at least at the outset, keep it simple. I deploy 'hybridity' as I first came to it; innocent and unadulterated by its ubiquitous constructions in academia, meanwhile appreciating the social construction of meaning as a process required for analysis of 'reality'. Although my perspective on hybridity has by now been caught up in a more complicated and interesting net, I retain the simple stoppage of essentialising my French and Japanese subjects, taking the Japanese and the French, compared the one to the other, as homogeneous, discrete and different forms. While acknowledging its difficulties, I retain this categorisation in order to focus the present analysis on the experiences of members of YamaMax; in effect to see what work the organising of a 'cross-cultural' corporation[31] performs on my informants' categories of purity and hybridity, homogeneity and heterogeneity. I further justify this position by observing that my subjects identify themselves as Japanese and French – they are, so, limited and make themselves 'different' from one another – and that they, to a significant degree, work through, and sometimes articulated to me, these categorisations. In short, it is a matter of fact that these distinctions were mobilised on many occasions by everyone at YamaMax, and so they should form a central trope in this study.

Obviously in essentialising the categories 'French' and 'Japanese' at YamaMax we are speaking of inter 'ethnic' or inter 'racial' relations. However, although I continuously use the terms 'the French' and 'the Japanese' in this book I purposefully do not press 'race' or 'ethnicity' into the theoretical foreground. I feel that 'race' and 'ethnicity' are so supercharged, or 'loaded', as to overshadow, or dominate, more subtle forms of analysis: analysis those focussing more broadly on the overarching process of mobilising *difference,* by my subjects and within social analysis generally. This should not be construed to infer that I do not think that 'racial' categorisations are important. On the contrary, rather, we are so predisposed to their central role in day to day discourse that they no longer cut the cake in *analytically* unpacking contemporary contexts. That is, we, appropriately, emote dread with regard to racialism, but such a position may not be the most productive from which to strive toward a balanced account of groups of persons trying to figure out how to, and often failing to get along. To make the point through an extreme contrast, how much use would I be able to make of correlating 'ethnic tension' built up of communications difficulties between Japanese and French engineers in a shared workplace situation and the 'ethnic tension' displayed in the horrific slaughter of Koreans in Japan by Japanese vigilantes, with the complicity of the Japanese police, following the 1923 Tokyo earthquake? While these acts may, similarly, flag up problems built up around the construction of categorical 'ethnic', 'national' or 'racial' differences they are, *contextually,* rather dissimilar in type. If I were to not make such distinctions explicit, which specific acts would I name as 'racist' or, the more academically neutral, 'ethnically informed', at YamaMax, a context that is never intentionally socially destructive but, rather, a context organised around the collaborative goal of mass production? Intentions matter to actions, as they do to interpretations of outcomes.

While I do not elaborate it further in this book, the by-now theoretically sophisticated and strongly historically informed literature on 'race' and 'ethnicity' in Japan itself powerfully makes my point regarding categorical *contextuality*. Ordinarily deployed via notions broadly attached to the idea of 'purity', it has become abundantly clear that the boundaries of the categories 'the Japanese', 'Japaneseness' and 'Japan' itself have been flexibly mobilised at different times in Japan's history for specific ideological purposes. To understand this more fully, let us briefly work backwards from our own familiarity with Japan's core 'postwar' discourse. Recent claims to a post-bubble birth of diversity in Japan notwithstanding – which are largely empirically-thin discoveries smacking rather uncomfortably of Western academic 'projections' – the problematic of Japan's postwar particularity, uniqueness and homogeneity – its 'monoethnic ideology' (Lie 2001: 125) – has been understood as a driving force behind Japan as an 'economic miracle'. This was articulated in Japan's early postwar re-emergence on the world stage, declared in the highly successful 1964 Tokyo Olympics, the desiccation of core Western industries through Japanese consumer electronics and automotive production prowess in the 1970s, culminating in the reactive hand slapping of the 1985 Plaza Accord, where Japan's effusive economy was structurally adjusted – the value of the Yen doubled – through the external intervention of Western powers. Imperial Japan had, however, constructed a rather more inclusive theory of 'the Japanese', for if there is one certainty to colonial projects it is the diversity of their subjects, ethnic and otherwise. That is, imperialism requires some kind of integrating discourse, or an overarching ideology, however far-fetched, to assist in explaining that which is, effectively, sustained at gunpoint: imperialism's hierarchical disaggregations and its natural propensity to splinter through the discomforts of colonial subjection. On Japan's colonial periphery were thus found 'incomplete Japanese' (Morris-Suzuki 1998: 175) but 'Japanese' nonetheless, be they Formosan Ryukyan or more 'domestic' subjects, the Ainu, all of whom to which Japan's imperial 'civilisation' was in principle made available should they alter their habits, dress and language use to mimic the higher, Japanese order. These inclusive notions were convenient and necessary colonial extensions – beyond the archipelago – of Meiji era pronouncements that aligned domestic Japanese as a singular, homogenous *minzoku* ('race', or folk) within *kazoku kokka*, or a 'family nation-state': 'an enduring essence, which provided the state with an elevated iconography of consanguineous unity, enhanced the legitimacy of new economic, social and political relations, and provided the Japanese people with a new sense of national purpose and identity' (Weiner 1997: 1). Later, under the expansive militarism of the 1930s this was expressed rather more tenuously in the extended international relations of Japan's 'Asian Co-prosperity Sphere' an 'imagined community' (Anderson 1983) with Japan again iterating, it might be argued, the traditional Chinese tributary *ka* [centre of the universe] pattern: as 'first among (Asian) equals' fighting against Western barbarian infidels led by the Americans.

Drawing the mere 130 years since the collapse of the Tokugawa regime into a conceptual package, Howell points out: 'The linking of Japanese identity to cultural essence antedates the ideology of Japanese homogeneity, which is a twentieth-century phenomenon. It can be traced to early-modern notions of a dyadic relationship between a central Japanese 'civilization' (*ka*) and a peripheral 'barbarism' (*i*), in which the objective criteria of 'civilization' could be adjusted to fit changing political exigencies' (1996: 172). Indeed, during the Tokugawa period, when Japan had supposedly isolated itself absolutely, its self-conscious positionality vis-à-vis the outside world included the desire to subvert China's (deeply weakened) position as the centre of civilisation and further subdivide its periphery into "foreign countries" (*ikoku*) – including China, Korea, the Ryukyu kingdom, [and] *Ezo* [the Land of the Ainu] ... [B]eyond that lie the realms of the 'outer barbarians' (*gai-i*), who [wrote] horizontally and [ate] with their hands' (Morris-Suzuki 1996: 83). Relative civilisation was thus literally a matter of proximity, i.e. distance from Japan, with its co-construction with Japaneseness (as *ka*), as above, 'symbolized, above all, in appearance and etiquette: [with] hairstyles and clothing, footwear and tattoos, diet and housing, festivals and ceremonies ... the parameters which defined the foreign ... "Japaneseness" was not a matter of race or inheritance, but something which could be acquired by the adoption of the "right" customs' (Morris-Suzuki 1996: 84–5). Meanwhile, inside Tokugawa Japan what are we to make of *hinin*, or non-persons – effectively untouchables, but clearly of Japanese 'genetic–racial' stock – floating usefully beyond the four designated castes of Tokugawa persons? I have argued elsewhere that having constructed 'Japanese' *hinin* in Tokugawa, a familiar form was available in Japan for the de facto transport and ideological transformation, i.e. the social psychological processing, of colonised subjects, i.e. Koreans in Japan (Sedgwick 1985). The overarching theme here, then, is that the core trope reproducing the idea of 'Japan' – the 'code of pure bloodlines' – has been entirely variable within Japan's historical development.

If this compact analysis of the cult of Japanese ethnicity seems somewhat jumpy, that is the point. For our purposes, if the racialist–ethnocentric content of what constitutes 'the Japanese' has been so flexibly mobilised in Japanese history itself, i.e. by the Japanese themselves, how useful would it be for us to allow 'the Japanese' categorical priority over other forms of 'making difference' in analysis of contemporary Japanese contexts? While it would be absurd, especially in contrast to other advanced industrial nation-states in the West, to not acknowledge that over 98 per cent of the population of Japan can and does readily identify itself as 'ethnically' Japanese, it would be equally absurd to suggest that this makes available anything other than a potential ideological 'force', among others, underpinning the actions of Japanese persons. I suggest, then, rather than fixing our gaze through the particularly dusty lens of race or ethnicity, focussing on race or ethnicity instead only when subjects themselves use it as a device to explain or understand their own experience.

Indeed, in the context of making sense of industrial enterprise, 'purity' of practices holds far more explanatory power than does the correlation of purity with race. That is, engineers pay a lot of attention to the technical aspects of how to get things done, and in mass production consistency of action is, obviously, a core value. (Japanese) engineers may believe that the techniques they have learned for accomplishing industrial production are the best, or have the potential to be most effective. In an overseas setting, for example, in working with French colleagues, they may then logically prefer that their methods remain unadulterated, or pure to form. In practice some technical industrial activities may remain unproblematically pure, or true to form, from the perspective of Japanese engineers; others may not. Such experiences of relative consistencies in desired practices are, however, some distance from Japanese managers' thinking that only Japanese can do these things. If, in frustration, they say so in France, I want to know about that. And I also want to know what they say in frustration in Yokohama when practice does not match ideal form.

Through examination of hybridity, then, this study explicitly scrutinises, in a thoroughly modern context, the permeation of the boundaries of the nation–tribe–(and occasionally ethnic) categories upon which anthropological analyses have traditionally depended.[32] While this approach coincides with the contemporary theoretical aesthetics of constructionism, it is empirically based in observation of an explicitly 'not-Japanese and not-French' place created by persons who call themselves 'French' or 'Japanese'. Thus, this is not a study of how Japanese cope when they find themselves in France, or how the French cope when they work in a Japanese firm. This is an effort to understand the work – across cultures, languages, hierarchy, personality and technical knowledge – that organising an industrial firm, that is 'hybridised' by processes of globalisation, performs on its members. I part company, then, with Iwabuchi's elaboration favouring, over 'hybridity,' a particular 'Japanese ... *strategic hybridism* ... that absorbs foreign cultures without changing its national/cultural core' (2002: 53) [italics mine]. It strikes me that, especially in explanation of the interactions of the Japanese with non-Japanese, such a renaming reifies a long tradition of analytically mirroring the uniqueness of Japanese cultural claims and dispositions, including in Japanese persons' interactions with all sorts of non-Japanese phenomena. Furthermore, granting such particularity to Japanese practices serves also to undermine a powerful, if occassionally troubled, theoretical effort to make sense of contemporary globalisation, i.e. through deliberations on 'hybridity'. Here that includes the hybridity work on French and Japanese identities that YamaMax's members, explicitly and implicitly, carry through their employment at YamaMax. Through close-grained analysis of organising a particular context or place, then, I believe that this ethnography may prove capable of addressing 'hybridity' more tangibly and more successfully than in its common academic use: where 'hybridity' is forwarded as a caricature of a qualitative, even 'revolutionary', shift in the present era due to an ill-defined but, apparently, particularly high rate of 'boundary-crossing' activity.

Methodological considerations for a globalised field

Reorganising knowledge of scale and micro–macro divisions

Analytic divisions of the micro and macro are artifice. If we are as of yet unable to arrive theoretically at a perspective or methodology which bypasses or unifies them analytically, then observation of those intensively engaged in networks of activities across both apparently proximate and apparently distant places should provide us with a preliminary impetus. A goal of this study is thus to demonstrate how what are called macro activities – macro-economic structural adjustments, for instance – are articulated and constituted of local interactions. If we need to use the terms micro and macro at all, and, as will be seen, I think it is important to discard them, then let them be understood in this way: not unlike Knorr-Cetina and Cicourel (1981), I would take 'the macro' to be analysed and understood through its articulation in densely studied 'micro-level sociologies'. I maintain that to do that analysis work requires close attention to what subjects understand to be the 'macro' and 'micro', 'the local' and 'the global'. Thus I seat the interests of a large Japanese corporation in establishing a subsidiary in France in an examination of the larger political economic context of the overseas expansion of Japanese industrialisation. A policy decision taken in Tokyo will come to be understood – albeit, and properly, indirectly – to implicate face-to-face interactions at production meetings at YamaMax, an organisation in rural France.

The point is an exposure not of scales, but of linkages, or of 'networks' that theoretically link phenomena across what are commonly understood as macro and micro scales. Properly deployed, actor–network theory may assist in 'making the links' through description and analysis of the network, not a totalised assumption of a network's holistic integration, nor reification of the micro or macro. I will expand on this more fully in Chapter 4 but allow me to put forward the flavour of this discussion. Latour, for example, a leading actor–network theorist, understands the establishment of scientific 'facts' as a process unfolding over years that corresponds with the capacity of specific scientists, their teams and their data to forward the credibility of their 'facts'. They are in competition with other teams' 'facts', in a game of power and authority in 'the' scientific community (Latour 1987). Each particular research activity, paper delivered, phone call made, may effectively involve 'cutting' out other possible activities or alternative perspectives.

Over a longer time period, these discrete incidents may be understood as a network of activities. Latour's (1988) discussion of the successful work of Pasteur, which is contextualised across French institutions, is a specific example. It treats period texts generated from a wide range of organisational settings that are understood, in the language I use, as tools, or vessels, containing the overlap of what might be commonly understood as separate micro and macro frameworks. This work shows that notions regarding the micro and macro are not necessary to explaining the proliferation of ideas about, in this case, antibiotics: rather penicillin was generated through a series of social relations organised across ideas and materials that created a network of associations. (At a practical level these associations generated, and, indeed, continue to generate, a massive improvement in health care.)

This approach does not imply that processes attributable to 'globalisation' do not exist unless they are *experienced* by persons. An anthropologist's interest in 'globalisation' etymologically requires consideration of the impact at a local level of 'global' affairs, but blanket theoretical acknowledgement of the interconnectedness of human and environmental activity across 'macro' and 'micro' scales, however those might be defined, does not suffice. Indeed, in conducting fieldwork among members of multinational corporations one is impressed with how keenly they act across these scales and, therefore, how important to the success of these organisations are their capacity to collapse the relevance of scale; scale is made to disappear through erosion of its very boundaries. These are actions they call, simply and mundanely, 'working'. Note the continuous, and practically instantaneous, movements of (claims on) capital throughout the globe which are generated by firms like the Yama Corporation. Note also, however, the lack of autonomy of these most 'liquid' – these most apparently 'detached' – of global movements. It is persons who make the decisions, and program the computers, that trigger the 'velocity of money'[33] and generate other economic 'facts' of the globalised economy that, whether we like it or not, reach directly into almost everyone's daily financial activities.[34]

In studying social dimensions of processes of globalisation I recognise the very numerous and complex subject matters potentially entailed. In methodologically prioritising relatively intimate activities however – that is, the observation and analysis of face-to-face activities that I understand as the defining feature of anthropological field practice – I do not feel that I am risking any perspectival loss. On the contrary. The experiences of members of a French subsidiary of a major Japanese consumer electronics corporation are filled, by any definition, by global processes. Furthermore, their practical relations to those influences resemble our own. For instance, while many of YamaMax's managers send and receive hundreds of international e-mail, telephone and fax messages per week and we, perhaps, make do with somewhat fewer, we are nonetheless performing the same kinds of communicative acts, using the same kinds of tools to extend relations. The contents may differ, the modalities are similar. I hope that this familiarity alone may serve to show 'global' work at YamaMax as intimate for them whilst, also, recognisable to us, and that, therefore, reflection on those intimacies may represent a strategy to ground analysis of globalisation 'in here', rather than floating untouchably 'out there'.

Staying connected

As a matter of methodology and theoretical import concerning research on organisations, it is crucial to note that my connections *with* firms are personal, not institutional; that is, I have relations with persons who work at several firms. As I lose track of those persons, they retire, or the progression of their careers moves them into other parts of a multinational corporation, my ties with and access to, say, a particular subsidiary disintegrates: assuming new relations with new members at that subsidiary have not been created. My own fieldwork access has, thus, had to trace *and* keep pace with the particular careers of particular persons willing to be helpful, in part because they became my friends. These persons, furthermore, recognise that their potential to be helpful is circumscribed by the structural imperatives of their firm's 'interests' and their own complex sets of relations inside their firm. It is perhaps unnecessary but I nonetheless at times find myself envious of anthropologist colleagues who seem to understand themselves as a (perennial) member of a stable community – say, a village where they conducted their Ph.D. research – to which they feel confident that they can return for years, perhaps observing their own lives evolve through such visits. While theoretically so anywhere, the very character of 'community' in a multinational corporation – or, especially for expatriate staff, a foreign subsidiary within it – built as it is upon the relations of persons 'at work', is amorphous, unstable and under constant professional and personal renegotiation. The quality of those relations negotiated between myself and the 'organisations' I study, then, is a key 'finding': it is part of the global work I too, like my informants, conduct.

Thus, when 'at home' – away from the field – and struggling to make sense of and write up material from earlier research projects I was also concerned about losing contact with the Japanese corporations, the 'communities', I had finally managed to study in Japan and abroad. Thus I began discussions with a key Japanese informant and friend from the Yama Corporation about the possibility of pursuing ethnographic research at YamaMax, Yama's 'magnetic products division' subsidiary operation, making videotape, in France. As I will discuss in the next chapter, each of the nine factories in this division is effectively in competition for resources from the huge administrative 'centre' based in Tokyo, so the spread of relative resources is a core concern for the success of each factory and, therefore, the careers of those working in each factory. Thus, senior Yama 'magnetics' managers often circulate among all the Yama magnetic products factories in Europe, North America, South East Asia and, of course, in Japan itself. At the subsidiaries, these visits are highly anticipated and tightly planned. While conducting earlier research projects, I came to know some of these senior managers, if superficially.

Presidents of the subsidiaries hold biannual meetings with their superiors and counterparts, usually in Japan, although I am aware of meetings in Europe and Hawaii as well. Having previously discussed the matter with him, at one such meeting my central Japanese patron/informant – who at this point had become president of a Yama 'magnetics' subsidiary in Thailand – privately queried his (French) counterpart as to whether I might be hosted by YamaMax for a study.[35] I do not know, but have grounds to suspect that other informal conversations with top Japanese managers from Yama, who had either met or knew of me, also served to indicate to YamaMax's French president (or *directeur general*) that I was reliable, i.e. he and his operation would not be put at risk by my presence. In any case, later it was indicated to me by my patron/informant that the matter was settled. I thus began a fairly formal correspondence by letter and fax with the French *directeur general* of Yama-Max, whom I had not met, to arrange my 'extended visit'. He stated in one such letter that he had a 'personal interest' in my project. This may have been genuine but, in any case, it cannot be separated from his own more important set of personal relations with persons at the Yama Corporation that made my 'extended visit' possible.

My route to the 'French' field site was, then, undeniably linked to my knowledge and experience of Japan generally, through which I have over a very long period of time been able to develop relations with members of the Yama Corporation, as I have persons at other Japanese organisations. As such, it would be unrealistic to pretend that I could provide equal analytic insight regarding the Japanese and the French. Conducting ethnographic research is challenging enough without fighting against the current of my own knowledge, experience and opportunities. That said, my initial cross-national/cross-cultural experience was on a year-long high-school exchange programme in France many years ago. Due perhaps to the kind efforts of my (very large) French family, with whom I am still in contact, I am fluent in French and feel quite comfortable, or 'natural', among the French. Indeed, it was due to this positive, youthful experience that I was keen to go abroad again and, rather by accident, only a year after my homestay in France, went to Japan to conduct the first of many research projects across a, by now, thirty-year period.

Thus, this study draws together into one context those two foreign cultures – French and Japanese – that I know best. I am not particularly interested in giving this personal matter any special analytic gravity, except to say honestly that I appreciate both and, so far as I can tell, I do not favour one over the other. At an academic level, however, I will not substantively engage the anthropological literature on the French as I am not a specialist in this area. However, this ethnography should be of interest to its scholars, as I hope that, at the very least, it manages to retain the sense of French persons in their interactions both with each other and with their Japanese colleagues.

Globalisation at a 'single site'

This is a 'single-site' study, but I purposely put that notion in brackets (cf. Marcus 1995). As suggested by my earlier descriptions of social relations among Japanese members of Yama Corporation, which effectively reproduce its magnetics division, I understand YamaMax, and any organisation for that matter, as a process, and so a real-world fiction constructed of social relations. I unpacked briefly my understanding of 'constructionism' earlier in this chapter, and will do so at a more fully theoretical level with regard to specific activities at YamaMax in Chapter 4. Not to belabour the point, but here let me state that I understand the physical plant of YamaMax, the legal devises and technical transactions, and so on, framing its work as constructed of social relations, and entirely void of meaning or efficacy without those social relations. YamaMax is an outcome of its members' – and those with relations with them – organising of their lives and work. It is a temporary set, a point or node in various and extensive networks of relations that move far beyond its own boundaries and which are, in this case, by the nature of the work conducted at YamaMax, explicitly global.

This 'single-site' study at an organisation does not share with most anthropological studies of particular communities the sense that when their members leave, they return, or when they leave 'permanently' – as, say, members of a migrant community – their 'diasporic' mindset is imagined to retain some fundamental relationship with that particular 'place'.[36] Here, I suggest that the 'process' I evoke theoretically to characterise 'the organisation' may be shared by its own members' characterisations of their own organisation(s): constantly changing, temporary, fluid, moving along; and/ or as a site of 'work' and somehow detached from 'life', as if they are visitors. As such, organisation may stand in as a proxy for (post) modern *anomie*, or, possibly, the conceptual ungraspability of globalisation. I caution, however, against taking this characterisation as a suggestion that the experience of the organisation is unreal nor, of course, that it does not have real-world effects. Furthermore, in spite of my longing for relations to a 'stable' site, it does not seem to me in theoretical terms that what happens to persons in the process of organising a factory is in any fundamental sense different from the process of organising the communities that anthropologists have traditionally studied. 'Diasporic' or otherwise, a 'permanent' relationship to a particular place is nothing more than an idea, among many, through which social relations may gain purchase, and I take it that analysis of how social relations gain purchase is a central goal of anthropology.

In this ethnography I might have mimicked the traditional anthropological style and feel of the single-site formula had I treated YamaMax – at least for its French members – as an 'external': something providing an impact upon, say, the 'eternal' French village on the periphery of which it is found and where many of its members 'live'. As such, analysis of work at YamaMax, which requires physical displacement, may have inverted – with similar analytic outcome – the typical intrusions of, say, government officials or development agency personnel upon the 'life of the village', i.e. temporary diversions from normal, real life. However such a (traditional) strategy would have undermined the very sense of contingency by which, in theoretical terms, I understand 'place' to be constructed, a sense which is so well displayed, if not exaggerated, by the comings and goings – the traffic in persons, goods and experience – that is an organisation like YamaMax. In its intimate referencing to activities among persons in a particular (organisational) location, I nod here to traditional ethnography, but hope to demonstrate how we might think ethnography away from the artificial stabilities often associated with (superficial) readings, say, of 'house', village or kinship, toward ethnography that moves in time and sentiment with the continuous negotiations endemic to organising social relations.

Day to day interactions

This study's introduction argued for leaving the meaning of globalisation open, at least at the outset, in order that its 'feel' might be examined without being troubled by definitional restrictions. This strategy does not suggest, however, that the study of globalisation can be dissociated from places. The 'foreignness' of analysis of the 'global' – that it seems ethnographically distanced from persons' day to day realities – is a major criticism I have of much anthropological work to date on this subject. Rather, I wish to show for instance that writing an e-mail *and* imagining its reception at a location 8,000 miles away is a local act. It may be something else as well, that may also make it 'assume' distance, but this is a secondary apprehension. Thus, as I have focussed on local acts, my day to day ethnographic labour was not in any particular way different in intent from any other participant–observation study. That it was conducted largely within a formal organisation did, however, give it particular twists.

It took an enormous initial effort across several years to gain access sufficient to conduct substantive ethnographic studies at Japanese multinational corporations. Perhaps this process was particularly challenging due to my determination, first, that I should not be employed where I was conducting research and, second, that I should for all intents and purposes be allowed to circulate freely in the organisations I was to study. These two points may at the outset seem quite separate, but they are fundamentally linked where the anthropological study of organisations is concerned. If one is employed in an organisation one obviously enjoys a real 'participation' in its activities, however 'observation' is necessarily focussed through one's particular position and role. Of course, earlier I discussed the theoretical problematics of 'objectivity', while the anthropologist's 'positionality' vis-à-vis the host community is a concern that has been well-vetted under the rubrics of 'orientalism', the 'reflexivity movement' and the 'new ethnography' which it has informed.[37] However that it is impossible to avoid intervention due to one's presence does not, at least on theoretical grounds, justify purposeful intervention. Anthropologists who have purposely 'tested' their communities, with or, usually, without their subjects' knowledge, have been appropriately criticised in the anthropological community for unethical behaviour. I am not saying that being employed in an organisation that is under study is necessarily unethical, I am suggesting that it skims the edges of an ethical methodological dilemma as it is necessarily, by the fact of employment, a purposeful intervention. (It is quite unethical, on the other hand, to be employed in an organisation for the purposes of conducting an anthropological study without informing the community under study to that effect. I am not aware of cases of 'undercover' ethnography conducted under the rubric of 'anthropology'. However, this approach to fieldwork is apparently seriously considered, and evidently in practice, in some other disciplines that claim to use 'ethnographic methods': a practice I consider entirely unacceptable and inappropriate.)

Clearly, most organisations are not interested in having an anthropologist, who may get in the way or otherwise muddle things up, on hand. And as many of the most interesting organisations are those in which an anthropologist would be, in Nader's incisive terminology, 'studying up', authorities in those organisations usually have no problem saying 'no' to anthropological enquiry (1974 [1969]: 284–311). Access is a difficult problem everywhere but perhaps especially so in modern organisations as they tend to operate within the types of, read modern, societies within which most anthropologists, also, live the bulk of their lives. That is, as members of modern societies we are necessarily 'in relation' to modern societies' organisations before we set foot in them, so an emotional 'angle' towards the organisation under study is ordinarily present before study begins. Under Nader's activist agenda towards very powerful organisations in the US, that emotional angle is as likely as not to be critical or, in any case, motivated by a compulsion toward, say, 'egalitarian justice'. With all these complicating factors at hand it is not surprising, then, that there are as many justifications – shared privately and, occasionally, for general consumption – for the particular relations between the anthropologist and the organisation as there are anthropologists who study organisations. (Perhaps the most honest one regarding being paid by the organisation under study would, hypothetically, be something like this: 'Studying modern organisations is expensive; I needed to work there in order to survive while I did "my" work'.) In any case, it seems that acknowledgment of the particular circumstances of fieldwork, including the organisational hold over

behaviour that an explicit role is likely to entail, could turn a possible problem of positionality into, at the very least, an interesting discussion, if not
an analytic asset.

That said, for myself, by the time I formally began my studies of
Japanese multinational corporations in 1991 I had already worked professionally in several large organisations and, as an employee, was deeply
familiar with their power to direct and constrain me. As a result, I felt
compelled to free *myself* as much as possible where fieldwork at my study
sites was concerned from the power over perception – the positionality –
that organisations I had worked in had wielded over me. Although that is
stated as though it were policy, it was a matter of constant negotiation that
created, as far as I was concerned, interesting, and analytically necessary,
tensions. I was in the quite unusual position of being the only person at the
organisations I studied who could not be called on to 'do' anything for it,
and yet I circulated largely at will. Formally, at YamaMax my activities fell
under the aegis of the authority of the French *directeur general*; that is to
say, he was the only person who could immediately 'show me the door'.
That said, I went to great lengths, I believe, to avoid abusing the spectacular
privilege of being in the position of having access to activities at all hierarchical levels within the organisation, a position which, of course, only the
directeur general himself could, also, *technically* claim, i.e. in terms of the
authority outlined by his position on top of the 'organisational chart', but
which he could never activate in practice due to his own positionality.

A great deal of my initial period at YamaMax was spent getting to know
French members of the firm and, I realised later, convincing them that I was
neither working for, nor relaying any information about them to Japanese
members of the corporation in YamaMax in France, the Yama Corporation
in Japan, the French *directeur general,* nor their superiors or subordinates.
Most of the French members of YamaMax were well-educated and generally familiar with socio-cultural anthropology. They were interested, or
amused, by my claim that I was there to study them in much the same way
other anthropologists had studied the 'primitive societies' familiar from
their schoolwork. Since I was studying a 'modern' site, which they associated with the concerns of sociology, rather than anthropology, some
engaged me in serious discussion about differences between the disciplines.
In any case, I was explicit in forwarding the assurance that knowledge
gained while working at YamaMax would circulate only in a somewhat
rarefied academic arena. And I think it was helpful that in French society
'the academy' is for the most part highly respected by the population at
large.[38] Since French members of the firm were aware that I circulated freely
and was the only person fluent in all three languages (French, Japanese and
English) in regular use at YamaMax, if they gave the matter any thought, it
would be clear that I had potential access to a great deal of information. In
Chapter 3 I will describe how this situation created particular tensions with
one French manager, Monsieur Marchalot. However, I believe that to the

members of YamaMax I was for the most part nothing more than an innocuous curiosity, and on this matter my study probably aligns with the local perception of the anthropologist in any fieldwork situation, 'traditional' or otherwise. Personally, I was constantly struck by the limitations of my own physical and mental capacity to organise what I was coming across. The field was extraordinarily rich, and I was fully aware that day to day choices of focus necessarily ruled out observations of other activities.

Given my interest in cross-cultural relations, one general choice I did make was to seek out specific contexts where the Japanese and the French were in direct contact with each other, for example, in routine daily, weekly and monthly meetings, where basic data on production and decision-making were presented and discussed. Such contexts also presented themselves within the framework of larger projects in the organisation which I might follow, sometimes over weeks, in real time. In these cases I would observe a very large number of regular and impromptu meetings between the French and the Japanese, as well as their many separate meetings. (In Chapter 4, I describe several such meetings set within the context of the production tests for a new product, a very intensive period for engineering staff at YamaMax.) Although there was a constant stream of visitors from elsewhere in the Yama Corporation, since there were only eight Japanese employed permanently on site and they were nearly all of high rank, they tended to interact with the highest-ranking French managers and engineers who were, in turn, my main French informants. The core of my observations were, thus, of 'managers' at work.[39]

While I was literally present, during meetings I did my utmost to 'disappear'. Though I did not want to give the impression of being surreptitious, I sat either in the back of the room or somewhat apart from others, if possible. I very rarely said anything nor engaged the meeting's members. In observing, say, a regular weekly meeting, it was clear to me – in retrospect – that my presence was noted for the first few weeks. However, invariably, some relatively serious problem would arise that would focus the attention of all of the meeting's members. At points such as this, I often felt that my presence had, from their perspective, evaporated. Following such an experience, I usually felt that my presence made very little impression at subsequent meetings: their de facto exposure of whatever had been closed from me by their (organisational, i.e. interpersonal) crisis, resolved whatever 'problem' my presence might have created. As far as my fieldwork was concerned, such denouements were ideal.

Such ideals, however, were not always realised. For instance the top Japanese manager, Otake-san, at times verbally bullied his Japanese subordinates. When particularly upset, he would not infrequently use me as an audience to voice his, fully audible, asides in Japanese describing their weaknesses. I did my best not to respond – i.e. I assumed the highly subordinate position in Japanese social contexts suggested by my utter silence, lack of expression and no eye contact, and slow and shallow bowing – hoping all the while that the other Japanese appreciated the awkward position I, too, was in. Most of the time, however, neither Otake-san nor the other Japanese managers seemed to care less if I was present among them while they discussed their work. Meanwhile, weekly meetings were held with the small group of four or five top French (male) managers, the *directeur general* and his female secretary, whom they all found attractive and with whom they were all flirtatious. Boisterousness, involving a great deal of teasing and wordplay, accompanied exchanges of information and decision-making in these meetings. While I did not volunteer any jokes, it would have been totally inappropriate for me not to 'laugh along' with them. In the event, these meetings generated the secretary's formal minutes, that within a week I could use in tandem with my own, handwritten notes. While not always approximating the ideal 'position' of 'fly on the wall', then, I did what was required to stay with such important meetings month in and month out during fieldwork. I also spent a great deal of time outside of work with both French and, especially, the Japanese members of YamaMax. This typically involved taking meals together, but also included drinking, attending local festivals, playing sports and generally hanging about with them, and, on occasion, their families.

At no point did I consider recording meetings or any other event at YamaMax, and only on very rare occasions did I take photographs, none of which I use in this ethnography. Perhaps I was being overly careful, but I felt that the idea of such 'hard evidence' might jeopardise my colleagues', or informants', trust in me or somehow put them off in meetings. Furthermore, to be frank, organisational meetings can be exceedingly boring; all the more so, perhaps, as during fieldwork the anthropologist has nothing emotional at stake in their outcome besides the abstract hope that in the general gathering of information some nugget of insight, or perhaps an unexpected drama to break the monotony, may emerge. Although I have a great deal of respect, in theory, for the uses of 'ethnomethodology' (Garfinkel 1967) I find the direction of much of its offspring – intensively detailed conversational analysis (see, for instance, Moerman 1988) – less analytically incisive than was originally hoped (Sacks 1992; Silverman 1998). Quite apart from my doubt over its academic merit, I have never been attracted to the idea of attending to a meeting by listening to a recording of it. If I were to rely on technology beyond my handwritten (or, sometimes, laptop-typed) notes and my memory, I would insist on 'total information': multiply positioned audio and video recording that could take in all participants, i.e. the total scene apart from the temperature in the room. (Obviously this would be impossible to achieve to say nothing of the conundrum of making sense of such simultaneous 'data'.) It may be deduced from my perspective on this matter that what most interests me in attending meetings, as well as in my overall observations, is gaining a general sense of the atmosphere of social interactions; something I also consider a key component of the explicit (technical–practical) topic at hand for my subjects, whether or not they are consciously aware of it. All of my meeting notes open, then, with a diagram of where particular persons sit in relation to one another, and often what each person is wearing. Notes about what is being said are accompanied by a notation as to what language is being used (at what level of competence) by whom, and at what time in the sequence of the meeting, and an impression as to how and towards whom statements are addressed and received. The dynamics of very intensive interactions were difficult to record in real time, but my notes also account for such things by their level of illegibility as do, of course, fuller writing about events after the fact.

Of course much of the detail of my notes concerns the matter at hand for the participants: I was aware of why meetings were held in particular places at particular times and what was at stake in the meeting's specific agenda. However, it did not necessarily negatively affect my analysis that I did not understand every detail of what was under discussion – especially the rarefied technical details elaborated by engineers – as it, perhaps, allowed me to focus on their 'communicative acts' with less distraction. When I followed particular issues over some time, however, I did make a serious effort to understand what was specifically 'going on' or, more often, going wrong at a technical level.[40] This would sometimes involve asking a French or Japanese engineer to spend some time explaining to me what was at stake technically. Perhaps I guided discussion inadvertently this way but in any case these discussions often led to descriptions, from his or her perspective, of what was happening socially/managerially as well, and thus were especially useful. My overall strategy, then, was to attend meetings, get an idea of what was under discussion, follow up on the details of what seemed interesting (in that, for instance, I might be able to anticipate that they would draw the Japanese and French into further interaction), follow the issue over time through joint (Japanese–French) and separate meetings, and discuss it, privately, with several persons actively engaging it throughout the entire process. It might be noted here that in any one day there were perhaps one hundred meetings held in the entire YamaMax organisation – thousands depending on the degree of informality one decides to ascribe to the notion 'meeting' – so I had to make hard, and sometimes retrospectively disappointing, choices as to where to focus my attention.

As I will elaborate in some detail in Chapter 5, I generally located myself physically in the engineering section of YamaMax, where the Japanese and the core group of French engineers had their desks. I had a desk in the communal office space that most of the engineers used, which was surrounded by the private offices of their superiors and the meeting rooms where they conducted most of their formal meetings.[41] Thus, when they were not 'in' the factory, for example, on the shopfloor, I could literally see what most of them were doing, and spent some time simply recording their activities. When a problem was particularly 'hot', their circulations, impromptu and formal gatherings could move at a very high pace. In these cases I sometimes simply followed someone around, hopefully picking up a sense of things, until I handed myself off to some other related gathering or person, or simply withdrew for reflection.

Interviews: getting together

I tend only to conduct formal interviews at the opening and closing of fieldwork. They can be helpful at the outset for gathering a general picture of the 'field' but are more likely to be useful as a story about a particular interviewee's perspective as told to a relative stranger. In practice in organisational settings, I find that interviews are more important for 'breaking the ice' than anything else. Outsiders who visit modern organisations on other than regular business tend to be technical experts or 'consultants' who rely on particular individuals to provide specific data and information. Therefore, members of private firms are accustomed to this form of interaction and, once they have decided they have the time, readily engage it.

From such initial interviews I have often been able to get a 'read' as to who might be able to be helpful in future or, perhaps more importantly, who may be willing or interested in spending time with me. Of course, where certain members of a hierarchical organisation are privy to information, i.e. at the top of the organisation, and/or have been able to gain particular perspectives that are of central importance to a study, one may feel obliged to work out a relationship of some kind. I would have been in real trouble, for instance, if the top Japanese manager at YamaMax – Otake-san – had decided that my participation in either formal or informal meetings with the group of Japanese engineer/managers was taboo. I was serious, painful as it sometimes was, in imposing myself upon the meetings of the relatively small Japanese group, in the hope that my presence could be normalised, as it eventually was. That said, however, with so much going on in any organisation I have not generally felt that any particular piece of information justified pressing too hard to engage an unwilling informant. One can usually move around the issue. For instance, I was interested in information regarding dismissals from YamaMax. This sensitive topic was, obviously, in the sphere of knowledge of the (French) director of personnel. We did not get on particularly well and, though in an interview he provided me with the printed text of YamaMax's 'rules and regulations', he was unwilling to discuss particular cases – and perfectly justifiably so – even where names would not be mentioned. It turned out, however, that he generally did not get on well with colleagues, so other members of YamaMax were not surprised at my lack of success in obtaining information from him. As a result, in confidence, some of them were willing to recount various, sometimes contradictory, stories about dismissals. Motivated by an interest in dismissals, then, the quality of the circulation of information upon it –

the types and timbres of stories told, and from whom – became far more interesting than the accuracy of the formal details of particular cases, which, whether I had 'formal documentation' or not, would be impossible to confirm as 'accurate' in any case.

My own practice during long-term fieldwork is to avoid, certainly at the outset, querying the usually compelling personal histories of members of the community under study. I prefer to observe them, as much as possible, without preconception and allow our joint experience, hearsay and documents to nuance my knowledge of them, i.e. I get to know them. Furthermore, at the beginning of my fieldwork at YamaMax although, given the intent of the study, I may have safely assumed that I would eventually want to interview the eight Japanese members, I had no idea who I would end up interviewing among the French. It was certain that I would not interview all of the over 400 French members, for my 'formal' interviews take at least 90 minutes – the set of questions I might ask extends to several pages – and are fully open-ended. Furthermore, these people are busy and while interviewing them, neither they, nor I, were 'in' the organisation, as it were. Additionally, I generally felt that neither they, nor I, would have the patience for more than one, quite lengthy and wide-ranging, formal interview. It thus made sense to wait until the final month when I knew whose stories I wanted to flesh out. For instance the educational background and career paths of the top French and Japanese engineering team was critical to my study and this information could be gathered relatively efficiently in an interview setting. Also, at the close of fieldwork I could query events witnessed during fieldwork about which I was unclear. Another advantage of waiting until the end is that at this point one is loaded up with largely unfiltered field information, so one can – far more easily than at the beginning of fieldwork – let go of examining events or exploring information that may generate more information.

Time, of which there seems to be so much – too much – at the start of fieldwork, seems so precious at the end. When, upon observation of something terribly uneventful, one can generate a sensible explanation about a community, one may be ready to leave. And it is perhaps then, when meaning has become so enriched, that it is especially difficult to leave. The 'interviews' I conducted were, thus, by this time – over seventeen months since my first arrival at YamaMax – private events. They provided an opportunity for some sort of closure, thanks, a summing up. One is chosen by and chooses good informants. My interviews served to get some specifics onto paper but were effectively a vehicle to open up space for wider discussions. The 'interview' was nearly always capped with two queries, 'Is there anything else that you think I should know?', and 'Is there anything that you want to ask me?'. It was not unusual that this would lead to another hour of conversation. And well it should; for in the serendipitous course of working together a great deal, one cannot help but become fascinated by the great stories that people have to share about their lives and day to day understandings. Years later one cannot help but grasp in vain to do justice to what was closely shared.

Notes

1 I choose these two particular types of organisation because they are typical of academic analyses of organisations, respectively, in France and Japan. For example, compare Crozier's *The Bureaucratic Phenomenon* (1964), based on fieldwork in France in a section of the national bureaucracy and at a wholly, state-owned enterprise, with Womack, Jones and Roos' *The Machine that Changed the World* (1990), on 'total quality management' at Toyota, a large, private Japanese corporation. The academic approaches of each of these studies would seem to correlate historically, and respectively, with the rise of the modern state and its bureaucratisation following the French Revolution, and the rise of Japanese industrial power in the post Second World War period. These are matters of profound historical significance nationally, internationally and, indeed, in terms of the analysis of modernity. However, analytic approaches to subjects – French bureaucracy, Japanese corporations – may become fixed even where they may have less empirical relevance in a different, perhaps less dramatic, historical period. It would be unacceptable, for instance, to write a book about the Japanese Government that did not intimately consider its relations with the private sector. Meanwhile, though perhaps slowly changing, the private sector is a relative sideshow in deliberations on French governance. Crozier relates the similarity in styles of behaviour at a public sector and an industrial organisation, but not how they are linked to France's political economy. State–private sector relations are structurally similar in Japan and France and, indeed, these relations must be conjoined in any analysis of contemporary capitalism, including analysis of any particular organisation, such as YamaMax.

2 Hypothetical analyses of the use of globalised objects – say, cans of Coke – in other, or more expansive, ways than they were intended by the Coca-Cola Corporation – as, say, jewellery – would remind us that local cultural contexts resist the apparently homogenising influences of 'global culture' by using such objects in new and unexpected ways. This may provide some relief and reaffirmation of human creativity. However, what I am referring to here is the deployment, however limited, of local knowledge in transaction with the 'reach' of Coca-Cola's corporate interests as, also, a global phenomenon. While, most simply, the Coke salesman is clearly at the end of a Coca-Cola's enormously expansive 'global' network, he is nonetheless part of that network as are, indeed, the consumer without whose purchases the corporation would not exist. (I will theorise such forms of corporate relatedness in Chapter 4.)

3 Hannerz's (1989: 211) full quote is as follows:

> The macroanthropological [*sic*] project entails a strategic selection of research sites which would take ethnographers to those interfaces where the confrontations, the interpretations and the flowthrough [*sic*] are occurring, between clusters of meaning and ways of managing meaning; in short, the places where diversity gets, in some way and to some degree, organized.

Hannerz's interests would seem to overlap with Marcus' call for a multi-sited ethnography in order to make ethnographic sense of the world system (Marcus 1995). Also see Hannerz (1986) for his related perspective on, and partial invention of, 'the problem of complex cultures'.

4 The classic sociological and anthropological literature on the organisation and management of large-scale private corporations in modern Japan is, Cole 1971; Dore 1973; Rohlen 1974; Clark 1979; Abegglen and Stalk, Jr. 1985.

5 'Informal' voluntary organisations nonetheless provide interesting cases for commentary on informal attributes in all organisations in Japan, as elsewhere. See Sedgwick 2003.

6 Three recent exceptions to my implicit criticism of superficiality with regard to analysis of Japanese media artefacts are Iwabuchi (2002), Miller (2006) and Condry (2006).

7 I would be interested to know from colleagues working in Sinology if this is the case for the study of China as well.

8 Perhaps all Asian nations have borne the scars of 'exoticism' from traditional Western academic perspective (see Said 1978). However, Japan may operate in an exotic 'class of its own' due to perhaps its relatively recently concluded over 250 years of isolation:1600–1867. This is a period, of course, during which every other Asian nation, like nearly every nation in the world, directly and substantively felt the impact of Western imperialism. That Japan's self-imposed isolation was in direct reaction to this process both acknowledges imperialism's global importance as it demonstrates – in an early setting – the radical means the central Japanese polity may take in order to achieve national political ends.

9 In my view this mode of operation in the social science of Japan culminated with the three-volume set, *The Political Economy of Japan*. I include the titles here as the approaches so represented are interesting: *The Domestic Transformation*, Yamamura and Yasuba (eds), 1987; *The Changing International Context*, Inoguchi and Okimoto (eds), 1988; *Cultural and Social Dynamics*, Kumon and Rosovsky (eds), 1992. The project was also notable for the explicit collaboration of Japan specialists from both Japanese and Western universities. Another excellent, and more critically informed, interdisciplinary edited volume is Gordon's (1993), *Postwar Japan as History.*

10 Ironically, both China and India, if less developed than Japan, have also traditionally been marginal in anthropology due to their 'complexity' (Appadurai 1986).

11 An exception here is Ruth Benedict's, *The Chrysanthemum and the Sword*, originally published in 1946, which has been reprinted time and time again over the years.

12 The revaluation of the yen in the 1985 Plaza Accord, which was the formal international agreement negotiated in order to redress imbalances of trade between the West and Japan, also accounts for the proliferation of new 'Japanese' factories abroad, such as YamaMax. The political economic context of Japan's international (business) relations will be treated in detail in the next chapter.

13 Official, that is, state-sponsored, programmes bringing native-English-speaking, recent graduates to Japan's middle and high-school classrooms has also been influential in inculcating a new generation of Japan scholars. Beginning in the late 1970s with a mere handful of participants, the original Fulbright English Fellows, and later the Monbusho English Fellows programmes, sponsored first by the US Government, and then taken over by the Japanese Ministry of Education, has expanded into the JET (Japan English Teachers) programme that now brings over 4,000 'teachers' to Japan each year. See McConnell (2000).

14 These successes notwithstanding, *nihonjinron* continues to be heatedly discussed among anthropologists of Japan. See, for instance, debate on the topic from 25 November 2000 to 5 December 2000 among members of the East Asia Anthropologists' discussion group at website: <EASIANTH@LISTSERV.TEMPLE.EDU.>

15 For instance, Kondo's (1990) and Ivy's (1995) work – which treat 'tradition' in modern Japan, albeit in quite different ways – is widely read outside of 'anthropology of Japan'. Both works have attracted criticism from Japanologists, some of it justified on analytical grounds, other based, I believe, on envy regarding the relatively broad readership of these books.

16 In an otherwise extremely interesting and thorough paper on the history of Japanese management, Gao (1998: 94–100) seems to fall into this trap.

17 At least one can take heart that as Japanese 'culture' is still under general discussion, even if dismissed by some as an irrelevant analytic vehicle, acknowledging intellectual tradition in the social science of Japan is taken seriously.

18 Not unlike 'globalisation' I consider that the ubiquity of the term 'culture' in general usage – in lay contexts, business, the media and academia – makes it more interesting. Although among anthropologists 'culture' has witnessed considerable slippage, *pace* Strathern (1995) (her title is 'The nice thing about culture is that everyone has it'), culture continues to be conceptually useful or, for the moment, not replaced as a shorthand for describing the phenomenon of context generating meaning for persons.

19 In addition to the new 'transnational' corporation, Westney (1999: 21) notes the similar 'multilocal form' (Prahalad and Doz 1987) and the 'heterarchy' (Hedlund 1986).

20 While technically I believe the term 'transnational' corporation most parsimoniously describes any corporation whose activities cross national borders, in preferring in this study to use the term 'multinational corporation', I am purposely using the commonly recognised term. I am thereby marking out non-engagement in debate over various definitions of 'multinational', or 'global', or 'transnational' or 'international' corporations, which is not central to this study. The term 'transnational' corporation is used by the United Nations Conference on Trade and Investment's (UNCTAD), Division of Transnational Corporations and Investment (DTCI); a research institute charged with studying the activities of these organisations. For definitions different from those used by the United Nations, see, as an example, Bartlett and Goshall (1989: 13–18, 48–71) as well as my discussion to immediately follow.

21 This was due to macroeconomic mismanagement in Japan, rather than any difficulties with the early stages of expanding Japanese overseas production. It was responsible, furthermore, for the collapse of the Asian market in 1997 from which the region has only slowly recovered.

22 While appealing in principle, in practice the transnational model does not take account of the relative structural power of the 'home'–headquarters organisation over its 'local–foreign' subsidiaries. The problem is that the hollowing out of the authority of the centre, while theoretically attractive, is difficult to realise. In short, 'headquarters' does not like to lose control of the resources, especially financial assets, that would be implied in an authentically decentralised model. This matter will be taken up broadly throughout this ethnographic study as it is sited at a 'local' subsidiary, and so includes analysis of its (financial, technological and personal) relations with its 'home' organisation(s).

23 I entertain the contrarian view that, while it is clear that Japanese firms are not matching the organisational shifts towards multinationalisation or transnationalisation of their Western counterparts, and thereby are simplistically perceived as unworthy models, they are, rather, operating on a different developmental/evolutionary trajectory – a separate continuum – from that of their Western counterparts. I will not be taking up this problem except to offer the following comment. Although Japanese corporations are subject to the same general set of structural pressures in terms of technological innovation and the global political

economy as any other corporations, that these structural facts should generate equivalent forms of organisation is the crudest form of reductionism. It has, furthermore, been disproved by the 'case of Japan' itself in analyses of the organisational forms generating its own 'modernity' from the mid-nineteenth century onwards. Perhaps the best look at Japan's early, modern organisational forms is Westney's (1987), astutely entitled, *Imitation and Innovation: The Transfer of Western Organizational Patterns to Meiji Japan*. What was witnessed in the 'boom' of interest in Japanese organisational patterns in the 1980s was a (temporary) reversal in the standard direction of imitation and innovation.

24 Indeed this is how Bartlett articulates it, and so acknowledges the extreme difficulties of matching conceptual notions and formal organisational structures and processes, as described above regarding hollowing out headquarters' authority over subsidiaries.

25 I include machines, documents and other physical and representational attributes of the firm as constitutive of these same cross-cultural and organisational relations, a theoretical point I elaborate at some depth in this study, especially in Chapter 4.

26 I am drawing on Scott's sense of 'resistance' here, deployed in his analysis of peasant labour–plantation owner politics in Malaysia (1985, 1976). To my reading, Scott does not understand accommodation except as a form of resistance: a means of temporarily gaining (limited) power or influence in particular moments of interaction across these two groups. While politically more radical, his position limits the analytic usefulness of 'accommodation'. I understand accommodation in a necessary, but contextually broader, dialectic with 'resistance' that *minimally* recognises the withholding of accommodation as a form of resistance but also understands accommodation as meaningful in less negative ways.

Let us note here, however, the contextualised character in the emphases deployed in the use of such analytical tools. The polarisation of peasants and plantation owners in Malaysia is far more extreme, structurally and otherwise, than that of French labour *and* French management and French workers and managers *and* Japanese managers at YamaMax. I am Marxist enough to not call them different in kind, but there are systemic distinctions in 'capital's' exploitations that allow for far more overlap of interests among all of those working at 'YamaMax' than in 'Sedaka', Scott's village/plantation site.

27 See, for instance, Werbner and Modood's (1997), *Debating Cultural Hybridity*. For commentary, see Narayan 1993; Papastergiadis 1995; Strathern 1996.

28 My intent in forwarding these particular pairs is illustrative. I am not claiming equivalence in terms of their capacity to bear analytic weight. For formulations that specifically understand 'globalisation' in terms of binary relations, see Robertson 1992: 178; Jameson 1998: xii.

29 Of course, this process is assisted analytically by the observation that those persons enjoying ethnographic scrutiny elaborately name themselves, i.e. articulate differences, in relation to other categories of persons and things.

Meanwhile within the anthropological discipline itself, the most extensive and least attractive form of generating and maintaining categorical distinctions has perhaps appeared under the rubric of hierarchical stages of socio-'Cultural' evolution leading to its pinnacle in Western 'Civilisation'. See Stocking (1987) for an overview of the Victorian anthropology implicated here.

30 I would add here explicitly, however, that rejection of the possibility of 'finding' empirically 'clean' 'data' does not in principle reduce the analytical power of 'scientific' method; it merely makes our understanding of its findings and processes more realistic (see, for instance, Shapin and Schaffer 1985), and it allows for other means and methods toward knowledge. My own view is that washing

down the drain attention to methodological rigour with the sullied waters of 'objectivity', is short-sighted, recently all too frequent and will, ultimately, undermine the credibility of openly sensitive, non-statistically based social analysis. Indeed, the means of gathering information and the technical parameters of argumentation deployed by those I have named above as constructionists – as well as such academic heroes as Foucault and Derrida – is thoroughly caught up in the *textual* prerogatives – at the very least – of scientific method even if, in some cases, their analysis is (appropriately) turned onto the foundations and implications of that very method itself. (See Derrida (1967), for instance, on the Greek roots of Western thought and theory.)

31 I will further examine, later in this chapter, the reasoning behind a focus on this particular type of ethnographic site in analysis of globalisation.

32 I, of course, acknowledge that this problem has attracted substantial interest (for example, Leach 1977 [1954]), although rarely in analysis of modernised contexts.

33 The 'velocity of money' is an economic principle demonstrating how access to credit generates greater quantities of economic activity, and therefore the assumption of a greater quantity of human welfare, than would be the case without it. In neo-classical economics this is a fundamental justification for the systemic preference of the moneyed economy over barter or other forms of exchange.

34 Nothing changes hands in such transactions except information regarding claims. As the most liquid of commodities money is purely representational until translated, usually at a very local level, into goods or services. This fluidity accounts for its communicative speed and its penetration right up to the point of translation. For an extraordinarily original, early analysis of the effects of money on sociality, see Simmel (1978 [1907]); and commentary on Simmel by Poggi (1993).

35 With the exception of subsidiaries in South East Asia, where they were Japanese, the top position in all subsidiaries of the Yama magnetics division outside of Japan, i.e. in Europe and North America, was held by local nationals. This particular finding shall be pursued in other research projects from the present study.

36 The reference is to claims about consciousness within 'diasporic communities'. For an efficient synopsis of the 'problem' with diasporas, see Clifford (1997: 244–78). In keeping with the limitations inflicted on 'diaspora' through its overuse, Clifford's article arrives at the term's analytical margins and diffuses altogether. To my reading the article is successful, but it would be extraordinary had its ultimate diffusion been deployed as an intentional textual proxy for contemporary usage of the term – 'diaspora' – it seeks to describe.

37 There is fuller commentary on what I call the 'new ethnography' in the final chapter.

38 I might note here that the 'academic' enterprise generally occupies a similarly high status in Japan or, in any case, that most members of large, Japanese industrial firms who I have met respect serious 'scientific' work and the important role of universities in their society. My experience of this matter, and its effects upon my research, has been quite different at both US and British firms. Here, to over-generalise, I have occasionally experienced hostility, especially from high-ranking managers, that is invested, from my perspective, with the feel of a 'class' divide between the 'practical' work of industry and the intellectual 'pretences' of academia. That said, I have not yet made the effort to organise long-term ethnographic fieldwork in either country at the depth I have experienced elsewhere. Should I do so, it will be interesting to see how, or if, my perceptions evolve over time.

39 I often spoke with those who worked on the shopfloor about their experiences. However, I did so away from 'the line' – where my immediate presence could

literally put their and my life in danger – interacting with them informally during breaks or after their work was finished.

40 The next chapter's general description of the technical work of YamaMax includes a general argument about mass production as a full time effort to 'create' regularity and repetition. In this context engineers' attention to what is 'going wrong' is an accurate description of how they focus their time, not a negative general outlook on the world.

41 Chapter 5 is devoted to a longitudinal, sociological analysis of this office space, as articulated by some of the French engineers who occupied it.

2 Japan's globalisations and a 'subsidiary' in France

Five rooms with five views (in a factory)

At 7.45 a.m., at a subsidiary of a Japanese consumer electronics firm in rural central France, four Japanese engineers huddle over a faxed message that was waiting for them when they arrived that morning at 7:30. They are distraught to learn that according to the R&D division in Chiba, Japan their new chemical formulation – the basis of the latest version of their videotape – is 'out of specification' in three of seven key parameters. Their own in-house quality assurance results, in hand for the last two weeks, had shown a tendency towards *supeku outo* ('spec out') in only one parameter. The fax is brief, written in a rather *teinei* (formal) Japanese. The chief engineer, Otake-san, is soon on the phone with his colleague in Chiba requesting a detailed report and his colleague's *feeringu* (feeling) concerning a revised schedule to move this new formulation into production. On the wall is a company poster with the letters 'c' and 's' in giant ink brushstrokes admonishing 'customer satisfaction'.

At 8.30 the French *directeur general*, Monsieur Cardin, hurries in from the front car park, reserved for general managers and above, to make a call he had arranged to his product division's chief of parts purchasing at Tokyo headquarters. Yesterday afternoon the French directeur received a solid semi-annual price from the Chinese firm that currently supplies 40 per cent of the plastic cassettes containing videotape. The price is 8 per cent lower than his other suppliers, all Japanese firms. In highly accented English, over the phone he tells 'Tokyo' that he wants to increase his Chinese share to 70 per cent. A long and largely friendly discussion takes place during which he explains to his colleague in Japan, 'After 10 years of production we have just broken even for the first time due to enormous cost-down efforts. We want to extend this effort to our case suppliers'. Three weeks later he is informed that he may increase his Chinese supply to 55 per cent. He tells me he is pleased, saying he expected less. He comments in his lilting, southern French, 'This sort of internal supply relationship between "Tokyo" and its subcontractors in Japan is part of our cost of doing business'. Later in our conversation he notes in an ironic tone, 'Now that we are "in the black" [making a profit] we have to pay a higher proportion of general advertising costs to the Europe Office'. Lining the walls of the hallway that approaches his private office are oversized copies of advertisements for Yama products that are currently appearing in over eighty-five European magazines and are backed up by television campaigns, specific to each national setting, that, it is estimated, are viewed by at least 36 million European households daily.

Watanabe-san, the Japanese accounts manager who has been at YamaMax for nearly five years, wears elegant Paris fashions and James Joyce-style, wire-rimmed glasses. He tells me of the struggle over his first two years to increase his fluency in French and so gain the respect of his local colleagues. (Those French managers who have been here throughout his stay acknowledge his efforts and successes with the language, as they implicitly criticise other Japanese managers for their poor French.) Both of Watanabe-san's children were born in France and his family has enjoyed a spacious and relaxed home life. He and his wife are bemoaning their imminent return to Tokyo. Watanabe-san recounts to me the history of the start-up of Yama-Max over a decade earlier. At the time he was still a student at Keio; an elite, private Tokyo university. The stories are complete with the embellishments typical of multiple retelling: larger-than-life individuals and circumstances. The practical details revolve around a local French politician's seduction, via fine food and drink, of one of Yama's high-level Japanese executives, who visited the area several times over a two-year period in the early 1980s. Watanabe-san tells me, with undisguised irony, 'Our executive chose this site, several hundred kilometres from the most practical port, and is now well into his retirement'. Almost angrily he states that French government officials have been made aware that the company would never consider another 'greenfield'[1] investment in France until the tax rates on foreign operations, out of sync with the rest of Europe, are reduced. Watanabe-san has clearly become a francophile, and draws me several maps over the next few weeks of the nearest city's best French restaurants, all unaffordable to me. Meanwhile, although the other Japanese managers are pleased that they can converse with me in Japanese, my conversations with Watanabe-san chart a trajectory based on time of day. We start out in French but as we fatigue move into the mutually more comfortable Japanese.

The young wife of a Japanese engineer tells me about her and her husband's journey last weekend to the nearest Japanese restaurant, which just opened in a city 150 kilometres to the south. She says that even though the chef was Japanese the ingredients and the flavour were poor. Although in the first year here rice made up much of their luggage on two return trips from Japan, they have found a shop in Paris that sells very good rice from Spain which she says is grown on a Japanese-managed farm. Along with two of the other wives of YamaMax's eight male Japanese managers, she has been teaching Japanese two hours per week to twenty-five interested French employees at YamaMax. Although she is studying French, she says that after a year and a half she has only made one French friend, one of her students of Japanese: Gonzalez-san.

Madame Gonzalez's mother is Spanish, as are both of her 'French' husband's parents. Her main job is to maintain the computer program that tracks all of the over 400 salaries in the firm. She has been very friendly and helpful in explaining the salary, flex-time, and extremely complex benefit programmes; especially so in clarifying the thinking behind programmes that are unique to the firm and were designed in-house, and the national programmes to which the firm is subject to regular inspection by the French authorities. She says that her (French) boss's current headache is how to cope with a warning from the Bureau of Employment. By law, employees may only work 40 hours per week with a maximum of 92 hours of overtime per year. Her boss suspects that someone in the firm has reported to the Bureau that several French production managers have been regularly spending 45–50 hours per week at work. She says that everyone knows about the fierce temper of the chief Japanese engineer, Otake-san, who has shaken up the production division since his arrival about three years ago. Human resources staff now has a betting pool based on guesses about Otake-san's next day off; whoever chooses the closest date is taken to lunch by the other six. It is now a standing joke between them that they no longer know each other: of seventy-five potential lunches they have only had sixteen.

These five vignettes are brief expressions of my sense that anthropological analysis of 'globalisation' should be seated in the general day to day experiences of persons; albeit in this ethnography persons directly engaged with a multinational corporation with truly global reach. I highlight, therefore, the 'global' as *produced* by, and productive of, local activity; that is, the external and apparently abstract resonances of the 'global' as 'macro' activity are rooted in the activities and perceptions of persons. I also understand, and will explore in this study, organisations as central 'organising' contexts between individuals and their understanding of the global. As such, the vignettes above seat quotidian experience within the context of an obviously globalised organisation. That said, I shall try to demonstrate finally that in theoretical terms the 'organising' of their perceptions of the global, while perhaps exaggerated by their membership in a multinational corporation, is not different in kind from that occurring generally in the contemporary experience of modernity.

The vignettes may also serve to suggest that large Japanese multinational corporations, especially manufacturers, are engaged in the most intensive global interactions among all Japanese organisations. Even as they stand, these slices of organisational life push the considerable domestic Japanese implications of such global operations through the sieve of a subsidiary of a Japanese firm in France. When we think of keywords relating to 'Japan and the world' then – for example, financial flows, government and private foreign relations, media, the movement of ideas (including technology transfers), labour, law, families abroad, careers, education – it is difficult to find any arena untouched by Japan's multinational corporations. And this is the case for Japan more than any other nation. In the language of political science it would be written this way: Japan's late-twentieth-century global interactions are dominated by the spread of Japanese capital in a mercantilist form driven by business–state coalitions. In other words, Japanese corporations are the central filter through which 'Japan' interacts with the world, collectively surpassing the Japanese state as an actor in international affairs.[2] These corporations are critical to analysis of a changing Japan.

Having forwarded their relevance, how is one to treat these grandiose subjects? As a consequence of their enormous complexity, large organisations, and especially multinational corporations, are indeed unwieldy subjects for anthropology, which has traditionally favoured analysis of far more discrete units. Let us begin our work, however, by looking into general globalising pressures upon Japanese multinational corporations and then making our way into the somewhat more discrete local frame of a Japanese corporation's subsidiary in France that is the ethnographic focus of this study. As I shall show, these pressures have in a very short period of time required formal acknowledgement by these corporations of higher institutional, read international, complexity than that which they had grown familiar. This acknowledgement has, in turn, generated organisational action. What, then, is the context in which Japanese multinational corporations have themselves understood, named and, so, attempted to tame their increasingly 'global' activities?

The political economy of Japanese investment in manufacturing abroad

The spreading in time, space and quantity of Japanese 'economic' exchanges has led to an expansion in Japan of the social capital of the notions of 'globalisation' and 'internationalisation' in domestic economic, political and social arenas.[3] By the late 1980s, with Japan's global economic work already in full blossom, Japan needed to tell the world and, more importantly, itself a story about its newly achieved worldwide influence. With significant cash reserves in hand, especially following the 1985 revaluation of the yen, the Japanese government became the world's biggest overseas development assistance (ODA) donor. Japan spread 'butter rather than guns' to the developing world via its own bureaucracy and in highly visible, and arguably disproportionate, economic support of the multilateral institutions; especially the International Monetary Fund, the World Bank and the Asian Development Bank, the latter of which always has a Japanese president. These moves coincided with a relative decline in US Government commitments to development, and so in filling a gap Japan could position itself as a major player in the 'development game' among its North American and Western European peers in the, at the time, Group of Seven (G-7) nations.

At the corporate level, surplus trade figures vis-à-vis most of the G-7 – and, except for some OPEC (Organization of Oil-Producing Countries) members, most of the world – exhibited explicitly Japan's relative wealth. By the early 1980s Japanese manufacturers, fearful of trade barriers into G-7 markets, moved into production abroad, especially in motor vehicles and electronics. In Europe, Japanese multinational corporations had recognised in the increasingly active moves toward a European Economic Community a threat to their global sales. The revaluation of the yen in 1985 generated more international political pressures for more private sector investment into these deficit countries. And here we begin to see highly visible investments of Japanese private capital into real estate, Hollywood and buy-outs of faltering industrial enterprises (such as Rover in the UK and steel firms in the US), while the Japanese Government assisted the US economy by buying a high volume of US treasury notes. Elsewhere, with government development aid behind them, Japanese corporations positioned themselves to benefit from huge profit-making opportunities in rapidly expanding markets, especially in South East Asia and China. Thus by providing investment, employment and/or development aid, Japanese entities became in a very short period of time important domestic economic, political and social players in a large number of foreign countries.

The material manifestations of globalisation for businesses of course depend on the 'sector' (the type of business) under discussion. In Japan's business media, for example, 'internationalisation' was for a long while the main attention-grabbing subject of pundits; it sold newspapers, magazines and television talk shows. Interest in 'internationalisation' also drove publishers to place more reporters abroad.[4] For its part, manufacturing has the particular characteristic of direct, high density and wide-ranging interactions with local environments. In the foreign context this has meant that compared with other types of Japanese enterprises, such as banks or trading houses, large numbers of foreigners and local institutions have been directly and intimately caught up in Japanese manufacturers' globalising processes. The vignettes that opened this chapter are an attempt to make real this sense of things on the ground in a Japanese manufacturer's subsidiary in France. And it is in this context that in the late 1980s there appeared a proliferation of terms such as 'internationalisation' and 'globalisation' in the slogans of Japanese corporations as well as the ministerial cajolings of the government and quasi-governmental organisations affiliated with them. As in government circles, these terms filtered down into Japanese manufacturing firms as overarching policies, reflecting 'goals' for what had in fact already occurred.

The case of the Yama Corporation is no different. The exploration for manufacturing sites and the planting of factory foundation stones in Europe trace an historical trajectory with the flow of international economic data and Japan's ever-increasing involvement in the high-level machinations of international politics and domestic economic conditions in a large number of nations. And in the coalition between business and the state that makes up the vast majority of 'Japan's' interactions with the world, factories such as YamaMax are the foot soldiers. While to stretch the analogy too far may be unseemly in a contemporary ideological environment favourable to the goals of liberal capitalism, I have heard Japanese businessmen from many corporations on any number of informal occasions use the phrase, *'Bizuness wa sensou desu'* (business is war). The potential for a 'Fortress Europe' was a threat that was taken seriously in Japan, and in the meeting rooms at Tokyo headquarters of the Yama Corporation.

Much of this battle is fought at the level of 'name recognition'. An early convert to placing marketing (especially advertising) at the core of its operations, Yama is one of the most well-known corporations in the world. Indeed the firm's 'name recognition' is probably only surpassed by that of Coca-Cola and McDonald's. In the accepted mores of commercial marketing this degree of 'global penetration' is understood within the firm as one of its key assets; as it is among its competitors.[5]

In public relations documents Yama claims that over '40 per cent of its products sold in Europe are manufactured there', up from 0 per cent fifteen years ago. Indeed, Yama prides itself as a globally oriented corporation and was indeed well ahead of its competitors in seeking out foreign markets for its Japan-manufactured products. A 1992 pamphlet entitled 'Yama and the new Europe' states that 'Global localisation, in principle, means that Yama aims to conduct as much business as possible locally, from product planning, to engineering and design, production, marketing, service and financing. Yama's operations in the European zone are staffed by local people, each one contributing to Yama's strengths and advantages as a truly global enterprise'. Be that as it may, as I have elaborated, Yama's investment in European manufacturing must be seen in the context of larger political economic forces at play in Japan.

Charting the Yama Corporation (in Europe)

Yama has some fifty 'companies' in Europe, but the site of this ethnography is one of its eight manufacturing plants. European headquarters, in a large German city, is supported by ten other companies (in Belgium, Switzerland, the Netherlands, the UK and Germany) which carry out such tasks as financial services, logistics (large-scale movement of goods), advertising, research and development (at centres in Germany and the UK) and computer operations for the entire group. At the centre of European operations sit the so-called, 'business group and manufacturing organizations'. These consist of: (a) consumer product manufacturing operations: including four factories, in the UK, Spain, Germany and France, where television, video and audio hardware is manufactured. This is supported, for example in logistics for the manufacturers, by two 'business group' organisations, in the Netherlands and the UK; (b) four 'professional products' organisations:

two in the UK and one each in the Netherlands and Germany supporting the technical requirements of clients using Yama products, predominantly imported from Japan, in the broadcast, medical and industrial sectors; (c) Yama's computers, semiconductors and peripheral components operations, are guided from European headquarters in Germany with the support of an organisation in the UK. The only European factory in this sector produces circuit boards in France; (d) the magnetic media division is overseen by headquarters in Germany and includes audiotape production factories in Italy and France, and videotape production in France.[6] Meanwhile, twenty-one 'sales and service' companies support the distribution of Yama products to retail markets. These companies can be found in Austria, Belgium, the Czech Republic, two in Denmark, Finland, France, Germany, Greece, Ireland, Italy, the Netherlands, Norway, Poland, Portugal, Russia, Spain, Sweden, Switzerland, Turkey and the UK.

In combining all of the above operations, the Yama Corporation employs 14,000 persons in Europe, and worldwide some 150,000. Year by year, company public relations figures consistently claim that 49 per cent of Yama employees are found in Japan, and 51 per cent abroad. Around 25 per cent of total sales are in Japan, with the US and Europe about even at 30 and 29 per cent each. In Europe sales consistently increased at 5 per cent per annum throughout the 1990s. Worldwide, video and audio products account for one-half of all of Yama's sales, with televisions the largest single other product, at 16 per cent.

My study site was the Yama organisation listed in the fourth category (d), above, that manufactures videotape in France, and called, as we know, YamaMax.[7] I have described it above in regional terms, for example, as a factory in Europe. It might also be described – in terms of the total global organisation of the Yama Corporation – as one factory among nine, within a worldwide network of five overseas subsidiary factories and four factories in Japan, all producing 'magnetic' products, and increasingly digital technology-based products. Meanwhile, as I have mentioned, each of the nine factories in Yama's magnetic products division is, effectively, in competition for resources, especially large capital investments, from the administrative 'centre' in Japan.

YamaMax might also be described as the product of social relations and career progression. That is, in an effort to focus engineering and manufacturing skills and knowledge, careers in large Japanese consumer electronics firms like Yama tend to track within particular product divisions. Most of the top managers in the Yama magnetic products division thus had years of experience of at least one or two factories as well as accurate knowledge about other subsidiaries in the network. They had perhaps been involved in decision-making regarding initial investments and, certainly, had closely tracked developments at those subsidiaries. Earlier in their careers they may literally have worked with particular machines that, in turn, were transferred to another factory, typically abroad. Indeed, every Japanese member of 'magnetics' manufacturing at Yama – whether they were just beginning, at mid-career or ending their careers – had personal contacts across its global manufacturing network and they could always recount stories, whether witnessed or not, about technical and personal issues that unfolded at other Yama magnetics factories.

Thus, although at the highest echelons of the Yama Corporation top directors might move across to head a product, or some other, administrative division in order to bring in fresh leadership, the vast majority of members of the Yama's magnetic products 'centre' was a group that shared extensive, in-depth knowledge about the technical work and social relations constituting Yama magnetic products organisations, having developed their careers within those very organisations.[8] Let us not understand the 'centre', then, as an arm's-length entity separate from the subsidiaries, but an organisation embodying those of high rank in a set of personal relations across the magnetic tape division. I raise this issue here to make the point that while I could reproduce any number of formal organisational charts of YamaMax's position within the Yama Corporation, these are limited to a particular perspective at a particular point in time and used to merely fit the purposes of managers at that particular time. Over the long run, it is the relations of members to each other, and their influences and decisions regarding technology, research, finance, competition with other parts of the organisation and other firms, and so on, that is the core source of activity and change at Yama.

Siting YamaMax

YamaMax is found in a predominately rural prefecture, indeed one of France's poorest and most sparsely populated, in the centre of the country. Unemployment is relatively high in the prefecture. Jobs at Yama attract many applicants and turnover is low. There is no significant history of industrialisation, nor industrial radicalism, in the prefecture. Efforts of labour in other parts of the country, and the French public's general receptivity to it, have essentially guaranteed that through government oversight the interests of labour are fully integrated into the tasks of every French corporation's human resources department. Nothing as extreme as Britain's Thatcher revolution vis-à-vis trade unions and the national structure of industry has occurred in France, and indeed compared with my knowledge of industrial relations in the US, Japan, Thailand and the UK, labour conditions are highly favourable. The French Government's moves to cap benefits and annual guaranteed pay increases in state-owned enterprises, such as the French National Railroad, and industries such as truck drivers – and so begin to align French industrial relations with the rest of Europe – have led to numerous strikes and slowdowns over the last few years. An indicator of the high esteem with which the 'right to work' is held in France is the government's negotiations with industry over the last several years for a four day work week or the reduction of working hours to thirty-five hours to cope with rising unemployment. It remains to be seen whether President

Sarkovy's regime in Paris will be able to make the changes in industrial relations suggested in his election campaign.

While my central concern is with the social dynamics occurring at YamaMax, a cross-cultural industrial organisation, government industrial (and taxation) policy forms an important backdrop both vis-à-vis the rights and attitudes of French employees in any industrial firm and the reaction of Japanese managers to it. As described in the opening vignettes, it is telling that the Japanese accountant at YamaMax, Watanabe-san, explained to me in no uncertain terms that French taxation policy on industrial activity was so out of alignment with the rest of Europe that Yama would never consider another 'greenfield' investment – the development of a factory from scratch – until the policy changed.[9]

Yama has sited many of its manufacturing operations abroad in relatively obscure locations, rather than following the pack of other Japanese firms into the same areas of foreign countries. It is true that land may thereby be obtained cheaply and that traditional labour problems of industrialised, unionised national regions in host countries potentially bypassed. However, in my view, Watanabe-san's impression that YamaMax's location was impulsive rather than 'strategic' – logically thought out in terms of business imperatives – rings true. High-level executives are given the responsibility to take individual decisions on such matters at Yama. Unlike manufacturing itself, there is no blueprint for this process and these executives are trusted to get on with it as best they can. It is true that good relations from the outset with local government officials may prove very significant to the long-term success of an overseas operation. Furthermore, however distant from ports or otherwise, transportation costs within Europe are a relatively insignificant factor in the calculations of manufacturers. That is, for example, as a videocassette is made up of some nineteen parts, a percentage point difference in the cost of producing or buying any one of those parts will far outstrip the cost of adding a few hundred kilometres onto the haulage of an entire truckload of either parts or completed videocassettes. In any case, such an unorthodox siting for YamaMax, whether planned or not, perpetuates Yama's professionally-managed image as a maverick among Japanese companies. As such, the siting of YamaMax will remain an interesting enigma, an event from the past available for wide interpretation in the present.

On the ground at YamaMax

A high metal fence traces the perimeter of the rectangular-shaped 100,000 sq.m. grounds of YamaMax, one mile from a village of around 3,500 inhabitants where many of its French employees live. Some 100 metres from a motorway, YamaMax is officially in an 'industrial zone'. However, beyond the fence on its west and north sides are extensive forests, on its east side a tract of several small detached houses, beyond which is found a small wood-processing plant. Although members of the local population – including those who are also employees of YamaMax – will often go about their daily chores in the village on bicycles, YamaMax is invariably approached by car or truck by the small road on its south side, virtually at the off-ramp of the motorway. The grounds are entered by passing a metal barrier gate, which is always open except after midnight and on weekends when it is reopened between shifts. Bearing left beyond the gate is a large car park where all employees (except for the four general managers and the *directeur general*) leave their cars. This is surrounded on three sides by a low fence. The side facing the plant itself has a substantial fence through which employees must pass on foot through a locked, metal revolving door released by the passing of their personal magnetic card through a sensor.

Driving to the right upon passing the metal barrier gate one comes to a guardhouse with drop gate that is almost always down, as it marks access to the grounds proper. Truckers must stop at the guardhouse at this gate in order to deliver materials or take away videotapes. Here they are invited to make their business clear, as are all visitors. Straight past the guardhouse an internal road system surrounds the interconnected three buildings of YamaMax, providing access at several points depending on the business at hand. Between this road and the high, secure external fence are around 10 metres of light forest, inhabited by a very large number of rabbits.

As they approach the guardhouse, the general managers' (one Japanese and three Frenchmen) and the *directeur general*'s cars are usually recognised by the guard on duty, who ordinarily manages to press a button that automatically lifts the drop gate without requiring that they slow down.[10] The general managers and *directeur general* then bear left, winding briefly through an attractively landscaped area of pine, low bushes, lawn and three flagpoles bearing, at equal height, the French *Tricolore,* the Japanese Rising Sun and, in the middle, a flag with the Yama Corporation logo embossed on a white background. The top managers, and their guests, park as they wish in a large circular space fronting the main entrance. Here double-glass doors are surrounded by glass panels, centred on the wide pine-shingled and glassed front of TP1, YamaMax's main administrative building.

The buildings

YamaMax's physical plant is divided into three distinct buildings connected by two hallway systems. (See Figure 1.) In the smallest – TP1 – are found the private offices of the French *directeur general*, his French secretary and another French general manager. The open-plan offices of the accounting, purchasing, shipping, computer systems and human resources departments are also found here. There are male and female toilets with two stalls each, as well four nicely appointed meeting rooms. One meeting room is medium sized, windowed on two sides, and comfortably seats twenty-five people around a u-shaped table. At the front a movie screen may be lowered in front of a large whiteboard around which are found a large Yama television set and various audiovisual equipment on a trolley, including a computer which may be projected onto the movie screen. The other three meeting rooms are smaller; two of them, including that just off the *directeur general*'s office, have large tables and hold up to eight people. The remaining room, just to the right as one enters TP1 has a low, glass coffee table surrounded by low couches, armchairs and a large television set. On a sideboard are found various trophies YamaMax has received from the Yama Corporation (generally as recognition for achieving production targets). On the coffee table may be found two photo albums of two ground-breaking and two production-starting ceremonies at YamaMax. On each of these four occasions, YamaMax was visited by very high-level officers of Yama Corporation from headquarters in Japan, managers from European headquarters in Germany, and regional officials of the French Government. On TP1's cellar level are found a small canteen and changing rooms for assembly line workers in TP2.

TP2 opened at the same time as TP1, in 1986. It contains about 40,000 sq.m. of floor space, most devoted to the latter stages of the videotape production process. (I will briefly detail this entire process below.) TP2 also contains two large storage areas where finished product is held until it is shipped, and parts and non-toxic materials are kept until used in the production process. TP2 has the plant's largest meeting room, holding up to 100 people if folding chairs are arranged in rows. There are also four separate open-plan offices of managers overseeing quality control for the entire plant, the final stages of production (which takes place within TP2), storage and shipping tasks.

TP3 was built in the early 1990s to accommodate the earlier, more technically demanding stages of the production of videotape. The vast majority of my research time at YamaMax was spent in this building, so I would like to describe it in some detail. We might begin the social organisational history of TP3 by examining its architectural design. While we understand 'floor space' as the starting point (the lowest common denominator) for quantifying space within buildings, we might call 'floor space' within the shell of TP3 a prior construction. TP3's 30,000 sq.m. of 'floor space' is an expression of potentiality: it is literally the floor space of its foundation, so should TP3 be divided throughout into three floors it would in fact have 90,000 sq.m. of floor space. However, the tape production machinery within TP3 is of enormous scale, some of it requiring 50-foot ceilings, and where this is the case the 'ground' floor is sunken to accommodate machines that reach the roof.

Before entering TP3's main 'production area', one must first don hooded, blue nylon 'bunny suits' and clean trainers, all of which are found in designated lockers, respectively, in male and, much smaller, female changing rooms. (There are always sets of multiply-sized bunny suits, shoe coverings and lockers available for guests.) Then, with the push of a button, a glass door slides open and one enters through one side of an air chamber. Once the chamber is sealed, after pushing another button, for 15 noisy seconds intense air blowers, gushing from every direction, clear dust and static electricity off one's suit. The other door of the chamber slides open, and one crosses metal walkways and descends a steep set of stairs to enter the vast production area. This is filled with the sounds of very large machines and the dry, high-frequency pulse of the enormous quantities of electricity required to power them. A sparse collection of workers and engineers in their blue bunny suits goes about their various tasks. This production area also contains the slitting machines of the middle stages of the tape production process, which only require 15-foot ceilings, as well as two very quiet, enclosed tape quality assessment laboratories, behind glass doors, each packed with electronic and fine optical equipment and an occasional technician intensely at work.

Because of the scale of TP3 machinery only one section of 'floor space' in TP3 is currently divided into three floors. The bottom floor has storage areas and a few machine maintenance shops. The top floor is a windowed, empty space; a repository for computer equipment boxes, old fluorescent light bulbs, files of production information at least two years out of date, slices of magnetic tape (now collecting dust while propped against a wall) that had been subject to 'visual' (microscopic) inspection (and thereby provided a physical record of the quality of tape produced), and the odd cigarette butt. Especially hot in summer, in my few visits I never saw anyone on this top floor. While its objects may represent an archaeology of Yama-Max, it is a social void. My interests focused, rather, on the middle floor where the engineers, managers and staff overseeing the production work of TP3 have their desks, computers, telephones and fax machines; their office lives. The layout (see Figure 8) is a large open-plan office surrounded on three sides by four single manager offices, two open-plan rooms with three or four desks, and three meeting rooms. The two larger meeting rooms, holding up to twenty people at u-shaped tables, are named, respectively, 'Arc de Triomphe' and 'Tour Eiffel'. This office area is the site of the detailed ethnographic descriptions in Chapters 3, 4 and 5.

The land out of which the YamaMax grounds have been constructed rises slightly from south to north. As such the northernmost part of TP3 is, by design, surrounded by a bunker of sand and dirt upon which sits the north fence. Within this bunker two towers of pipes and ladders have been built. Fed by a series of enormous tanks, these towers are positioned to spray automatically appropriate liquid chemical compounds (or water) on TP3 should there be an explosion or fire from the many toxic and highly flammable materials used in production.

Producing videotape

Industrial production is not governed by seasonal, or daily, weather variation, nor marked day to day by what appears, comparatively, as ongoing sociality in hunting and gathering, or traditional sedentary agriculture. Especially at highly automated factories such as YamaMax, colleagues on the shopfloor are dispersed. They may be within visual range but the machinery is invariably loud, dangerous to life and limb, and where one, rarely, works directly with others it is in order to carry out technical procedures or, more likely, coping with machine failure. Sociality with shopfloor colleagues is thus confined to formal 'breaks', the changing rooms where the dustproof 'bunny suits' are donned, before and after meetings, meals during working hours – although many employees return home to take meals – and occasional after-work activities.

Although among managers and engineers breadth of responsibility requires more flexibility in activities and far more meetings, work is understood by everyone at YamaMax as a series of interventions upon a continuous cycle of production. Thus, for example, maintenance of a machine on a dual assembly line is preceded by increased output of both lines in order to create stocks so that total production goals are sustained. When, for instance, a segment of the production process is taken over for a test of a new product – which in the short run will produce no sellable output – managers of other segments become extremely anxious when planned 'downtime' is exceeded. It is as though every activity at YamaMax is conducted upon a moving walkway of production. Inside the factory one is reminded – through sound, sight and artefacts such as statistical charts and graphs – that regular production is inexorable. 'Production' is the primary noise, literally and metaphorically, through which every other aspect of work is pressed forward at YamaMax. My repetition of this point is intentional.[11]

There are several steps in the production of videotape, each with its own set of machinery. Each step is worth describing, if extremely briefly, as the manufacturing process preoccupies the French and Japanese engineers who are the central day to day subjects of this study: the technical foundation of work and skills through which language, organising and other aspects of communications at YamaMax are articulated. Each one of the eight steps articulated below is in itself a technical specialisation, with the complexities of the first five in particular, built up over decades of industrial science and experience (see Figures 2, 3, 4, and 5).

1) Mixing: magnetic particles in powdered form are dispersed in tanks containing a heated solvent of binders, dispersants and additives. In the course of its fabrication the composition and technical characteristics of the resulting liquid are permanently stabilised into a liquid magnetic paint.

2) Filtration and thickening: the magnetic paint must be perfectly homogenised, corresponding with a precise index of fluidity. A system of filters eliminates all particles or lumps larger than one micron. (One micron = 0.001 millimetre, or approximately one-twentieth of the diameter of a human hair.)

3) Induction, or painting: this is the most delicate part of the production process. It consists of spreading the magnetic paint to an exact thickness across a polyester film backing which is unrolled slowly and mechanically from spools – which look like giant paper towel rolls – 1.22 metres wide. Each spool holds 10,000 metres of polyester film backing. Depending on the type of magnetic tape being produced, there can be two stages to this painting process. The first places a non-magnetic band across the backing which increases the mechanical and electrostatic qualities of the tape, while the second applies the magnetic paint. In any case the painted ensemble – of magnetic paint on film backing – subsequently passes through a magnetised channel which orients all of the magnetic particles in the same direction.

4) Drying: the painted and magnetised tape is dried as it passes at around 350 metres per minute through hot, dust-free tunnels in an atmosphere of inert gas. Highly toxic solvent vapours in this step are recovered through vacuuming into a solvent-regenerating tank. Now dried, the 10,000 metre by 1.22 metre magnetic tape is rolled onto a bobbin.

5) Calendering, or resurfacing: in order to gain appropriate mechanical characteristics the magnetic tape is compressed by passing it through several sets of highly polished metal rollers, each 1.3 metres wide and heated to 60°C. It is then rerolled onto a bobbin, at which point it is called a 'jumbo roll'.

6) Ageing: in order to stabilise the chemical qualities of the magnetic tape, the 'jumbo roll' is stocked for 30 hours in an incubator at 15°C. and controlled humidity.

Once ageing is completed, the jumbo rolls may be stored until the next stage of the process begins. Indeed, during its first six years YamaMax began its manufacturing at this stage with aged jumbo rolls shipped in that had been manufactured at a 'sister plant' in Japan. In 1992, however, with the completion of TP3, YamaMax began its own manufacture of jumbo rolls. (The sociological significance of this event will be elaborated in Chapter 5.)

7) Slitting: the 1.22 metre by 10,000 metre jumbo rolls are unrolled and divided, making two rolls of 5,000 metres. Each 5,000-metre jumbo roll is unwound and 'slit' lengthwise by 49 razor-sharp knives, thus creating 48 'pancakes' around two feet in diameter and of exactly the width of the videotape with which we are all familiar. 'Pancakes' may then be processed into the next stage of production, or they may be stored.[12]

8) Winding, packaging, labelling, storage and shipping: moved to TP2 the pancakes of videotape are then wound – at various lengths corresponding to 60, 120, 180 and 240 minutes of playback time – into plastic video cases. As

described in the vignettes that opened this chapter, at YamaMax, plastic cases, or cassettes, are imported from both Yama subcontractors in Japan and a subcontractor in China. The loaded videocassettes are then labelled, packaged in brightly designed cardboard slip cartons (upon which 'Yama' appears from 10–15 times), heat-wrapped in cellophane, and boxed, ordinarily in sets of ten. About fifty boxes are then placed on a single pallet, which is wrapped automatically in plastic and taken by forklift into designated locations in the storage area. These pallets of fifty boxes of ten videos each, or 500 videos, are YamaMax's sales units for accounting purposes. The stockage area has three bays fitted to the size of the backdoors of the large trucks which carry them to markets throughout Europe, or to ships which disperse them throughout the globe.

The formal organisational structure of YamaMax

With the tasks occurring in the physical spaces of TP1, TP2 and TP3 in mind, the general logic of YamaMax's organisational chart emerges (see Figure 6). Apart from the movement of personnel listed on it, the design of this chart shifted several times during the eighteen months that I followed YamaMax's activities. In any case, the basic tasks involved in the activities of the plant are consistently represented on this organisational chart. Essentially, below the *directeur general* are tripartite task divisions: (a) General Administration and Control, (b) Production and (c) Quality. As indicated in the above descriptions, general administration is located in TP1, the administration of 'quality' in TP2, while its laboratories are in TP3. Manufacturing takes place in both TP3 and TP2, where production engineers also have their offices. The *directeur general* of YamaMax oversees general administration, with one general manager below him. There is one general manager in charge of quality, and two in production. Some 70 per cent of lower level managers, however, are in the production division, which takes up the vast majority of the time, expense and is understood as YamaMax's *raison d'être*.

Equality in local conditions of work

Some 440 persons are employed, in three general categories, by YamaMax: around 300 are workers (of which 37 are women), 97 technicians and administrators (of which 16 are women), and 42 managers (of whom two are women). (All eight of the Japanese managers and engineers at the plant are male and are considered 'managers'.) The average age of men is 32, women 34.

Salary levels are broken down along five grades of employee which generally correspond with education levels. In the French education system students are tracked from around age 12. The lowest achievers move into training programmes at age 14 for potential employment from age 16. (At

YamaMax such persons are likely only to be among temporary contract labour.) The next higher group would have passed a general exam called a bep, two or three years before the *baccalaureate*, or *bac*, which I recognise as an exam system between GCSEs and A levels in the British education system. These two latter groups make up (a) *'operateurs'* with salaries of 85,000–102,000 French francs (ff) per annum (£9–11,000);[13] (b) *'regleurs'*, who have passed the *bac*, but probably in a limited number of subjects. Their salaries are 102–50,000 ff (£11–16,000); (c) *'techniciens'* have at least two years of education or training beyond the *bac*. *Techniciens* make up the majority of the mid-level technicians and administrators at YamaMax, their lowest positions being foremen on the factory floor. Salaries are between 140–200,000 ff (£15–22,000); (d) *'chefs de service'* are managers. At a minimum they have two years of education beyond the *bac* plus extensive experience. If engineers, they usually have five years of education beyond the *bac* or, in our terms, a university degree. Salaries are between 200–350,000 ff (£22–39,000); (e) finally, the *'directeurs'* are general managers and the *directeur general*. They have the same minimal qualifications as *'chefs de service'* but more extensive experience, and salaries between 300–450,000 ff (£33–50,000). (I was unable to gather where the *directeur general*'s salary stood. My impression, however, is that his salary was certainly at the upper end, and probably exceeded, this scale.) If we assume that the *directeur general* was paid 450,000 ff (£50,000) per annum, his salary was, then, 5.3 times that of the lowest-paid worker.

Meanwhile, Japanese staff are paid according to their ranking as though they were in Japan. This is an entirely different pay scale which would place all of them well within, if not above, salaries comparable to category 5, French *directeurs*. Japanese staff are given complete moving expenses in going abroad, generous housing allowances, other special monetary benefits and their own car. As a result, they 'bank' most of their monthly salary. They are paid in French francs, which means they are vulnerable to exchange rate fluctuations as most of their pay is transferred to Japan where it is, usually, used to pay off mortgages. Even if difficult and challenging in other ways, the economic advantages to Yama's Japanese employees of an overseas posting are obvious.

Among all French employees the only difference in benefits is that each *directeur*, or general manager, is given the use of a company car as are, as noted, each of the Japanese managers. The canteen is subsidised, and all employees get 25 per cent off the retail purchase price of the extensive line of Yama products. Of course the amount going into pensions and social security depends on salary itself, the proportion varying according to complicated schemes concerning length of service designated by the French Government. Bonuses are paid in a fixed formula if total profits exceed the expectations of the original budget for the year. Unlike Japan, where bonuses may account for two to three months of salary, they are not significant in France, where pension and bonus systems are tightly regulated by national law. The Japanese managers, however, like their colleagues in Japan, are paid a large bonus directly into their bank accounts in Japan.

As mentioned above, YamaMax is found in a rural part of central France where unemployment, and underemployment (due to seasonal agricultural work), is relatively high. Among the 300 *operateurs* and *regleurs*, drawn largely from the local population, ten left their jobs in 1993, seven in 1994 and twenty in 1995. All were replaced, virtually immediately, from among the twenty-two temporary workers, on short-term contracts, among the 300. Temporary workers are, in effect, a valve to cope with the many unexpected turns of manufacturing. At YamaMax temporary workers made up a very low proportion (7 per cent) of workers and were generally on three- to six-month contracts. After at least three months, although in some cases this can be 12 months, temporary employees were eligible for permanent employment. *Technicians* and higher-level personnel are drawn from all over France. Turnover rates are very low indeed at these higher levels in the organisation; usually only two or three persons per year.

YamaMax is not unionised. However, by law, it has a *comité d'établissement* with annually elected representatives from each of the three general categories of employee. There is an official meeting every three months during which the concerns of employees are raised by the *comité* with representatives of the firm, led by the human resources director. The *comité* also organises *club* activities (typically, sporting events, including hunting on local estates), feasts, cut-rate group trips for employees (including in the years of my fieldwork, tours of Thailand and the east coast of the US), and manages a small store where goods, including champagne, are sold to members at wholesale prices. YamaMax provides around 50 per cent of the costs for *comité* activities. The rest is accounted for with a general charge to employees and, more significantly, direct charges to the participants of any particular activity, especially trips abroad.

Apart from national holidays, all employees have 25 days off per annum. Japanese are also given the right to 25 days off per year, though few use their full quota. French staff, in alignment with French labour law, also have the opportunity to take unpaid sabbaticals, usually to care for infant children, for up to one year with a guarantee to return to their jobs.

Distinctions in locations of work at YamaMax

Administrative and managerial staff must work eight hours per day, on 'flex-time' between 8 a.m. and 6 p.m., five days per week. The assembly line of TP2 is in operation 350 days per year, twenty-four hours a day. In TP2, three shifts work from 5 a.m. to 1 p.m., 1 p.m. to 9 p.m. and from 9 p.m. to 5 a.m., with a 30 per cent increase in pay for night work. The teams on each shift are stable, cycling internally for their two days off per week. In TP3, work is continuous, 365 days per year. Five teams work shifts in cycles of three days on, two off. After fifteen weeks, each team in TP3 has worked through the entire cycle of shifts.

The physical division between TP2 and TP3 has considerable sociological implications. As described above, the earlier-established TP2 continues with its original tasks of assembling and packaging videocassettes, while TP3 is involved in the far more technically-demanding production of magnetic tape, or jumbo rolls: steps 1–7 in my description of the production process. General skills levels of workers and engineers are higher in TP3, where the environment carries the hum of high technology, with employees maintaining dust-free, computer-controlled machinery. In TP2 the loading of 'pancakes' into videocassettes is, similarly, conducted under dust-free conditions. However, the rest of the work of TP2, especially packaging, is noisy and dirty. It is conducted by the least trained, with the highest proportion of temporary employees and the highest proportion of industrial accidents. As one would expect, shift work makes interactions between TP2 and TP3 shopfloor employees relatively circumscribed. Engineers at Yama-Max, however, are expected to operate within a general paradigm of overview of 'total production'. Here each stage of the production process is understood to be fed from the previous stage and, in turn, to feed the next. The 'progressive' metaphor in Japanese manufacturing firms is to understand each stage as a 'customer' for the next; thus internalising into the activities of the factory the notion of 'customer service'. If articulated as a principle, the technological and sociological divisions between TP2 and TP3, however, made this sort of metaphor largely irrelevant in practice at YamaMax.

While necessarily 'mechanical' in places, this chapter has presented the structural outline of our core ethnographic site: YamaMax. Through vignettes describing the day to day concerns of some of its members, I have briefly reviewed the value of conducting research in organisations in order to come to terms with global phenomena, a theme elaborated throughout the book. The position of the Yama Corporation and YamaMax within the political economy of Japanese international political economic relations has been elaborated, as has the physical plant, production of goods, hierarchical labour relations and formal organisational design.

Notes

1 A 'greenfield' is an industrial building site which has never had a building. A 'brownfield' site had buildings on it that have been demolished or transformed by the current owner.
2 While one does not want to overstate the potential cooperation of the wide range of interests engaged in Japanese business abroad, the argument can be soundly made that these entities represent a far more unified force than the corporations of any other of its peers in the, so-called, 'Group of Eight' (G-8) 'advanced industrial' nations.
3 'Internationalisation' is written in Japanese in *katakana* (Japanese's phonetic alphabet for foreign words) and in Chinese characters (as *kokusaika*). 'Globalisation'

has remained largely a *katakana*-based term, when it, and its derivatives (e.g. 'global,' 'globalised') are not romanised.

4 'Internationalisation' and 'globalisation' continue to engage much media attention in Japan. In the headlines, however, they were eventually superseded by more personalised subjects; such as discussion of *karoshi* (death by overwork) (based on several reports of businessmen who, without particular medical problems, had collapsed and died at their desks), and, later, by 'the decline of Japan's lifetime employment system'. Following this were found surprisingly ironic Japanese media reports of 'tearful' apologies by corporate leaders whose financial institutions had failed.

5 I put these terms in inverted commas as they are typical of the language used to describe these features at multinational corporations. While their promotional methods may vary greatly, nearly all corporations, regardless of their home countries, place great value on name recognition. This is especially so among corporations producing for 'consumer' markets, as opposed to 'specialist' markets. (An example of a huge specialist market is the defence sector.)

6 Based on 'old' technology, the generation of profits in the production of analogue audio and videotap is increasingly difficult as its worldwide manufacturing shifts to less-developed countries. Thus YamaMax is in the process of – 'temporarily'– converting its operations to mini floppy discs and, more fundamentally, the production of digital tape. The technology and manufacturing experience of mounting either analogue or digital media onto tape continues as the core know-how of this division.

While it may seem that in producing an ethnography of a factory that produces videotape I am studying a 'dead' technology, the details of producing particular products are relevant here to the extent that they generate a 'language' in the discourse of my informants, which we need to understand to get our bearings on their day to day concerns. I have also studied micro-chip manufacturers, and automobile companies, and can confirm that the central matters regarding cross-cultural relations (in factory settings) that I am concerned with in this book, and elsewhere, do not vary in any significance according to the particular products produced. Also, I am currently involved in a separate project that considers longitudinally the impact on persons and organisations of the decline of technologies for which particular persons and organisations have built up significant 'know-how'.

7 Viewed from the perspectives of other disciplines, it may seem an anachronism of anthropology that my field site, in this case the name of the multinational and its subsidiary, is disguised. The disadvantage is that there is a popular comparative literature that I cannot cite concerning the company. Overall, however, the advantages far outweigh this disadvantage. I could not have enjoyed the degree of access required for in-depth study without this foundation of anonymity. Negotiating access to this company was a difficult process – as described in the last chapter, it was arranged over a period of years – and their final acceptance of my day to day participant–observation came to be based on their belief that I could be trusted to sustain their anonymity. Once this occurred I was no longer 'handled'. Indeed, I was often surprised that no effort was made to shield sensitive matters from me. To date, critics of this anonymity have been consultants and a small number of academics; usually individuals with a greater interest in filling in their knowledge of specific firms than in generating general analysis. While the motivations of the anthropologist and the businessperson are quite different, business-people, familiar with the logic of screening information, have generally appreciated the value and intent of this aspect of my methodology.

The ethics of the matter, of course, stand for the study of modern enterprises as they do for the more mainstream communities of anthropological inquiry. At the level of intimacy required for sound ethnographic work, it would simply present too great a risk to individuals within companies if even the company were named, to say nothing of the potential damage to the firms vis-à-vis their competitors. This is not a study of the past, but of firms and careers in process.

Apart from matters of ethics and methodological taste, there are other advantages in disguising the names of companies as fieldwork sites, of which I have studied several. They are so well known that mentioning them inevitably pushes forward images of products and, among specialists, notions as to specific corporate styles. These conventional wisdoms are extremely difficult to dislodge, in spite of claims that we are willing to start fresh with new data. While I am at times sorely tempted to debunk publicly held notions as to how particular corporations are run, this is not the goal of this research project. I will continue to simply tip my hat at the successes of these firms' public relations departments.

8 I shall elaborate upon the dynamics of personal/professional progression as experienced by individual members of YamaMax in the next chapter.

9 Toyota's construction of their main European manufacturing plant in France reveals, however, that there is variation among Japanese firms on this matter. I would guess that Toyota's choice was based on France's ideal geographic position at the centre of Western Europe and relatively highly skilled industrial workforce. Of course, it can also be imagined that Toyota cut a very favourable 'behind-the-scenes deal' regarding investment incentives with the French Government.

10 When they had the opportunity to pass through, this 'gate raising' phenomenon was a matter of interest to some of the regular Japanese engineer/managers, who suggested that a guard's capacity to raise the gate without their having to slow down was a measure of his intelligence.

11 For an evocative description of the feel of repetition in assembly line work, see Turner (1995: 229).

12 Pancakes are sometimes sold at this stage to other manufacturers who will carry out the latter stages of production: the assembly and packaging of videocassettes. These purchasers are, by definition, competitors with Yama. Indeed, in an interesting twist to our understanding of proprietary arrangements and the fierce public competition between consumer electronics firms, though the final packaging of a video tape must hold the label of the final 'producer,' say '3m' (an American company), the tape itself may well be made at Yama. Pancakes are also sold to companies that mass produce prerecorded videos, who in paying close attention to costs want the length of tape in their videos to correspond exactly with, say, the length of a movie. Both 'jumbo rolls' and 'pancakes' are, therefore, points of production at which sales can be, and are, made.

13 Salaries are recorded as they stood during the period of fieldwork in the late 1990s. They can be expected to be 50 per cent higher, at a minimum, in 2007.

Part II
Organising persons in places

3 Personalising socio-technical relations

Introduction

Although Japanese expatriates at subsidiaries of multinationals manufacturing abroad are proportionately few in number and many occupy 'adviser' positions on the margins of factory organisational charts, they are in the highest positions of authority in these firms. I describe this as a complex form of 'ownership' and will elaborate how this unfolds in practice in a processual analysis of several days of activity at YamaMax in Chapter 4. In structural terms, the point is that information about what is to be transferred down this de facto, if perhaps not formally articulated, hierarchy is making its most critical cross-cultural leap in the communications between expatriate and top local managers. While there is a literature, largely focused on North American and European cases, addressing shopfloor activities at Japanese multinationals abroad,[1] very little is written on local management and their interactions with Japanese supervisors. As my perceptions evolved during fieldwork it became clear that exploring local management and its interactions with Japanese management would ultimately yield the most comprehensive explanations of my specific observations on the shopfloor and, thereby, underpin my general analysis of how organisations adjust to cross-cultural conditions. That is, the capacity of local and expatriate personnel, typically at an upper level, to share information strongly affects the development of capabilities to successfully handle technology closer to the production line among lower level, local staff. In Chapter 6 I will provide evidence of difficulties in fixing into place the 'Japanese shopfloor model' at YamaMax in France. I suggest that these findings are indicators of problems of communication at the higher managerial level at YamaMax which I examine in this chapter.

I begin by briefly recounting biographical stories of several French and Japanese managers. These persons are typical of the unique individuals constituting an organisation such as YamaMax. I describe their backgrounds, the circumstances leading to their arrival at YamaMax, and some of their particular features; in effect using their histories to assist in explaining how the corporation works as an organised and a personalised place throughout, and indeed beyond, the careers of its members. In the process I seek to substantiate the claim that Japanese *salaryman* are not the automatons led by the nose of corporate ideology that we are popularly led to believe. Thus, here I shall flesh out *salaryman* as producers of corporate ideology and its constitutive behaviours *as they are* producers of other conflicting ideologies and behaviours. In the process I also, at least implicitly, contrast Japanese *salaryman* with French managers. Having done so, the patterns of interaction between these persons, who work closely with one another, will be detailed. While much of this commentary suggests preoccupations with hierarchy, to the detriment of other factors, I intend to make explicit that the dynamics of hierarchy, while important, should be recognised as one among other important features of social relations in formally organised contexts.

Otake-san

Forty-seven years old at the time of the study, Otake-san had worked at the Yama Corporation for twenty-eight years. He had come to YamaMax three years earlier as the highest-ranking Japanese, and the only Japanese among four 'general managers' (*bucho*) working immediately under the French *directeur general*. At Yama in Japan, however, he held the highest level within the lower rank of 'manager' (*kacho*). During his tenure in France he made the significant achievement of being promoted (by the Japanese reckoning) to the lowest level of *bucho*; equivalent perhaps in British universities to a promotion from senior lecturer to reader.

Otake-san is the son of a mid-level bureaucrat in Japan's Ministry of Construction, and to accommodate his father's work moved frequently during his childhood: once while attending lower school and twice in his high-school years. His high-school years, before entering Yama, aged 19, are significant in his telling. All that Otake-san wanted to do was travel. He had no desire to join a 'normal' high-school, so took the exam to enter a merchant marine school (*shosen gakou*) and go to sea. He found out several months later that he had failed, and thus entered an 'industrial' (vocational) high-school. Utterly disinterested in schoolwork, he socialised with a rough group apparently involved in petty theft. However, he excelled in sport; joining rugby, judo and rowing clubs, where he was a member of a nationally ranked schoolboy crew. Though Otake-san worried his teachers by his disregard for homework, he recalls that his '*mission*' was to gain the 'part' (*yakuwari*) of assistant to his classroom teacher. He achieved this goal. Obviously highly intelligent, by merely paying attention to class presentations he tested well and was ranked fifth in a class of eighty. Although he apparently had the opportunity for sport scholarships at private universities, fewer than 10 per cent of his classmates were college-bound, and Otake-san had no desire to go to college, unclear what he would spend his time studying for four years. Instead he imagined taking many different jobs, in order to make enough money to support various travels. Since his school results (*gakou no seiseki*) were good, his chemistry teacher suggested nonetheless that he take the Yama Corporation's all-day entrance exam. He did so and, although he 'did not feel that (he) had passed it' (*ukeru ki ga nakata*), he had passed, and so joined Yama's magnetic products division.

Although, he claims, new entrants nowadays would not have the same broad exposure, over his initial three-year period at Yama Otake-san gained skills as he rotated through jobs in the mixing, coating and, finally, the R&D (*kaihatsu*) sections of Yama's main tape factory. He 'made a lot of friends in his third year', but still held on to the notion of travel, squirrelling away much of his (low) entry salary. After these rotations, Otake-san had the choice of remaining on a more permanent basis in either tape R&D or the production (*seizou*) *saido* ('side') where new coating machines were just being installed. Describing himself as a 'natural' (*natsueru*) at tape coating, Otake-san chose production. However, the decision was also based on 'not being a good member of the R&D team', and not getting along with his department manager (*kacho*), where Otake-san held the lowest rank in a team of nine. In further explaining the move out of R&D as motivated by the importance of 'moving around and changing colleagues', Otake-san flagged his dislike for the acceptance, typical among members of Japanese organisations, of working for years with the same, small group of people.

> I don't ever want to do the same job for more than three years. It becomes boring being around the same *menba* [members]. When a new *menba* comes it makes new *karucha* [culture] and makes new *kaze* [wind; 'brings fresh air']. I wanted to do this throughout my career: changing a lot to be around different people.

In expressing this attitude we might note here that at Yama, as in most large Japanese organisations of both the private and public sectors that have implicit 'lifetime employment' policies, the invariably male *salaryman* all move formally between jobs, and so colleagues, in three to five year intervals throughout their careers.

Engineers at Yama join the corporation upon graduation from university or, as was Otake-san's case, high-school. In such large-scale and hierarchy-conscious organisations how this distinction might affect both career progress and more general social relations was a matter of interest to me, especially as on several occasions managers at Yama and other firms I have studied had suggested there were sometimes intra-organisational and inter-personal tensions based on this factor. Length of service is also of central importance to pay scales and ranks in most Japanese organisations, so university graduate entrants would logically appear to be disadvantaged as they would likely join the company three to four years later than employees who had terminated their education at high-school. Otake-san's reflections on the period when he was joined at Yama by university graduates, follow:

At that age everything is the same. Everyone with a university degree, they were just people then. There was no feeling of difference at all among the entrance group from age, say, 22 to 25. Whether or not there was later, depends on the person. They had a degree as they'd studied for four years. But we had all worked; I using my body and they their heads. There is no problem. My feeling is that everyone respected each other [*sonkei shita*] as we were all there together [*issyu*]. We were *issyu*. Later when we took tests for promotion, we all took them together.

The problem of length of service was resolved by high-school graduate employees becoming official entrants – at the same salary – with the 'class' of university graduates of their same age. Thus, work on the shopfloor was, in effect, equated with university training at Yama.

Otake-san recalled without hesitation that among the thirty-two members of his 'class' at Yama's magnetics division, sixteen were women – 'only five of them married Yama men' – none of whom is currently working at Yama. Only one out of the sixteen men had quit the corporation. Among this group of fifteen men, Otake-san held the highest rank. I asked him to account for this:

Progress depends on each person's use of his potential. *Tama-tama* [by chance, unexpectedly [humble form]] I am doing things for my own self-respect [*sonkei*]. In *mai peesu* ['my pace'; though it usually suggests 'taking it easy'], I want to finish soon. I am fast; I have the next job to do. I expand my capacity in that way.

Otake-san tells me, 'the only way I can remember my work history is to look at the documents showing all of my official positions at Yama', which are contained in a large manilla envelope that he promptly pulls from a sideboard in his office at YamaMax. He points out the statement in one of these documents indicating that – from age 26 (his third 'post') – he officially reported to two bosses in the tape production division: one directly concerning engineering, the other an administrative position. During this period Otake-san also received a 'special request' from one of the directors (who occupy positions at the tightly squeezed top of the corporate hierarchical pyramid) to conduct a special test of a new material. Otake-san recalls:

I was feeling good; working up to my limit in a situation of 'must do by tomorrow'. It was the end of the year [*nenmatsu*] and everyone was on vacation. My boss actually gave the presentation of the test data to the directors, but it was fun to have done this sort of thing.

Indeed, opportunities literally to gain recognition by members of upper management in a large firm such as Yama may anoint the career of a *salaryman*. In the context of 'internationalisation' of large Japanese firms, I will expand below upon the interpersonal aspects of career progression.

Career time: away from Japan, towards the organisational centre

Otake-san's bosses also changed several times during his third post – 'So I was able to learn a lot' – and he spent six months supporting the 'start-up' (*tachiage*) of a Yama tape factory in a rural area of the US. He was 27 years old at the time.

> About thirty-five Japanese were putting up the factory. One of my extra jobs was to take care of the food for the Japanese (along with formal technical jobs). For five days in advance I arranged for the food. I took care of all this on one schedule. The person hired to take care of the Japanese was the Japanese wife of an ex-US Army soldier. (The husband and wife presumably had met in Japan during the Occupation.) I helped them a lot. The husband was very friendly. And we were very close. I have no letter from them these days. I see them if I go to visit the tape factory in the US. We have a 'get together'. Last time we did this she was crying a lot when we talked about the period setting up the factory and all. They seemed well [*genki mitai*].
>
> When I was working in the US, top managers from Japan came often, so I had a lot of contact. A lot of '*top*' came over; the *nihonjin* [Japanese].

Otake-san's earlier 'special project' indicates that he stood out in the eyes of his seniors for his technical capacity and energy in Japan itself. However, a posting abroad is advantageous to any *salaryman* of any age in that it structurally focuses the attention of high-level managers upon them, and as such represents an important opportunity.

The attention that Otake-san gained while abroad is indicative of how shifting organisational structures and processes reflect the shifting political economic fortunes of Japan generally. From the close of the Second World War until the late 1980s Japan produced the vast majority of its manufactured goods domestically. With the exception of 'listening post'[2] positions in the major world capitals, especially in the US,[3] postings abroad were generally reserved for those *salaryman* overseeing trade and local distribution. These persons were in effect marginalised as they were displaced from central (*kihon*) organisational action in Japan. As elaborated more fully in the last chapter, following the oil shocks of 1973 and 1979, hostility to inexpensive Japanese products led to a substantial increase in trade barriers among Western nations. To protect the overseas markets deemed essential to the Japanese economy Japanese industrial firms were increasingly forced to invest in new production outside of Japan, a move which coincided with tremendous strength in the purchasing power of the Japanese yen especially from the mid-1980s. Huge investments were witnessed in North America and Europe, and the East and South East Asian countries from which 'Japanese' products could be imported into North America and Europe with relatively fewer trade constraints. Thus, Japanese organisations such as Yama 'internationalised' along with their investments, as economics and politics dictated. The oversight of foreign operations therefore became a central activity for Japanese firms, increasingly requiring the attentions of its most promising *salaryman*.[4] The current understanding at major Japanese corporations is that a serious career must include overseas experience.

'Distance' in organisational context

The physical 'displacements' witnessed by large Japanese corporations due to foreign investments have had significant effects upon their organisational communications. In contrast to the interest in 'flat organisations' in the West – often used as a 'strategic' tool to lay off mid-level managers – in Japan organisational hierarchies continue to be crammed with positions. As a result there is considerable interpersonal distance between directors and middle management (to say nothing of factory shopfloors). Directors, however, often visit overseas subsidiaries and spend a good deal of time with the Japanese middle managers posted there. This is especially so with a 'start-up', where huge sums of 'upfront' capital are 'at risk': invested in a venture that cannot be expected to 'turn a profit' for many years. Such 'bottom line' anxieties are compounded in a foreign environment where a company such as Yama may have little experience beyond involvement – in many cases superficial – with trading and marketing their 'final' (completed) products. Directors also circulate internationally more frequently when an established subsidiary is performing poorly.

However, all is not work. Overseas subsidiaries also attract prodigious attention in that tours of subsidiaries provide high-ranking executives the opportunity for relative recreation compared with extremely busy schedules in Japan itself.[5] Fine food and drink, and golf feature during such visits while, though certainly nerve-wracking to those responsible on the ground at overseas subsidiaries, 'work' as it would be understood by Westerners often consists of relatively superficial reporting on current subsidiary conditions. Though no significant decisions will be taken during such visits, per se, this does not imply that they are not important. These opportunities for face-to-face interaction provide a 'voice' for carrying, and personalising, the praise, concerns and/or cajolings of headquarters to members of subsidiaries. In turn they are a source back at headquarters for explanations of disappointing 'data' and other information, especially information that is influential in personnel decisions regarding Japanese managers who are posted abroad.

YamaMax, well established by the time of my fieldwork, has at least five visits by directors per year. Each provides the opportunity for all eight of

YamaMax's Japanese members to interact professionally and socially with directors, and during some visits to hold individual, private discussions behind closed doors.[6] Thus, for instance, at the extremes, a 25-year-old Japanese engineer at YamaMax will meet, and possibly explain his concerns, to an executive 35 years his senior who in Japan occupies a netherworld of distant and unapproachable authority. Merely having participated in such a meeting, even if its contents are utterly superficial and predictable to both parties, is valuable to a *salaryman* in that its form alone may display a distinction from those in his 'class' against whom he measures himself, as we have seen in Otake-san's case, and against whom the organisation measures him. A sense of confidence may result from such an opportunity for interaction, as well as a sense of further commitment to the firm if one's voice would seem to be heard cross-generationally, that is, cross-hierarchically.

Personnel department negotiations inside the firm (in Japan) concerning new postings may draw the nod of a director if a particular individual is personally remembered. This may also not occur, especially in the hypothetical case of a new posting for a 25-year-old *salaryman*, but that it *might* be seen to have occurred assists in what I can only describe as fierce, intramural battles for career progress in a firm such as Yama. That upon joining the firm a male is likely to believe that he is joining colleagues 'for life', adds to the intensity here. It is perhaps a universal that gossip can seldom be corrected; over time it may become irrelevant. However, in a single organisation, significant professional or personal events may hold a 'shelf life' of decades, personal animosities simmer throughout careers and strategies for advancement are as equally full of intrigue, if less literally deadly, than any royal regime. A high level of competence is expected (and attained) in a firm such as Yama, but significant advancement requires serious technical knowledge, social coalitions and, crucially, the skill to generate recognition of both.

Up in, and out of, Yama

Except perhaps for the very top two or three executives in a corporation such as Yama – who in occupying such positions would simultaneously wield substantial influence in the highest-level industrial and government advisory circles in Japan – patronage ends with the retirement of a director. *Salaryman* who have achieved the rank of *bucho*, the crowded rank beneath directors and vice directors, are especially vulnerable as new directors usually carry with them an entourage of trusted underlings who will be granted positions that displace others at a high level. Thus, the culmination of careers at the thin end of an organisational pyramid serves to supercharge an already competitive and interpersonally-saturated atmosphere.

The system at the sunset of a career in a firm such as Yama operates as follows. Though the Japanese enjoy one of the longest life expectancies in the world, official retirement comes at 55. While low achievers at that point find themselves unemployed, most are retained, often on temporary contracts with lower benefits and fewer guarantees, until age 60. While the most capable remain in the firm after age 55, others move on to positions for a few years in 'subsidiaries' (*kogaishya*): companies that are in effect owned and controlled by the main firm, but legally incorporated as separate firms. (Thus, they can offer less generous benefits to employees.)[7] At Yama, directorships may be occupied before age 60 – for especially high flyers – but it is rare indeed for a director to be employed past age 65. A directorship can be removed at any time, either through retirement or becoming the 'president' of a *kogaishya*: a fine title, but essentially out of the loop of activity in the main firm and, therefore, of minimal patronage value to others.

The close reading of director-level organisational machinations among *bucho*-rank executives of Yama (as at other firms), some of whom I came to know well, is impressive. Their interest was obvious, yet detached and somewhat bemused. They recognised, in some cases quite ironically, that except for doing their own jobs competently, and so putting a minimal brick in the technical foundations of their patron(s), they had virtually no influence over decisions regarding promotion at the directorship level. Relationships of confidence built up over years of joint labour, and transformed into patronage in the context of career development, could suddenly become organisationally, and so, effectively, meaningless in terms of personal advancement. The sense of loss of control is perhaps under-standable among persons engaged throughout their working lives in actively deploying knowledge and information in the transformation of raw materials into completed objects, as well as in the manipulation of an organisational system that they understand deeply. Thus, through the knock-on effects of little more than the apparent whim of retiring a director earlier than might have been hoped, whole swatches of promising futures could be erased, others brightened. In a gesture at the personal significance of this state of affairs, all *salaryman* at Yama Corporation are required, when they are in their fifties, to attend a retreat concerning psychological coping skills in retirement.

Otake-san was the highest-ranking Japanese at YamaMax. Thus, he personally took charge of the arrangements for each visit by directors. Organising schedules to the minute of all of his YamaMax Japanese (and top French) colleagues, his secretary booking hotels, reserving restaurants, visits to wineries, possibly casinos and, in his case, avoiding the inclusion of a golf outing if possible,[8] Otake-san greeted and sent off each director at the airport while he rode with them between each occasion. These personal contacts were important, as Otake-san, in occupying at a relatively young age a high rank (*bucho*) that acknowledged his skill and hard work, had entered a realm in which personal patronage was increasingly important.

Otake-san's efforts regarding directors of the Yama Corporation are not displayed here to suggest the machinations of power-mongering. They are – and are so articulated and understood by Otake-san and persons throughout organisations such as Yama – the 'naturally' polite, pleasant and appropriate organising activities of a top local manager 'taking care' of his seniors in a hierarchical setting. That said, off-the-record conversations among confidants as to the politics among directorships or, at a lower relative level, *bucho* or *kacho*, and their influence on careers in Yama, are rife, as such conversations are at other large Japanese organisations. Seniors' musings, during daytime breaks or, more often, drunken evening outings, temporarily refocus the attentions of juniors. Thus it was not unusual that Otake-san paid particular attention to his superiors when they visited. On the contrary, to not to have done so is thoroughly unimaginable.

Otake-san's mid-career malaise

I return to tracking Otake-san's career before he came to France. While in his late twenties and on his third post, and enjoying the visits to the US factory by Yama '*tops*', Otake-san took the opportunity to explore the US. Whereas 'everyone (the Japanese) there played golf both days of the week-end, I went around travelling everywhere and enjoyed American football'.[9] Returning to Japan after six months, Otake-san explained that 'he had nothing to do'. His job had shifted, and he could not take the test to become *kakaricho* – assistant manager – as he had not been able to prepare while abroad. He considered quitting the company to travel throughout the US. He stayed on at Yama, however, and as a 'process engineer' helped out (*tetsudai shita*) on 'the new machines and support of the factory. *Nan demo* ... (Whatever ... I would do it). Not so much from the directors as before'.

Although he eventually made *kakaricho* rank, Otake-san seemed to enter something of a bleak period in his career. However he enjoyed a project in which he was charged with overseeing the development of materials supply (*shizai maata*, or, literally, 'materials matters') of the plastic base film for magnetic tape. He conducted audits of new supplies immediately, and often went to suppliers to make a *kureimu* ('claims', or complaints) when he discovered faults. Otake-san seemed to enjoy recalling that managers at the supplier firms were a bit shocked by his frequent and forceful *kureimu*.

From the manilla envelope in which he kept originals of the official documentation tracking his career course, Otake-san pulled out a card announcing his fourth posting – aged 32 – to a Yama company in southern Japan that supplied the main factory with chemicals for 'mixing': the first stage of tape production. With the move the Otakes bought their first house. Their eldest son (*chonan*) was in his first year of school. The company was a domestic Japan 'start-up' but, poorly organised, the machinery arrived later than scheduled while there were too many staff on hand for too little work. 'This was not a normal situation'. Otake-san oversaw eight or nine, of the staff of thirty-five, whom he engaged in 'fruitless' (*fukekka no*) work, such as 'cleaning the building' (*tatemono souji*). Most of his subordinates were formally employed at a local, subcontracting firm to Yama. They were quite young – 'only their body was adult' – and they got into trouble – 'we had to chase them down in the city and everything' – a situation that risked tainting Yama, and Otake-san's own, reputation. (Reflecting briefly on the importance of age to mature behaviour, Otake-san mentioned that at the start-up of YamaMax, the local French employees were also young, although he did not elaborate on the point.) One of his charges in Japan was apparently mentally unstable, so Otake-san arranged for him to see a psychologist. He told me:

> It is hard to do this sort of thing in Japan; the privacy situation is different than here [in the West]. I learned a lot from this situation, though. Now, of course, we have a counsellor on permanent staff (at the main factory in Japan). I broke a lot of rules for this guy; and I might have gotten fired. He had stolen from the petty cash supply in the middle of the night and I had to arrange the return of the money. But we have this sort of responsibility as a *Yama man*. It is my thinking anyway. Like a family, this kind of thing comes first. We also employ the deaf in Japan these days.

At 36, after four years away, and now a *kacho hosa* (lowest rank of regular manager), the Otakes moved back 'home' to the main factory. Although Otake-san had described himself – artificially humbly – as a simple 'production side' (*seizo saido*) person and not particularly good at research or start-ups, he began work on the metal evaporation process in the production of magnetic tape, a position which intimately combined both R&D and mass production concerns (and which during our discussion he elaborated at a level far beyond my technical comprehension). These days, in Otake-san's view, Yama's by-now far larger R&D department is not thinking of the practical aspects of production and is thus out of touch with how new things should be developed.

After eighteen months at 'home' he was asked to take a long post (3–5 years) at the US plant, where he had earlier assisted the start-up and which was by this time on a firm footing of regular production. He was disinterested in another move, and furthermore had a second son with some medical problems. He thus managed to avoid the US posting and continued work instead at the main Japanese plant on coating (his 'natural' skill) and mixing. He eventually was made project leader on the development and integration of a sophisticated industrial computer system at the factory, a post that involved visits to computer firms in Japan and Germany.

From age 40, Otake-san was again posted to regular production. However, two years later in December he had an 'end-of-year dinner' (*bonenkai*) with the director of tape production – and one of his main patrons – who told him, 'next year to Europe'. He discussed the possibility with his wife over the New Year's break. Her mother was dying of cancer, and his father was becoming ill. Otake-san's mother could not believe that he – the eldest son (*chonan*) – would move away under the circumstances. (Otake-san's younger brothers had left the local area years before; one to Hokkaido, the other to Yokohama.) He was also reticent to break up his young family by going to France on his own. YamaMax, however, was having serious difficulties – it was about £6 million 'in the red' – and Yama was keen that Otake-san help to sort it out. In April 1994 he had visited YamaMax for a week to assess the situation and returned from Japan in May for a month with three Japanese 'turnaround' specialists. Otake-san had heard from his Japanese colleagues at YamaMax that communications among the top non-Japanese managers were highly strained. The general manager charged with production – an American who had worked for many years in Yama's US tape plant – apparently would not even meet with the French *directeur general*. The American felt threatened by Otake-san, sensing that he was there to replace him, although Otake-san explained that he was merely there for 'support'.

Several months later, Otake-san returned to YamaMax for a four to five year posting without his family, replacing the US production manager, who returned home. The French *directeur general*, in his sixties, was forced to move to a lower position in a French components factory, also owned by Yama. The Frenchman who occupied the position below the *directeur general*, and who was in his late fifties, moved to a German Yama factory for a couple of years before he was retired (and returned to France). The responsibilities of both *directeur general* and his immediate subordinate were filled by a promising young Frenchman, Monsieur Cardin, who was in his forties, and had worked for many years as number two in a French Yama audio products factory. M. Cardin was, thus, catapulted upwards.

The story of this organisational transition at YamaMax has been recounted here in terms of YamaMax's internal dynamics. However, a Japanese manager, Yamada-san, who was present at YamaMax at the time, understood it as rooted in director-level transitions at headquarters in Japan.[10] In his telling the new Japanese director of magnetic products, who had formerly worked in audio, had a fierce reputation for shake-ups. His appointment was welcomed with some trepidation among magnetic product employees, who assumed that he would 'bring in his own "mafia"' (*torimaki ga kuru* ('hangers on' would come)). Indeed, the new, young French *directeur general* at YamaMax was well known to the new Japanese director of magnetic products, as audio products had previously fallen under his responsibility.

Like Japanese *bucho* in Japan, then, the top one or two positions held by non-Japanese at Yama overseas subsidiaries may be understood as directly subject to the machinations of director-level patronage in Japan itself. However, my sense is that since top foreigners' employment at Yama is relatively brief, they are not Japanese and they literally occupy the outer reaches of patronage networks, they are far more likely (compared with Japanese *bucho*) to be able to move opportunistically under the wing of a new Japanese director should the interests of that Japanese director be served by it. My purpose, however, is not to belabour politics at Yama at director level. In that my contact with these persons was only occasional, they do not feature as subjects of the ethnography. Rather, they serve to describe how stories of those in high positions of authority are 'worked' by my more local subjects at YamaMax, both Japanese and French, to organise their understanding of the corporation and their place within it. Such an explanation might also help us to personalise the multinational corporation and, perhaps, gently erode the common perspective upon them as hard, mechanical and hyperrationalised.

Working with Otake-san

While perhaps logically contradictory, if psychologically comprehensible, Otake-san's personal history seemed to recycle both aggressive individuality and a profound emotional desire for commitment to others. My perspective on this matter, however, was informed more importantly by our shared general experiences during my fieldwork than by the details of our only formal interview, which occurred only days before I left the field. As I anticipated, the arrangement for the interview with Otake-san was not straightforward. He was aware that, in my final month of fieldwork, I was in a cycle of lengthy interviews with others at YamaMax, both French and Japanese, and I was not surprised that he explained that he was 'too busy'. Having been asked, he could largely determine if it would happen. I was prepared to let go of the interview as, although Otake-san was a central character, I had more than enough material for my work.

One day, however, a couple of weeks after initially asking, I dropped by his office upon returning from lunch to ask if he had any time later that afternoon. He said, 'No, I have a meeting at 3, but we can chat now for a while'. It was not much time, but I gathered my things nonetheless and we began in his office at 1:40 p.m. Around 4, my notes recall that I was glazing over with fatigue. We ended at 7, met again at 8 for dinner at a Spanish restaurant we both liked in the large town 15 miles away, and ended at 11 p.m. I later wrote to one of my mentors (an anthropologist) that I estimated that I had spent around 15 minutes talking during our eight hours of 'discussion'. His story was fascinating to me of course, while our final joint event, if anything, reinforced my knowledge of his personal intensity.

Yamada-san

Yamada-san's father, who ran a small construction firm on the coast of Japan, left the family when Yamada-san was 14, and he has had no contact since then. His mother was remarried to a mid-level prefectural official when he was 18. Yamada-san joined Yama, aged 20, having completed a technical college degree in chemistry, and for four years analysed the mixing process at Yama's main tape factory. He spent his next four years as a member of the R&D division until in his third post he returned to production where he was involved in the design of production processes for professional videotape. Having worked in Yama for eight years at this point, Yamada-san took a test to become a *kakaricho dairi* (sub-assistant manager). The six-hour test involved: (a) writing an essay concerning what was at stake in a (hypothetical) dangerous situation; (b) specific questions regarding Yama's internal accounting and quality control systems; (c) a test of his general knowledge; and (d) an English listening-comprehension exam. Six months later, he was informed that he had failed. Yamada-san described the situation as 'next year at the Olympics'; that is, he was like a failed Olympian who would prepare himself for another four years with the intent of winning a medal. Indeed, Yamada-san passed the exam the following year.

Four months before Yamada-san came to YamaMax, aged 31, he received a call suddenly from the secretary of a very high-level production general manager (*jigyo bucho*), who wanted to discuss something with him. Yamada-san asked his direct boss (*kacho*) about it, but he denied any knowledge. (Yamada-san's *kacho* had actually heard of the posting offer for the first time the previous day.) Yamada-san was surprised during his 30-minute meeting with this distant, high-ranking *bucho* to be asked to go to France, where he would work in customer service and in quality assessment (QA). No one from his current section had been posted to France, but his *bucho*, who had already completed the appropriate form for the personnel division to approve Yamada-san's new posting, explained that it was a *chiansu* ('chance'; a good opportunity for him). Yamada-san asked him to wait a while for his decision.

Yamada-san needed to discuss the opportunity with his wife of three years. Mrs Yamada was his same age and also employed at Yama working on the development of high-technology computer discs. As a university engineering graduate, she was more highly educated than was her husband before entering Yama, although she had not been promoted as quickly over their first ten years there. Without children, Yamada-san explained that they were living well as DINKs (double income, no kids), and the move to France would require her to quit her job at Yama. As an ex-employee married to an employee posted abroad, she would have the opportunity to register for first priority for a Yama job, once they returned to Japan. However, even should she get such a position, Yamada-san explained it would 'only be for a woman's job', such as working in a lab providing technical support to engineers, and not possible to develop her career in any meaningful way. While she thought going abroad was attractive, she was reticent to quit Yama. However, she joined her husband two months after his posting to YamaMax began. Yamada-san explained, 'Now that we have children the situation is changed, but before, when we were DINKs, she was thinking of going back to work'.

Two days after meeting with his high-level boss, Yamada-san had discussed the matter with his wife and agreed to take the job at YamaMax. A week later, Yamada-san received a formal offer from the personnel department for the new post. In anticipation of the transition, the personnel department began visa preparations and arranged for Yamada-san and his wife to study French for two hours, once a week, for three months. In retrospect, Yamada-san regretted there was no more extensive formal training. He explained that when he was 22 he had participated in a Yama-sponsored English-language training course during which he was isolated ('with six *kacho*') for a month where no Japanese could be spoken. Yamada-san told me that 'during my (*pro forma*) returnee interview', once back in Japan, he would suggest such training for his France-bound colleagues. However, in spite of the paucity of formal preparation, Yamada-san aggressively sought out information on the technical and organisational aspects of YamaMax in France, and the situation that Japanese wives found there. This involved checking through documents and, more importantly, discussion with colleagues who had spent time in France. He explained:

> Kimura-san had just come back so I had some time to chat with him and look at stuff, though a lot of it was at the tech centre [and not easily accessible]. I got documents together myself and studied about what kind of machines they have here, the organisational chart, what jobs the Japanese were doing, how the organisation had evolved, communications with local people, and so on. I asked a lot of people who had been here. By the end I was looking at some documents in French. During this period Nagata-san [who was a Yama engineer who had worked at different times with both Yamadas, was a good friend of both of them and was later posted to YamaMax himself], did a lot of my official work for me as, especially just before moving, about 50 per cent of my time I was looking at stuff having to do with France. I was not nervous about it, but I wanted to know what they were doing here as I only had experience with professional tape, not the standard VHS tape [that they were making at YamaMax in France].

Once in France Yamada-san, like all the Japanese managers except Otake-san, studied French at company expense on Saturday mornings with a 'very kind' local French woman who was a high-school English teacher. (Most of the Japanese wives studied with her as well, though during the week.) Yamada-san also boosted his general reading about France, eventually compiling an impressive collection of books (in Japanese) on French history, politics, art, wine and food. Indeed when one of his Japanese colleagues mentioned that he was taking his family to Paris where they planned to visit the Louvre, Yoshida-san delivered an impromptu five-minute lecture on the highlights that should be seen, and in which rooms they could be found.

What is a salaryman*?*

Like three of his seven Japanese colleagues at YamaMax, Yamada-san was aged 34 years and held the rank of *kakaricho* (assistant manager) when I conducted my research. In France Yamada-san had cultivated a lifestyle that would be seen to contrast with our typical understanding of Japanese *salaryman*. For instance, when he was queried specifically as to the relevance of golf to Japanese business, he replied:

> I play a little but I don't like it. It's awful, isn't it [*Ya desu nee*]. It is recreation; should not be for business.[11] Especially, since I came to France I feel this way. I think it is part of Japanese life to do this but if I were a *bucho*, I would try to change this for sure. I am the type of person who hates corporate drinking occasions and overtime work [*enka, zangyo ... kirai*]. I don't like hostess bars and discussing business after work.

Nonetheless, as part of his 'customer service' role, Yamada-san was obliged once or twice a month to host European clients of YamaMax for dinner. Always taking place at restaurants, these were social events during which business was never discussed. Sometimes Yamada-san would be accompanied by YamaMax's French *directeur general*, and on occasion Mrs Yamada would be invited along as well. By his presence Yamada-san in effect embodied the technical commitment of Yama to its products; any problem (a *kureimu*, 'claim') would be handled personally by him.

Day to day Yamada-san maintained an interesting distance from the six other Japanese engineers at YamaMax. His position was somewhat distinct from the others on three grounds. First, he was vested with the authority of 'local knowledge' as he had been the longest resident in France among them and, as we have seen, had fairly substantial knowledge of 'French civilisation'. Second, involved with QA and customer service, i.e. 'claims' from customers who had purchased YamaMax products, his tasks were not concerned with the engineering and oversight of production that engaged the others. Third, Otake-san, his senior, was highly confident of Yamada-san's ability and, thus, effectively allowed him to be his own boss. The smooth and non-interventionist relations between the two was, according to the other Japanese engineers (who did not share this experience), strongly influenced by Otake-san's appreciation for Yamada-san's being very helpful when Otake-san first arrived in France.

Yamada-san rarely got together with the others after work during the week. He usually returned home for dinner, played with his infant child, bathed and sometimes 'played on the Internet', looking for news of Japan and Europe, and 'information on F-1' (racing-car competitions). He explained:

> On the weekend I am under the control of my wife. Last Saturday we went shopping. On Sunday we went to the Gotos' house for dinner with them and Sato-san and his wife. That Sunday night Tanaka-san and his wife were at Nagata-san's for dinner.
>
> When I first got here I wanted to make friends with the French but usually I just hang around with the Japanese, getting together for barbeque parties. Now to make good friends is really difficult [since he has a small child]. I like to meet and do something together, I don't really like drinking every night and the like. I've always felt that way.

In reflecting on his life as a *salaryman*, Yamada-san told me:

> I will always work as a *salaryman*. I think so. But if I think that way I get sad. I think it is boring. I have security but . . . [he pauses, sucks his teeth]. Sometimes I think of starting my own business, but I don't know. What kind of business would that be? Maybe I could import French *foie gras*, or something like that, to Japan. I have ideas but I have no money. I have no choice recently because I have a baby and a family. If I can minimise the risk to start a business by myself, I'd want to try.

All in the family

One late afternoon while sitting at my desk, I heard Nagata-san's phone go unanswered as he was on the shopfloor. Immediately after, the phone rang on Goto-san's desk, next to mine, a sign that the Japanese were being called in rapid succession. Goto-san answered and immediately expressed his concern. It was Mrs Yamada calling, seven and a half months pregnant with their second child, and apparently in great pain. Yamada-san himself, away for the day on business, was unreachable. Goto-san hung up and sprang into action. He immediately called his wife who, as they lived close by, went to the house by car to take Mrs Yamada to the hospital. Then he literally sprinted across the large communal office, into a smaller office shared by two of his Japanese colleagues where they and Otake-san were having a discussion. All were immediately on their feet and within seconds it was decided, as they exited into the main communal office area, that Otake-san would stay and wait for Nagata-san to come off the shopfloor, while Goto-san and Susumu-kun[12] would go to the hospital. As they stripped off their Yama vests and gathered car keys and shoulder bags, Otake-san recalled (in Japanese) to everyone present that Mrs Yamada had had some difficulty during the first birth, using a technical Japanese medical term (which I did not understand) to describe a malaise of the lower back. The few French employees in the communal office had no idea what was going on and, accustomed to sudden activity among the Japanese, paid no particular attention.

By chance that day I had YamaMax's small delivery truck parked just outside – it was loaned to me from evening until morning, so I could travel to and from my home – so to save them a few minutes I drove Goto-san and Susumu-kun to the lot where their cars were parked. Susumu-kun, who when off-duty (and away from the concerns of hierarchical relations) was always quick to deliver somewhat inappropriate and, thereby, often amusing remarks that expressed his true thoughts (*honne*), mentioned to Goto-san that although it 'could not be helped' (*shigata ga nai*) this was unbelievably bad timing given the work they were in the middle of doing on the calendering rolls. That said, both he and Goto-san seemed very nervous. I was concerned as well, and muddled as to how I should conduct myself in this surprising circumstance. I related to them that as I spoke both Japanese and French I might be helpful in interpreting at the hospital. Seeing the sense in that, they paused, and took my home phone number on a matchbook, while we acknowledged that they could reach me easily at YamaMax. Thanking me, they clambered into their cars. I returned to my desk where I fought a battle of affection for them, envy over their commitment to one another, and disaffection with myself for the self-absorption and pretentions of 'professional', methodological reticence to impose myself onto what seemed a private matter. I left for the hospital a few minutes later, reflecting during the 15-mile drive that in this – unusual – case of my presence possibly making a positive and important difference, my 'ethical' dilemma was absurd and entirely misconstrued.

Yamada-san arrived at the hospital five minutes earlier than I and was in the emergency ward with his wife. His car had been spotted on the motorway and was flagged down by Goto-san and Susumu-kun as they drove in opposite directions. The Gotos were in the waiting room, Mrs Goto having brought to the hospital several pillows and blankets, in case they were to spend the night. Susumu-kun's wife arrived a half hour later with a box full of rice balls (*onigiri*), snacks and drinks. Yamada-san came out about a half hour later saying his wife seemed all right and was asleep, having been given a sedative. He looked shocked, recalling in a glaze the start of events when he was turned around dangerously by his colleagues on the motorway on his way back to YamaMax. Asking if I could help with translation, he thanked me saying that the doctors, who had spoken to him in English, did not think there was anything to be alarmed about. Nagata-san, old work mate of both Yamada-san and Mrs Yamada in Japan, and good friends with them both, arrived thirty minutes later. When the French obstetrician-gynaecologist came out to speak with Yamada-san again, I clarified with the doctor what Yamada-san had understood about his wife's condition. Well out of danger, after a couple of hours Yamada-san wheeled his wife out of the ward into the waiting room where she found all of us. Groggy but excited, she described her terrible pains, and apologised to us, and especially to me, for being inconvenienced. The Gotos accompanied the Yamadas home, with Susumu-kun's wife's *onigiri* in hand. The rest of us returned home separately.

Nagata-san

Among the Japanese, Nagata-san had most recently come to YamaMax. He grew up in Tokyo, where both of his parents were professionals: his father was a gerontologist and former *bucho* in Tokyo's Ministry of Social Welfare; his mother an official of the YWCA. At present, his parents were retired from these posts and both held university teaching posts in social welfare, albeit at different private universities.[13] Nagata-san recalled the household of his high-school years as 'a bit unruly' with his mother and father trading off cooking duties every other evening but inconsistently delivering meals. Nagata-san's sister, who married young and was subsequently divorced, now lives with her teenage daughter at his parents' house and does most of the cooking. Nagata-san reports that though the family rarely shares dinner together as they are too busy, his parents are happy in their professional lives and the atmosphere at home is good.

Nagata-san attended a top public high-school in Tokyo, but failed his exams to enter Tokyo University and spent a year out as a *ronin*.[14] The next year he entered Waseda, an elite private university in Tokyo where he read physics. Although he contemplated an academic career, Nagata-san opted for Yama where upon graduation he was immediately posted to Yama's main tape factory in northern Japan. He recounts with lucidity that his Tokyo birthplace (*Tokyo no ningen* (literally, a 'Tokyo human being')) and elite education drew the attention of his generally more rural and less highly educated colleagues at the Yama tape complex. Overall, Nagata-san seemed to me to have cultivated his distinctiveness including, when I knew him, wearing garishly bright clothing, for which he was evidently famous at Yama in Japan. Of more recent significance, however, he remained at age 35 a bachelor. As such, he was the only unmarried Japanese manager at YamaMax.

When he first joined Yama, Nagata-san worked for a couple of years under Inukai-san who would later become a senior vice-director of the tape division of Yama. He was also working in this post in a high-technology engineering lab with the future Mrs Yamada, and in his next post with Yamada-san himself in mixing. Rising relatively rapidly through the ranks, he was already a full *kakaricho* after ten years at Yama. Two years later, and five months before he was posted to France, Nagata-san got a call from Inukai-san. According to Nagata-san, given the wide gap in their statuses this call could only mean a discussion about a new posting; either in Japan or abroad. Their meeting took less than ten minutes. It was brief so that, as Nagata-san explained it, 'If I declined the offer, Inukai-san could deny that the discussion had taken place'. If Inukai-san heard nothing from him within twenty-four hours, he would assume Nagata-san would take the post at YamaMax.

Nagata-san was surprised by the posting, as Yama rarely sends unmarried personnel of his age abroad. Although he described the offer as a 'mystery', he imagined that he had been requested by Otake-san (his future boss at YamaMax) following the recommendation of a Yama colleague who, although they had not worked in the same unit, knew of and respected Nagata-san's expertise. He explained to me:

> The tape plant in Japan is a small [*semai*; literally, 'thin', but implies 'socially dense' or 'intimate'] organisation, so we all know each other. Not so bad performance at the time. Now my performance is not so good: with so much to do, I can't get finished.

Nagata-san had seen the photographs and videotapes taken by Yama colleagues working in France and the US, and was not unpleased that he was being posted to France. He thought the US plant, where the only 'lifestyle' option seemed to be golf, would be boring, while in Europe he would have better opportunities for travel and skiing. The latter was important to Nagata-san although he had suffered a serious leg break while skiing a few years earlier that left him hospitalised for several months and with a permanent limp. Not disadvantaged in this sport by his short height, Nagata-san was apparently a very good skier and enjoyed the flashy outfits that went with it. Nonetheless, once in France his workload could only accommodate one skiing trip per year, although in winter one could ski within two hours' drive of YamaMax.

Starting at YamaMax two years after Yamada-san, Nagata-san was better trained for his overseas posting. The company sponsored his study of French nine hours a week for six weeks. He also had a three-day 'intensive cultural training' at Yama headquarters in Tokyo. The training consisted mainly of role-playing concerning 'safety' and 'trouble' (*turaburu*) while abroad, such as what one should do if there was a thief in the house, pickpocketed or one's car tyres were slashed. Also, details concerning the crime situation in each country to which the Yama participants would be posted were covered. Nagata-san explained, 'It was useful, but around here it's very safe'. A month before he left for France, the tape factory in Japan was visited for a week by a Japanese working at YamaMax who was accompanying three French engineers on a training mission. Nagata-san thus had a chance to ask his Japanese colleague about 'work and lifestyle' aspects of life in France, and even went out drinking with the Frenchmen and other Japanese who had earlier been posted at YamaMax. Although apparently less intensively than had Yamada-san, he studied the technical aspects of the machinery and production methods at YamaMax about which there was plenty of information available to him in Japan.

Getting personal

Nagata-san's surprise at being posted abroad as a bachelor were mirrored in, what seemed to me at the time, an extraordinary focus by his superiors at Yama on his private life. The concern was not entirely unfounded. Nagata-san had been given wide responsibilities and a heavy load of tasks. He was working very long hours indeed, and often under great personal pressure, as well as the direct and aggressive criticism of Otake-san. It is possible that Nagata-san also came under the special scrutiny of Otake-san in that, while bearing formal responsibility for overseeing the well-being of all his Japanese subordinates, Otake-san was also, though married, alone in France. The potential for them to spend private time together may have thus seemed natural. However, in practice, this was obscured by differences in rank, age and the fact that, while Nagata-san found much of Otake-san's behaviour towards him 'unacceptable' and he could do nothing about it at work, he could manage to avoid Otake-san outside of work.

Both single, Nagata-san and I in fact shared a fair amount of 'social' time; meaning, in practice, taking an occasional meal together. It was clear to me that he was not eating well and was exhausted. The Japanese, and Nagata-san in particular, who had no other obligations, often went into work over the weekend to catch up. I was at work with them many weekends and recall inviting him to my house for a meal one Saturday. He obliged but, almost literally, fell asleep in his pudding. On a couple of occasions when he had picked me up on his way to work early in the morning I noted whisky on his breath. Fairly heavy drinking is common among Japanese *salaryman*, and though it might draw their scrutiny would not necessarily be disapproved of by Nagata-san's colleagues. However, it was certain that Yama was closely attuned to the overall situation. The solution was that Nagata-san should be married which, in effect, put additional strain on him.

Nagata-san had a 'friend' in Japan – who had a good position at Japan's foremost telecommunications firm – but their relationship was not well established before his departure for France and, in any case, she had not given any indication, and Nagata-san had not requested, that they should understand each other as a couple. The fact that his Japanese colleagues at YamaMax, and especially their wives, asked me if I knew if he had a girlfriend suggested just how minor the relationship with his 'friend' was to Nagata-san: if it had been important he would have gladly admitted to it – they would not have asked me about it – and, thus, he could have possibly evaded some of their scrutiny. Instead, Nagata-san's bachelorhood was a source of amusing teases during social occasions where his colleagues' wives were present; a sign of both their affection and concern. It was not unlikely that they might have invited potential marriage partners from Japan – friends or relatives – to meet him, had he expressed interest. Indeed, this was discussed openly if, in order to avoid embarrassment, jokingly. Nagata-san, however, had experienced an arranged meeting with a potential marriage partner (*omiai*) in Japan some years earlier. She was willing but he declined the opportunity. It had embarrassed his parents so, from then on, Nagata-san resolved to sort out the matter of marriage on his own, without external intervention. Nonetheless, although Nagata-san had seen his 'friend' when he was home again for the New Year, he reported to me – in confidence – that while they had the opportunity to see each other more than once when he was home, they had not done so.

A couple of months later, YamaMax was visited by one of its directors, Nagata-san's former boss Inukai-san, who, as was to be expected, took the opportunity to meet with each of the Japanese managers. Nagata-san admitted to me afterwards, with some disgust, that the only thing Inukai-san queried were his intentions for marriage: he had not even asked how his highly stressful job at YamaMax was going. In retrospect, the explicit intervention of his senior colleague, which had included the suggestion that he could arrange, through Yama contacts, a meeting with an appropriate marriage partner, appeared to drive Nagata-san to action. He increased his e-mail correspondence with his 'friend' in Japan, building up the anticipation of his visit to Japan for a week a couple of months later. On this trip they saw a good deal more of each other and he proposed to her when he visited Japan again several months later. Although she accepted, perhaps as a matter of pride he kept the proposal private from his Japanese colleagues at YamaMax; at least until her impending visit to France to stay with him for a few days made it impossible to further carry forward the evasion. Although they were both from Tokyo, their wedding was held in the city where the Yama Corporation has its main tape factory, where Nagata-san had worked before going to France. The vast majority of guests at the wedding were from the Yama Corporation. She gave up her promising career in Tokyo and joined him in France.

Monsieur Marchalot

M. Marchalot had been at YamaMax from its beginning, twelve years earlier. Aggressive but utterly unpretentious in style, I was surprised to learn that he was the most highly educated member of the firm, having gained the British equivalent of a Master's degree in engineering during earlier employment as a manager of training at a French electrical equipment firm. Directly before joining YamaMax he had been a high-school teacher in mechanical engineering and, happy to be back in industry and with a higher salary, while at YamaMax he gained a second Master's degree, in business administration, on a part-time regional programme which only required his attendance twice per month over sixteen months. He and his wife were both *de la region* ('from the region'/locals), born in a middle-sized city some 80 miles from YamaMax, where she remained as a primary school teacher. M. Marchalot returned home on weekends where his 19-year-old son – who was working and, so, not pursuing higher education – lived as well. During the week M. Marchalot kept an apartment in a town 50 miles from Yama-Max where, an active and well-known local personage, he coached a regionally ranked women's water polo team.

Indeed, M. Marchalot was a socially keen and affable character; perhaps abnormally so. This was suggested by his immediate interactions with me on my first day at YamaMax, when all the other French members of YamaMax remained politely, but reservedly, engaged until they knew more of me. Before I had come to France I had been asked by the French *directeur general* of YamaMax to be in contact with his secretary regarding my accommodation. Eventually it was arranged that I would stay in a small village some 10 miles from the plant. It is telling that M. Marchalot, who shared this secretary with the *directeur general*, let me know, that first day, that he had largely organised my housing, a matter about which I was of course appreciative.

Meanwhile, M. Marchalot was naturally aware before I came to YamaMax that I had gained access due to connections through the Japanese side of the Yama Corporation. Indeed, once I was conducting my fieldwork this could be deduced by anyone who paid any attention to my activities at YamaMax. I did not pretend otherwise. For M. Marchalot this fact was reinforced day to day by my (apparently to him) easy interactions in Japanese with Japanese managers at YamaMax. I also often attended 'Japanese-only' meetings, as I did 'French-only' meetings, while I was perpetually present during the – usually more formal – meetings when the Japanese and French at YamaMax held joint discussions, officially in English. For a hearty communicator like M. Marchalot this was perhaps unnerving at times, especially as his own relations with Otake-san, the highest-ranked Japanese at Yama-Max, were wrought with tension.

Otake-san and M. Marchalot were of the same age – a matter of special significance among age–stratification–conscious Japanese – and they occupied the same hierarchical rank (at YamaMax) – a matter important both to the Japanese and the French. Indeed, when M. Marchalot was promoted he took over Otake-san's position as general manager of production, while Otake-san was moved laterally to become an 'adviser' of engineering, effectively formalising M. Marchalot's position as the superior to the Japanese engineers who were in this department. The adjustment was organisationally rational: Otake-san had come to YamaMax to assist in getting control of day to day production, and it was thought appropriate that eventually a French person should take over this role. This would also allow Otake-san the 'advisory' role formally and publicly encouraged by the Yama Corporation for its Japanese managers in its overseas subsidiaries. Thus, while M. Marchalot ran routine mass production, Otake-san could concentrate on keeping YamaMax responsive to the continuous pressures for higher efficiency and quality in magnetic tape by liaising with technical developments in Japan and coordinating the efforts of his Japanese staff.

This shift of roles occurred before my arrival at YamaMax, and it is unclear to me whether these formal hierarchically-oriented organisational changes were a source of difficulty between Otake-san and M. Marchalot. In any case, Otake-san, who was not subtle, hardly disguised his dislike for M. Marchalot. This made M. Marchalot's work doubly difficult. Perhaps promoted out of his (technical) depth, M. Marchalot needed access to Otake-san's detailed technical knowledge and substantial production experience.

Meanwhile, M. Marchalot was unaccustomed to difficult interpersonal relations. Indeed, he was to my knowledge well liked by his French colleagues of nearly all ranks throughout the firm for his friendliness, accessibility and, especially relevant on a functional level at YamaMax, for the fact that he trusted people to take control over and responsibility for their actions. This latter point is important. Analyses of French industrial, and bureaucratic, settings indicate that the French are highly conscious of hierarchical–positional authority (Crozier 1964). Indeed the psychological authority of French institutions, among the general public, and French 'organisations', for those within them – what I might call 'system respect' – is built upon the collapsing together of organisation, ascribed positions and persons or, in more contemporary parlance, a powerful 'embodiment' of 'position'. It is this same constellation of sensibilities that among French persons makes consciousness of class, or other notions available to carry ascribe hierarchies, especially acute. Within organisations – when there are difficulties or when mistakes are made – such social configurations, however, tend towards personal displacement of responsibility onto others or onto other 'positions' in the organisational structure. That is, while responsibility is desired as a marker of sought-after authority by members of French organisations, when things go wrong responsibility is 'too hot to handle' and quickly divested. M. Marchalot's sensitivity to French forms of sociality and his attractive personality, however, seemed to short-circuit these general tendencies and lead to responsibility-taking among his French colleagues, including those below him at considerable hierarchical distance.

Meanwhile his 'chumminess', when viewed by Frenchmen ranked above him (especially, during my fieldwork, by the *directeur general*) was personally appealing, it might also be recognised by top management, more abstractly and functionally (that is, 'strategically'), as a powerful managerial tool for the organisation. For M. Marchalot, this meant promotions and increasing levels of formal authority, that were perhaps incommensurate with his technical experience, even if he did have two advanced degrees. In some cases colleagues at an equal or slightly higher rank perhaps enjoyed his 'spell', but might also be envious, perceiving him as a threat and, in turn, be obstructive. In addition, while not to be addressed in depth here, there are limits to a 'winning personality' or the 'human touch' in a large organisation. Time and energy allow one person to 'reach' only so many others. This is all the more so when based (as in M. Marchalot's case) upon genuine interpersonal contact; as opposed to a 'winning personality' or the 'human touch' constituting aspects – along with, say, 'knowledge', 'business acumen' or 'strategic vision' – of symbolic formulae attributed, routinely in corporate contexts, to 'organisational leadership capability'.

Allow me to flesh out this point. That Jack Welsh, the famous former CEO of the General Electric Corporation, may have been understood to be a 'good person', along with possessing evident 'business savvy', was no doubt a powerfully motivating image for GE employees, that was generated both within the organisation and reflected back into it from the publicity that surrounded him. However, only a very small proportion of GE employees ever had the opportunity to 'get to know' Jack. His 'personality' was an organisational commodity, reinforcing ideas of how GE employees could do more of what they did well already, while it was a means of giving GE a public face, or 'personality', which, it was presumably felt at GE, as at other large corporations, strengthened consumers' desire to engage in 'economic' transactions over washing machines or nuclear power plants. While in a far smaller organisational context, what was at stake in M. Marchalot's personality and interactions were social operations that reinforced some French persons' possibilities for action *outside* French organisational norms. In this case the configuration required, perhaps literally, M. Marchalot's 'human touch', among other means of trust building, that could lead to original and potentially instrumentally successful forms of social action in the organisation. Thus, as M. Marchalot was promoted, the networks, the size and the strains of his interpersonal responsibilities expanded.

M. Marchalot's social relations were, thus, sincere; not specifically instrumental, but expectant of others' response. Our relationship was no different. As a result, on more than one occasion, especially during difficult periods in the workplace for him, I was queried directly by him as to what the Japanese, and usually Otake-san, were either saying or thinking. As the core of my research interests lies in analysis of such cross-cultural communications and social relations, I was keen as a matter of principle not to, in effect, 'interpret' for M. Marchalot, or any other of my French or Japanese subjects, and thereby risk skewing any situation further than I did already by my day to day presence. Indeed, throughout at that point nearly four years of fieldwork in subsidiaries abroad of both Japanese and Western corporations I had managed to very rarely find myself obliged to do so. M. Marchalot, however, was not easy to put off course by my tendency in such cases to listen seriously (rather than speak), or engage with generalisations on matters cross-cultural. Indeed, even if he understood no Japanese, I expect that M. Marchalot's own perspective on cross-cultural social relations at YamaMax was generally more astute than my own; after all, he had been 'in the field' for twelve years. I also understood that for someone like M. Marchalot the problem with me (exacerbated by the pressures upon him) was that I *might* know more about what was unfolding in a particular situation than he knew. Like almost everyone, I liked M. Marchalot, so our social relations were complex and challenging.

Monsieur Legrand

As chief of production, M. Legrand reported directly to M. Marchalot, who had interviewed him twelve years earlier, just after YamaMax had been established. M. Legrand is from the small city 15 miles from YamaMax, where he studied through to a *bac* (A levels) in sciences. He did military service for one year and then received a salary from the government for one year of training in chemical engineering. From there, M. Legrand went to work as a technician at a computer company in Bordeaux, but after three years away was keen to return 'home' and responded to a newspaper notice for a position as technician in production at YamaMax. He passed a basic technical examination and two weeks later was called in for an interview. According to M. Legrand, the interview went badly, but M. Marchalot and another French manager who interviewed him asked M. Legrand to wait in the hall while they called a French colleague charged with overseeing quality control at YamaMax. This interview was apparently far more technically oriented, and M. Legrand was informed by post shortly thereafter that he was offered the job. He happily accepted and joined YamaMax two months later, aged 24.

At YamaMax, M. Legrand worked as a foreman in the quality control (QC) department for four years, spent two years in quality assessment (QA) and, rising quickly in the YamaMax hierarchy, became chief of quality control, a position he held for four years before he became chief of production. He had been in the latter job for two years when I came to YamaMax. Although M. Legrand was happy for the change, as the routine of QC had become dull for him and production generates a far more variable workload, he admitted that he found the work at times quite stressful. This was not indicated in the slightest in his demeanour, however. Always ready to exchange a friendly joke even under highly pressurised circumstances, M. Legrand was generally so laconic and mellow that, while it seemed to me that others – both French and Japanese engineers – might implode from the pressure, at times I wondered if M. Legrand was fully up to speed with his work. This possibility, however, was never suggested to me by anyone at YamaMax.

According to my interview with M. Legrand, Otake-san, who as we know was originally sent to YamaMax on brief missions to try to sort out the situation when production rates and quality had fallen badly, apparently handpicked M. Legrand for production, recognising in him someone of talent. Soon after Otake-san took his 'permanent' position at YamaMax, displacing the US production manager, according to M. Legrand, Otake-san put pressure on the new French *directeur general* to give M. Legrand the new, and highly responsible, position of production manager of mixing and calendering: the initial, and most technically demanding, stages of tape production. In this position, M. Legrand had six engineers directly under him who, in turn, controlled 110 technicians and workers. M. Legrand, thus, worked directly under Otake-san for two years in production until Otake-san moved over to the role of adviser of engineering, essentially for-malising his position at the top of the Japanese engineering team and making a place for a French manager to take greater responsibility. As we know, with Otake-san's move, M. Marchalot became general manager of production.

M. Legrand clearly recognised his period under Otake-san as an appren-ticeship, mentioning that Otake-san held him 'under his wing' and that he had made M. Legrand's training his 'mission'. He told me, 'Even now, when Otake-san is no longer my direct boss, he still puts pressure on me, often disapproving of my production choices, stating to me in English, "That is not what I taught you"'. With his gregarious attitude, M. Legrand took such comments with a grain of salt, aware on the one hand that pointed comments by Otake-san were his way of being friendly, while on the other, he thought Otake-san might be correct. He was also aware that, formally, unless it went terribly badly – and M. Legrand knew that it had not gone badly – day to day mass production was no longer the responsibility of Otake-san. During my fieldwork I had noticed nothing particular between them and was, indeed, surprised when I learned that they had spent two years working intimately, day in and day out.

During my interview with M. Legrand, it was clear that he was somewhat relieved to be free of Otake-san's direct tutelage. Their close relationship had meant at times that M. Legrand attracted Otake-san's negative atten-tions. M. Legrand was clear on the point that Otake-san's interpersonal behaviour was debilitating to anyone's desire to work hard. Nonetheless, he appreciated Otake-san's insistence on exacting work. If he asked for some-thing the next day, Otake-san expected M. Legrand to stay up all night, if need be, to get it done. (It is unclear to me whether M. Legrand ever actu-ally did this.) M. Legrand felt that on occasion the tasks that Otake-san required were not essential, and delivery unrealistic within the time frame suggested, but nonetheless understood – correctly – that this was the type of request Japanese managers often made of their subordinates in Japan. The form of such tasks in Japan have everything to do with proving willingness to work hard at the request of the boss, and often little to do with the intrinsic importance of the work itself.[15]

M. Legrand contrasted work under Otake-san with that of his new boss, M. Marchalot. M. Marchalot would ask for things in general, without saying exactly what was required, and then later would change his mind about what was needed. On the one hand M. Marchalot's vague orders gave M. Legrand room to manoeuvre and, indeed, he admitted that he often did as he saw fit in his work, with the thought that he could justify it later. How-ever, overall I had a sense that M. Legrand was uncomfortable with the de facto flexibility he was afforded by M. Marchalot, and found that Otake-san's exacting orders more closely matched the prerogatives of engineering. In the next chapter I will present further evidence suggesting this interpretation but, frankly, no sense of dissatisfaction with M. Marchalot was evident day to day where M. Legrand was concerned.

M. Legrand seemed a 'small town kid', who had done well. He had had a bit of luck in being promoted up the ranks very quickly, as YamaMax grew. He now had an excellent and secure job, especially by the economic standards of the hard-pressed agricultural community in which he lived, where he had held an unpaid but elected position of municipal counsellor for the past six years. M. Legrand went about things entirely unruffled; he was well-mannered, respectful of authority, friendly and genuinely helpful to everyone.

Organising persons, cultures and hierarchy

Through descriptions of some of YamaMax's Japanese and French engineers, I hope to have counterbalanced common perspectives on formal organisations, and their members' lives, as mundane and empty, uneventful and uninteresting. The textual strategy employed here – a focus on life histories – has allowed a free-flowing and comparative commentary on career progression, as well as persons' relations to each other and to the Yama Corporation. In examining 'individual' histories one can see that members of corporations such as Yama reproduce powerful corporate ideologies and appropriate behaviour as they also, by their varied personal experiences as persons, implicitly and explicitly seek to challenge those very forms.

The remaining sections of this chapter analyse the intertwining of hierarchy and cross-cultural relations among YamaMax engineers. I begin with the claim that in organisations communications are articulated along with knowledge of hierarchical relations. I am explicitly not saying 'communications are articulated *within* knowledge of hierarchical relations' because I am not claiming the precedence of knowledge of hierarchy over the entire repertoire of communicative forms of members of organisations. Thus, for instance, a member of an organisation understands the communicative efforts of his superior through a hierarchical context that influences, but does not control, that comprehension, just as hierarchy affects but does not necessarily determine the quality of his response. Let me add to this claim regarding the play of hierarchy upon organisational communications the natural dynamic of cross-cultural relations which so obviously pervades YamaMax, as it does an increasing proportion of contemporary, modern organisations. My overarching point is that we should not consider that any particular factor – hierarchy, personality, cross-cultural dynamics nor, in YamaMax's case, technical knowledge – dominates an organisation's social relations. Rather, they are all cooperative and conjoined in the social repertoires of persons organising places like YamaMax. Such matters are best understood by reflection on actual social interchange in such places.

In my discussion and interpretations below I focus to a considerable degree on communication patterns between and among the Japanese and

French engineers at YamaMax in light of difficulties both groups had in dealing with Otake-san, the top ranked Japanese at YamaMax. By all accounts, Otake-san was a difficult person to work with. Rather than skewing the data, however, I am confident that the pressure of his activities rather exposed his interlocutors' notions as to what expected behaviour should consist in, albeit overlaid, as we shall see, by complex cross-cultural dynamics. My discussion below will, I hope, suggest that their struggles with Otake-san effectively dragged them toward more explicit knowledge of proper form, often expressed through implicit actions, than perhaps would have otherwise been revealed in normal office situations. That is, while at times a worrying presence, Otake-san's exceptional behaviour served up the rules. Let my analysis itself speak for this interpretation, however.

The prerogatives of extremities

I begin by contrasting the hierarchical, social and interpersonal positions of Otake-san, the highest-ranking Japanese at YamaMax, and Susumu-kun, the lowest, vis-à-vis their French colleagues. As will become immediately clear in a verbatim transcript in the next chapter, Otake-san's English was disjointed at the best of times, while he spoke practically no French. According to his Japanese colleagues, as well as my own experience, he was not an articulate speaker of Japanese either. He was not speech-*less*; he was unconcerned or unable to make himself comprehended thoroughly through words. And he could dispose of the niceties of linguistic communication while the technical content and emotional implications – the meaning – of his communications were ordinarily keenly sought. This was so because both Otake-san's French and Japanese core audience of mid-level engineers were aware of three points relating to Otake-san. He was in the highest hierarchical position, he had enormous knowledge directly pertaining to the production techniques used at YamaMax and he was feared for his aggressiveness toward the other Japanese engineers but also, occasionally, his French colleagues.

Meanwhile, the lowest-ranking Japanese engineer, Susumu-kun, was also a poor speaker of French and English. Although he was ten years younger than most of his French colleagues, they shared similar technical knowledge and formal authority over workplace activities taking place on the shop-floor. Susumu-kun was for the most part mute in work time meetings with the French and, quite unlike Otake-san, was not expressive in other ways, such as 'body language', in such contexts. During Japanese-only meetings he similarly contained himself, and so acted as should the lowest-ranking member of the group while paying close attention to the proceedings.[16] In meetings with the Japanese Otake-san explicitly defended Susumu-kun's demure attitude and, unlike all the Japanese engineers but Yamada-san, never made him a target of his aggression. If Susumu-kun fell short in his work, it was explained by Otake-san as due to his youthful lack of experience, further made visible by his lower rank compared with his Japanese colleagues. I am unaware if any shortcomings in Susumu-kun's technical or managerial abilities were evident to his French colleagues but, in any case, such matters were never acknowledged or implied in joint Japanese–French meetings: the assumption was that all of the Japanese were experts.

When Susumu-kun spoke in English or, extremely rarely, uttered a word in French, he spoke poorly, which meant that his communicative forms were 'difficult' for the French who, meanwhile, spoke no Japanese beyond the most basic greetings. Unlike their relations with Otake-san, however, it was unnecessary for the French engineers to seek out Susumu-kun's 'meaning' – in this context, his technical knowledge – and when they did, it pertained solely to topics on which they were aware that he had quite specific information. That is, not communicating with Susumu-kun held no risk in terms of jeopardising relations with those who held more tangible hierarchical power. Information Susumu-kun held could be collected elsewhere or, when necessary, directly and privately with him, and so largely out of range of other organisational activities where communications difficulties with him could affect other matters. Thus, in comparing the experience of French engineers' relations with Otake-san and Sumusu-kun, standing as they were at the two relative hierarchical extremes of relations with the Japanese for the French engineers, while communications through more efficient linguistic forms largely fell out with both of them, efforts to communicate were sustained with Otake-san due to his hierarchical position, authority and enormous corresponding knowledge base.

Communicative density, and complications, at the hierarchical centre

Meanwhile, what about communication between the other four Japanese mid-level engineers, among them Yamada-san and Nagata-san (whom I described in the first section of this chapter) and the French engineers? The mid-level Japanese engineers could not luxuriate in the linguistic inaccessibility enjoyed by Otake-san and Susumu-kun vis-à-vis the French engineers. When I say 'could not' I am not literally saying they had no choice. I am saying that, compared with Otake-san and Susumu-kun, their choice was radically limited by the relative correspondence of their hierarchical positions with the French engineers. The Japanese engineers were hierarchically clustered quite tightly to one another in terms both of formal ranks and correspondences of age, as they were on both counts with many of their French engineer colleagues as well. Further, their relations with the French were densely framed by the technical discourse of production. That is, they could not be inaccessible from their French colleagues if they hoped to get their work done. The quality of the pressures on them will be made clearer in descriptions below of their patterns of communication with their French colleagues, placed, as I have claimed they must be, in the context of technical, interpersonal *and* cross-cultural relations.

Recalling that the principle vocabulary of social interaction at YamaMax concerned the organisation's explicit technical problems with continuous industrial production, these mid-level Japanese engineers depended on their French engineer counterparts to organise the enormous quantity of information so focussed. Meanwhile, the French engineers' relations with their mid-level Japanese counterparts was their only means of access to vast stocks of information – now-historical technical documentation, and collective experience held by persons in Japan – which might assist their oversight of day to day production in France. (In industry, while technology may change, historic patterns of production provide ideas for organising production in future.) Similarly, these mid-level Japanese engineers were burdened with the responsibilities of being 'positioned' to carry questions and information regarding technical aspects of production between the French to their superior, Otake-san, who embodied an enormous store of experience and knowledge in his own right.[17] The more powerful – that is, in this context, accurate, timely and expansive – the French and Japanese engineers' exchanges regarding technical information, the stronger their collective (and personal) successes in sustaining high-quality production and output. Thus, they were important 'stakeholders' in each other's knowledge. Let us be clear, however, that the seeming equality inferred by the notion of sharing 'stakes' in each other's knowledge does not mean that they were equally positioned in terms of the flow of information. As mentioned already, and as I will detail ethnographically in the next chapter, the Japanese engineers were positioned to, consciously or unconsciously, filter what was, effectively, information controlled by Japanese members of the larger Yama Corporation. Meanwhile, the de facto authority of the Japanese at YamaMax meant the French engineers had no grounds for restricting Japanese access to whatever formal information the French engineers had gained.

In studies of organisations much is made of the dilemmas of middle managers, who cope with substantive hierarchical pressures from both above and below. In cross-cultural organisations such pressures are not unlikely to become far more complicated. These Japanese middle manager engineers are persons, and so – in spite of the technical emphasis of their 'mission statements' – not automatons nor machinery, nor entirely autonomous nor mechanical. Their communications, and thereby their burden of carrying information 'in between' themselves and their French colleagues, could not confine itself purely to technical matters. In order to achieve their technical goals, it seems that they bore the responsibility, for instance, of explicitly explaining to their French colleagues the meaning and implications of the abrasive communicative style in which the knowledge that Otake-san held was often delivered. We have noted that both the Japanese mid-level engineers and the French engineers were dependent upon Otake-san in ways that they were not dependent upon Susumu-kun's far more technically limited, hierarchically irrelevant knowledge. Thus, had they been able, or even attempted, to explain Otake-san's behaviour, it is likely to have served to make their communications with their French counterparts more effective personally and, so, technically effective as well.

It might be argued that these mid-level Japanese engineers had the opportunity to expand coalitions of information-sharing through the construction of alliances with French engineers regarding the 'problems' they shared with Otake-san's communicative style. They did not do so, however. Indeed, they maintained silence on the topic, an indication within Japanese social relations that they were embarrassed and incapable of justifying Otake-san's behaviour. Effectively, conditions of solidarity among the Japanese group as a whole made it impossible to risk its own splintering by communicating outside the group where 'difficult', personal problems were concerned. Allow me to unpack this dynamic further for, as an example, though dramatic, it puts us right at the heart of the type of issues arising as a matter of course in cross-cultural social relations.

As a practical matter these French and Japanese engineers shared offices and so the majority of their direct communications were conducted physically apart from Otake-san himself. In other words, there was no explicit risk within this physical space to articulating the view, which everyone implicitly held, that aspects of Otake-san's behaviour were disagreeable.[18] Actually, and this is a critical point, separately, the French engineers periodically discussed it among themselves, while the Japanese entertained silent but implicit understandings of his behaviour, that were communicated bodily, perhaps unconsciously, and often; perhaps, as they were ordinarily its target, in order to brace themselves against it. (Such forms of in-group communication – spoken and/or silent – are commonplace among subordinates regarding their superiors in both Japanese and French organisations.) Between the mid-level Japanese and the French engineers, however, avoidance and social distance prevailed over what would have to be articulated as personalised – as opposed to common technologically-oriented – interactions; for reaction or consolation regarding Otake-san's 'episodes' was *personal*.

In practice the pattern and logic of their communicative taboo operated as follows. The mid-level French engineers, more often than not observers of Otake-san's extreme behaviour, would not raise the matter with a particular Japanese target of Otake-san at risk of embarrassing the victim. Nor, meanwhile, would they raise the matter with the other mid-level Japanese engineers.[19] In the event a French engineer was targeted he would later be consoled by his French compatriots, at least to the degree of brief acknowledgement that he had experienced a 'hard time'.[20] Thus, the French engineers' behaviour regarding Otake-san was keenly reflective of their sense of *hierarchy* over technical *knowledge*. They felt subordinate to their Japanese colleagues' knowledge of this matter along two grounds. On the one hand they perceived the Japanese as holding more de facto structural power in the organisation than they did, which was accurate when one thinks of

YamaMax's primarily Japanese vocabulary of production – technical information and the control of its flows – as well as the broader picture of financial control. Meanwhile the French mirrored their own understanding of cultural knowledge and behaviour vis-à-vis their expectations of the Japanese. They were, thus, reflecting (or projecting) upon the Japanese their 'cultural' authority as Frenchmen to provide whatever explanation or interpretation of French behaviour might be required. That is, they deferred to the principle of self-reflection and public presentation; the authority of their culture to explain itself both to itself and others. Thus, from the French engineers' cultural perspective, initiative on explaining the complicated and important matter of Otake-san's behaviour rested entirely with the Japanese mid-level engineer colleagues.

Meanwhile, the Japanese engineers, forced by various hierarchical correspondences to the communicative vortex – 'in-between' – similarly acted in ways consistent with the prerogatives of their own cultural knowledge: they avoided altogether articulating the topic with the French. In fact, perhaps as they were embarrassed, over time they seemed to fold themselves ever further away from the French and, therefore, the content and meaning of Otake-san's knowledge as they understood it, even while they may have otherwise thought this was inadvisable as it might influence the technical aspects of their work. Among other ways of deducing this, both the Japanese and French engineers told me that over the years they spent less and less time socialising together outside of work. For Japanese *salaryman* such settings – made more fluid practically *and* symbolically by alcohol consumption – are, as we know, the only place where interpersonal matters of this kind can be discussed.

Interestingly, however, the Japanese engineers did not often discuss Otake-san openly among themselves, even during informal social occasions. It seems to me that Otake-san's leverage over each of them was so potent, their number so few, and they were so much in practice in competition with one another (as they were at similar age and rank), that their capacity to elicit and articulate compassionate sympathy on this issue with their 'own', was quite limited. In any case, it was far less potent than the opportunities produced as a norm in organised settings such as those of the Yama Corporation in Japan itself, as I shall further examine below.

Nagata-san was serious and his expression deeply felt when he related to me, after a particularly difficult two week period, that he was 'treated worse than a dog' by Otake-san. However, he could not articulate his rage to his Japanese colleagues who, present as they were in observing Nagata-san's experience, were themselves driven to hope, simply, that it would be some time before they were so targeted. This process of silencing suggests perhaps a dismantling of the power of Japanese group coalition. Yet, the silencing itself rearticulated and reconstituted that very coalition, if not through the medium of language itself then through other routings of authority and power. Examination of the communicative experience of the French and Japanese engineers and Otake-san condenses into a single organised setting their cross-cultural, as well as general organisational, dynamics and – from an apparent perspective of failure of communication – the process of reproduction and embodiment of the Japanese corporation as a 'seamless whole', a matter I take up at depth in Chapter 6.

Recirculating productions

At the tape division of the Yama Corporation back 'home' in Japan, Otake-san had a reputation as a difficult manager, but a brilliant and hard working engineer. However those who worked with him in Japan had other resources at hand to defuse or cushion his hard-edged interpersonal style. Among these were simply a larger population of similarly-trained and experienced Yama personnel, an older and structurally more complex, that is, a deeper, organisation which, furthermore, included persons senior to Otake-san who could implicitly, and explicitly, hold his behaviour in check. At YamaMax, far away in France, there were few restraints. Social and hierarchical relations between the Japanese themselves were overheated by their small number and their de facto alienation from other kinds of local, read Japanese, support. Though they might not much discuss such matters in any case, the Japanese managers in France did not, for instance, get much relief when they went home, where wives and children with little French language ability were lonely, coping with distance from extended family and friends, and a minor French city's schools and neighbourhoods. These cross-cultural conditions thus threw the YamaMax Japanese managers and their families together with more dependency or, perhaps, in an altered form of dependency compared with what they were familiar in Japan. As we have seen, their relations were intense, necessary and highly strained, but they understood each other, at all costs, as together.

My analysis, stressing that the mid-level Japanese engineers – embarrassed – did not take on the emotional, that is the personal, side of their communications with their French colleagues, may appear a one-sided and unobjective criticism. I believe, however, that I have related the situation accurately. Note, also, that I have pointed out that due to their own lack of language ability and the inflexibility of their own cultural vision, the French engineers effectively, and perhaps irresponsibly, turned over the reins of authority on this matter to their Japanese colleagues. Let me mention here, as well, that working with Otake-san was important but was not the only issue about which the Japanese and French engineers interacted with each other. Nor were relations with Otake-san the only platform upon which the Japanese engineers' relations as a group were seated. The case of Otake-san and the engineers around him is merely a superb vehicle for focussing our attentions analytically upon the organising of cross-cultural dynamics in organisational settings.

I have argued that the Japanese engineers were at little risk according to a logical social equation regarding the building up of an information flow about Otake-san with their French counterparts, a matter that would have greatly benefitted both parties – technically speaking – over the long run. This risk refers however to whether or not Otake-san might observe them sharing information. I have suggested that Otake-san is unlikely to have cared, and I expect that had the Japanese engineers thought about it, they would have recognised this. The reason there was nothing for Otake-san to observe, in practice, has nothing to do with a logical social equation, however. It was based on fear of a perception of cultural duplicity among the Japanese engineers; that is, jeopardising the idea of communicative integrity within their own Japanese group. I stress the term 'idea' here for, as we have seen, they did not, and perhaps could not, much communicate – explicitly – about Otake-san with each other. In short, a crack in the notion of their own relations was evidently a far greater risk than a rift with the French regarding the technical communications upon which their formal 'work' depended. While in practice divisiveness and embarrassment clearly affected the Japanese engineers, by not discussing or acknowledging it, divisiveness and embarrassment were banished from the vocabulary of their social relations. It affected them but did not exist as a threat to the idea of what they should be. A 'seamless whole' was, so, reproduced among them.

Of course, at YamaMax itself all of these factors served to recycle perceptions of 'difference' from French colleagues; persons who were nevertheless formally named as members of, as part of, the Yama Corporation. The principles surrounding the creation of boundaries, necessary to the production of 'seamlessness' and a source of organisational strength in powerful Japanese organisations, therefore gained a particular expression within their own organisation. The question arising here, of course, is who may participate informally in what it is that reproduces the Yama Corporation as a 'seamless whole' as it is known to its Japanese members. That the French and Japanese engineers at YamaMax could not speak of their joint experience of Otake-san is suggestive of the processes defining their inability to move their relations beyond its formal, technical and work-laden parameters. Their relations were thus largely emptied of the meaning and commitments that might carry them beyond their merely contractual obligations, precisely the kinds of commitments between persons that reproduce large, powerful and domestically-successful Japanese corporations.

Conclusion

Japanese managers' domestic Japan experience 'naturally' encourages an expectation of similarly dense and high quality organisational information flows from committed members of the firm when posted to subsidiaries abroad. However such flows appear to be arduous to recreate abroad, as they depend, of course, on language but also on similar backgrounds and assumptions about social interactions which serve to further prop up circulations between images, products, 'the company' and persons. Poor information flows are likely, in turn, to increase the desire of Japanese managers abroad to keep decision-making under their control and to fine tune the work of their foreign colleagues, especially among engineers at structurally similar levels. In practice this encourages the presence of large numbers of Japanese expatriates.[21]

It has been suggested to me by some Japanese managers that a high density of interactions between Japanese engineers on-site and their French counterparts would encourage what I call 'managerial technology transfer' by multiplying the contacts between teacher and pupil. While in theory this appears reasonable, there is some evidence from my observations of Japanese engineers in several overseas settings that 'understanding' why a task needs to take place may be confounded with 'carrying out an order'. Japanese managers consider, as a matter of principle underlying their notion of work force competence, that a staff member is made more capable by understanding, for example, the impact of a particular task on a flow of tasks, rather than turning screw 5 at time X; or the chemical implications of mixing an element with another at a specific temperature, rather than merely being sure that A is at 89–91°C when mixed with B. Indeed, as I will elaborate further in Chapter 6, the education of shopfloor labour – mobilising their thinking while using their mechanical skills – is the core distinction between 'Japanese' and 'Fordist' shopfloors. The issue at stake in cross-cultural settings, then, is that, at least until persons learn to do so otherwise, understanding and learning take place within the culturally specified frames associated with linguistic, ethnic and/or national differences. At YamaMax, the Japanese often seemed to project meaning from a Japanese context onto the French frame; and vice versa. This problem may perhaps be best understood by way of example.

In Japan a highly trained and experienced worker responsible for maintaining robots on the shopfloor will verbally report to his superior the successful completion of a purely routine repair. A written record of this repair appears on the maintenance worker's daily report, which is perused by his supervisor and acknowledged by signature by a production manager. It becomes a permanent record. The verbal report to the supervisor of the repair has no instrumental effect on production output for the day, but is loaded with meaning. It is a statement both about a hierarchical relationship (respect for the authority of his supervisor) as well as co-participation (equality) concerning jointly working for the success of the firm. In an extreme example of this transcendence of 'co-worker's' hierarchical relations, I once observed at a factory in Japan a Japanese maintenance engineer describing to a robot the tasks he was performing upon it, as though they were mutually responsible for getting the job done.

In my experience, Frenchmen working in manufacturing settings would find such anthropomorphising of machines ludicrous. Meanwhile the effort to transcend hierarchy, such as appealing to abstract goals to justify joint activity, is especially threatening and disruptive to an endemic respect for formal aspects of hierarchy in French organisational dynamics (Crozier 1964). Thus a Japanese engineer may think he is 'transferring knowledge' through the projected kinship of, for instance, joint participation in the slog of relatively routine activities of a French maintenance engineer. However, unless his French colleague has learned to consider the act otherwise, before they have together turned the first screw this 'joint participation' indicates to the Frenchman that he is incompetent and unable to do the job independently, that is, without interference, as would befit his position in the French organisational framework.

As is clear from our discussions in this chapter, on the ground at Yama-Max a French engineer who has regular contact with the Japanese would hold relatively high rank and, through experience with the Japanese, may understand, and possibly appreciate, the intentions of his Japanese colleagues. His reticence in the 'public' social arena of the (French) shopfloor, however, would remain intact, for he must consider that his observers, French subordinates 'on the line', would account for this interaction as a demonstration that the Japanese manager did not respect the French engineer's knowledge. His day to day authority over his French subordinates might be hollowed out in practice by intimate cross-cultural events such as these.

In effect, through the best intentions of a Japanese manager to assist a local colleague in the most committed way he knows how, I have observed French managers in cross-cultural double binds which exponentially complicate the classic problems of the middle manager. On the one hand the French manager has likely gained a position that puts him in direct contact with the Japanese due to his educational background, technical know-how and/or skills in understanding the Japanese. However his hierarchical position, in combination with awareness of de facto Japanese 'ownership' of the firm, restrains him from suggesting that the Japanese might, also, work differently. On the other hand, he is a victim of his own success vis-à-vis his local subordinates, potentially obliged to conduct himself in ways with the Japanese that may effectively undermine his authority by local standards.

In addition to the structural strains they experience as managers,[22] then, we can recognise here the considerable pressures on French managers to act either as cultural brokers in Japanese firms or, in order to evade certain sociological problems altogether, avoid the process of interacting with Japanese colleagues as much as possible.

I opened this chapter by recounting stories of several Japanese and French managers at YamaMax and so attempted to undermine common perspectives on organisations, and sociality within them, as dull and purely functional. The elaboration of life histories has also allowed comparisons of careers between Japanese and French managers, as well as a description of tensions between the corporate and personal prerogatives of members of YamaMax. I then described in some detail the general patterns of relations between Japanese and French engineers of YamaMax. Here I sought to acknowledge hierarchy but treat it as one among several other features organising their social relations. The final section of the chapter addressed more generally the importance of focusing upon cross-cultural communications between Japanese and non-Japanese managers in order to account for differences in the ethos between domestic and foreign 'Japanese' firms.

With data to hand that has clearly articulated the relevance of cross-cultural and cross-linguistic dynamics, technical knowledge and personality to understanding how YamaMax organises itself, it may not seem at all radical to describe organisations as constituted through these features as well as through hierarchy. This move is, however, surprisingly unusual. It is more parsimonious to claim that hierarchy structures organisational communications, and parsimony fits what in some circles is recognised as the appropriate methodological thrust of analysis. From another (explicitly less analytical) perspective the idea that hierarchy structures or controls organisational communications is *intuitively* attractive: we notice in ourselves differences in emotional anticipation and content in engaging persons in superior or subordinate positions relative to us. This may be recognised in our language use as well: we describe apparently non-hierarchically informed social relations with our peers as 'relaxed', thus inferring that hierarchical relations, usually read as those taking place in organisations, tend to be tense, uncomfortable and, thereby, negative. Either move gives artificial precedence to the idea of hierarchy. If we prioritise hierarchy, we cannot help but oversimplify our subsequent interpretive task by looking through it at social behaviour, and thus cut away important subtleties of social relations in formally organised settings. Here I retain an analytic perspective that demands attention to the multiple features engaged in any set of communicative acts. Through the example of the engineers of YamaMax I hope to have demonstrated that hierarchy, technical knowledge and cross-cultural dynamics are cooperative, while also conflictual, in organising persons in such places.

Notes

1 On the UK, see Oliver and Wilkinson 1992; Garrahan and Stewart 1992; Williams 1994. With the exception of Kenney and Florida (1993), reports critical of shopfloor activities at Japanese plants, especially in the automotive sector, in the US are numerous. A good deal of this has been driven far more by negative opinion than by sound analysis within factories (see, for instance, Fucini and Fucini 1990). Negative press reports in the US, often about assembly line conditions, were especially numerous in the late 1980s and early 1990s. This followed the decline of the US northern 'rust belt' and a honeymoon period of investment by the Japanese in economically depressed, predominately white and traditionally non-union southern mountain states. (Indeed, this is not unlike what occurred in the UK, though locating in non-union areas was more difficult.) From the late 1980s many US states competed with each other to offer incentives to Japanese industrial investors; many of them maintaining expensive 'representative offices' in Tokyo.

2 Japanese managers at private corporations use a term equivalent in meaning to 'listening post', with its connotation of the information gathering in foreign countries of government intelligence agencies.

It might be noted that especially when compared with the minimal support traditionally provided to US businesses by US embassies abroad, Japanese embassies gather and distribute to Japanese firms a great deal of economic information as well as assisting with legal and political matters.

3 The US has been Japan's most important trading partner and main source of foreign technology throughout the postwar period. Major Japanese firms have extensive 'liaison' offices in Washington. They provide a major source of funding to US legal and political consulting firms that are often staffed by former US government officials.

4 Though less pronounced, this pattern is mimicked in the career structure of the bureaucrats of Japan's most important ministries, especially the Ministry of Economy, Trade and Industry and the Ministry of Finance. Both of these ministries post career bureaucrats within Japanese embassies abroad, while in the more important countries they establish their own offices separate from the embassy.

5 Indeed, I have invariably been impressed by the sheer physical endurance and vitality of director-level managers, who carry a daunting range of responsibilities.

6 With the exception of the French *directeur general* of YamaMax, to my knowledge no French managers had the opportunity for individual discussions with visiting Japanese directors.

7 Interestingly, overseas subsidiaries such as YamaMax are referred to as *kogaishya*, while their 'sister' factories in Japan, undertaking largely equivalent technical work, were in most cases considered part of the main firm. In terms of the jobs of Japanese Yama employees, as accounted for by the personnel department in Japan, overseas subsidiaries could be considered either as at the main firm or at a *kogaishya*, depending usually upon the individual's previous post in Japan. This categorical flexibility is a further demonstration of overseas subsidiaries' liminality due to their physical distance from Japan and the fact that the membership of overseas subsidiaries is predominately non-Japanese.

8 As indicated in my descriptions of his high-school years, Otake-san had been a serious athlete. He thought he might take up golf once he was retired, but did not consider it sport. To my knowledge the only physical activity in which he was engaged in France was swimming in the (gorgeous) public pool during summer in the nearby city where he and all the Japanese lived.

9 I do not have this impression in Otake-san's case, but among highly driven Japanese *salaryman*, 'leisure' itself often becomes an obsession. A *salaryman* I knew in Bangkok had no fewer than twelve complete sets of golf clubs though he was, admittedly, an extremely talented golfer and indeed 'traded' on his skills within the firm and in the Japanese expatriate community in Thailand. Another, from a major Japanese domestic energy supplier, set as his *'mission'* a visit to all fifty US states during a ten-month 'research associateship' at a think-tank at a major US university. I was associate director of this think-tank, and responsible for overseeing his research output. He and his Japanese colleagues kept his plans secret from me until a pleasurable evening out, a few days before he returned to Japan. He managed forty-two states (and a very insightful paper).

10 All of these events occurred two to three years before my fieldwork at YamaMax began.

11 Yamada-san was, however, a serious tennis player and was known to be the top player in the Yama tape division at home in Japan. Though entirely out of shape, I was interested in a game, having played tennis competitively years before at the University of California. In the event this could only be arranged once during my

fieldwork. A perfectly friendly match between us – witnessed by his wife and small children, who occasionally wandered onto court – the ever-competitive Otake-san apparently took an intense interest in the result.

12 A note on the use of *kun* with the Japanese manager named *Susumu. Susumu* is this individual's (pseudo) first name, and *kun* a marker of a lower or younger-ranking person, with whom one can interact with comparative familiarity. With all other Japanese persons in this study I use their surname and the marker *san,* which designates either formality, same or superior rank vis-à-vis ego. I use *Susumu-kun* because this is what all the other Japanese used at YamaMax in referring to him, as did, in following the Japanese lead, all the French managers on site.

13 In an extraordinary incidence of serendipity, I had met Nagata-san's father during my first visit to Japan in 1974. (Again, Nagata-san is a pseudonym.) A leading authority on the condition of Japan's elderly, he was instrumental in arranging contacts that made possible my research at an old folks' home outside of Tokyo, my first site of anthropological fieldwork. Beyond a letter thanking him for his help on my departure the following year (1975), I had not been in contact with him since.

14 Literally, *ronin* means 'masterless samurai', but refers to high-school graduates who have failed to enter university (and are, thus, masterless) and who usually 'cram' at special schools (*juku*) for the following year's entrance exams.

15 The stereotyped pattern is the following. When a requested report, requiring a large amount of (often highly tedious) work, is delivered by hand to the superior, he reviews it momentarily and then rips it up on the spot, while ordering it been done again – and better – without advice as to what was wrong with the original. Nearly every Japanese *salaryman* I know has either experienced or observed something along these lines in their company.

16 As mentioned in discussion of Mrs Yamada's hospitalisation, in contrast to formal settings, in informal contexts Susumu-kun was very 'familiar' inter-personally with all the other Japanese engineers, except for Otake-san. These included lunch, evening or weekend meals and drinking parties, as well as coffee breaks, invariably combined with cigarette-smoking, and other opportunities for non-formalised discussion with Japanese colleagues during work. Indeed, he had a cutting sense of humour, which in informal contexts he freely displayed towards me as well. At 25, and having grown up deep in the countryside of one of Japan's most rural prefectures, Susumu-kun's posting to France was his first overseas experience. It seemes he found the overall situation entirely bizarre. Interpersonally, and in terms of his cross-cultural interactions, he made practically no effort to venture beyond the company of his Japanese colleagues except where his work specifically required it.

17 This portage also at times included Susumu-kun's limited but, where needed, exacting knowledge.

18 Had such direct communications existed and had Otake-san known of it, I do not think he would have been bothered by it.

19 Interestingly, only the very top French managers ever explicitly raised the issue of Otake-san's behaviour with the Japanese engineers at YamaMax. They did so rarely, only rather superficially, and largely as asides. The Japanese 'in between' engineers were invariably entirely mum in response.

20 Only on one occasion during my fieldwork did one of the top French managers at YamaMax – the oldest, though not in the highest-ranked position – experience Otake-san's wrath. This was a form of public scolding in a French–Japanese meeting of around twenty persons. This manager responded by stating, in French, and thus beyond the understanding of all of the Japanese present, 'I will retire early before I will take any more of this abuse'. He left the meeting wrought

emotionally, his face a deep red. Although no one else left the meeting before it was finished, it was related to me later by some French members that there was concern that the older manager, severely overweight and known to have high blood pressure, might suffer a heart attack.

21 Here I focus on the 'pull' factor, i.e. conditions on the ground in overseas subsidiaries, in explaining the presence of large numbers of Japanese managers and engineers. I continue to consider this the key explanation. However, the phenomenon is certainly not discouraged by an important 'push' factor. Most large, Japanese manufacturing multinationals are now confronted with a flattening in domestic production of consumer goods while a high proportion of skilled Japanese managers and engineers, who expect 'lifetime employment', remain on their payrolls. Sending them abroad as 'advisors' helps to justify the situation, though it is enormously expensive.

22 Over the years I have come to understand managers as, literally, *entrepreneurs*, that is, as persons who carry information (or things) between persons.

4 Translating power in hierarchy
Seen and unseen organising

> The ideal of an organization as a smoothly running machine, clean and austerely effective, becomes *dangerous*. Rather, from the present perspective, organizational survival depends ultimately on the insinuation of polyglot, immersion in metaphor, and the prevalence of creative confusion. Rather than autonomous, self-directing managers, we find the emphasis on thoroughgoing interdependence, and the quality of relatedness replacing the character of the individual as the centre of concern. [Italics mine.]
>
> Kenneth Gergen (1992), 'Organization theory in the postmodern era'

Introduction

Organisations are sites of interdependence in the schema of contemporary theorists, both in the academy and at the top of formal organisations, especially large, private corporations. These two sets of theorists are aware that organisations are subjected to increasingly diverse impacts deriving from ever more complicated, global sources. Gergen's statement above, then, concerns how he thinks that activity within organisations ought now be thought about. In turn he asks managers within them for spontaneity and flexibility to creatively cope with new levels of confusion. Acknowledging their inability to control exogenous impacts, leaders of large organisations pick up such conceptualisations and mobilise them as ideological 'designs for the future'. That said, and 'dangerous' as it may be, the middle and high level managers and engineers, administrative staff members, technicians and assembly line workers who I have come to know at headquarters and subsidiaries of multinational corporations around the world tell me that they would be pleased if day to day their organisations could be made to 'run as smoothly' as their machines. While their mechanistic language may be especially pronounced as these informants work in industrial settings, they hold, like most persons, thoroughly modern, progressive conceptions of organisations and the processes of organising. Indeed, within these conceptions they may have experienced 'the character of the individual', i.e. themselves, as suppressed or, at least, pressed into the service of the 'character of the organisation'. These are artefacts of their hopes, perhaps not often attained, that things might run smoothly.

Perhaps all contemporary organisations demonstrate what we might call modern practices.[1] As Law puts it, '[the theoretical] turn away from dualism doesn't mean that we should ignore the ordering *strains* towards dualism built into the modern project' (1994: 138) (emphasis mine).[2] Thus, as much as we might hope for organisations that are ('postmodern'?) level playing fields displaying reflexive interdependence, opening up explicit space for individual volition, equality and open-mindedness regarding creative confusion, such as that described above by Gergen, organisations, whether 'successful' or not, nonetheless continue to enmesh us in the thoroughly modern project of explicitly and implicitly designing and mobilising our activities. They are sites that allow us to generate extremely subtle theories of contemporary social relations because organisations are sites that reproduce, indeed magnify, the very modernity in which we continue to live.

The present discussion of Gergen's ideas might set us at the centre of debate over what 'postmodern' organising may look like. I am more interested, however, in what *analytical work* any particular set of ideas or intellectual inclinations may achieve in explaining a world they claim exists, and, perhaps more importantly, what forms of analysis particular approaches *cut out*. I wish, then, to examine traditional organisational analysts' tendencies to generate, and exaggerate, theories of 'rational' organising when, as we know, because organisations are human productions, our non-rational, or perhaps 'irrational' behaviour also, necessarily, takes place within them. As may be deduced from my presentation thus far in this book my goal is to encourage the systematic linkage of organisation and society through an explicit focus upon persons, and to articulate a notion of 'power' in making the linkage. That is, to understand organisation as 'in the world' with the rest of society; organisation as perhaps a focal or concentrated point of social relations, but not something 'out there,' distinctive and analytically particular. Actor–network theory (ANT), which is most closely identified with the French scholars Callon and Latour, and is based for the most part in sociological studies of science and technology (S&T), may be helpful in unpacking the linkages of persons, power and organising. Like the general organisations literature, however, ANT limits our analysis by not accounting intellectually for a core ingredient forwarded empirically in our discussion of YamaMax; that is cross-cultural relations. The systemic hierarchical 'strains' (Law 1994: 151) apparent in any large organisation's activities are greatly complicated by cross-cultural and cross-linguistic divides. If a common language (as well as, therefore, the cultural understandings implicit in it) is assumed, a priori, by ANT, or other theorists, as a central platform through which organisational activity is played out, what are the implications to organisational behaviour where this foundation is itself divided? This is a matter of both substantial theoretical interest and pervasive relevance, for cross-cultural organisations, and the sorts of sociological problems they engender, will proliferate as the boundary-crossing effects of globalisation are inevitably carried forward.

The purpose of this chapter, then, is to examine ethnographically and in a substantial theoretical manner the problem of cross-cultural and cross-linguistic divides in the context of the day to day mobilisation of organisational power by the very small number of Japanese *salaryman* at YamaMax. As suggested in the previous chapter, and to be further detailed here, language use and ethnic identity will be recognisable as means, among others, for constituting and sustaining control at YamaMax.

Diversions of production: reviewing a test

While industrial 'research and development' may to an extent mimic pure science's goal of 'discovery', industry is dominated by mass production's search for predictability, consistency of output, automaticity and internal organisational stability. While maintaining consistency – or creating 'seamless' products – seems mundane on the surface, it is, rather, an extremely challenging and complicated process, subtle and analytically interesting. In industrial settings, explicit efforts to normalise daily practices characteristic of mass production may, however, be intentionally broken. In the case to be recounted here YamaMax is – that is, members of YamaMax are – trying to learn to make a 'professional' tape of far higher technical 'specification' than they by now routinely produce. To do so, they shut down normal operations for a time and push to the limits of their collective ability. Both expensive and out of the ordinary, in that they usually only occur over two or three periods per year, these tests deeply stress the social relations underlying standard day to day production. In the process, and accompanied by considerable emotion, implicit forms of social relations seem to, temporarily, reach the surface or, in any case, become more obviously exposed. The following event thus concerns dismantling, suspending and, in turn, reinforcing organisational order through tests in which members of the firm are literally trying to *create* new forms of continuity. They are technically building the procedures around which regular, mass production will subsequently be channelled. Such organisational learning is difficult work and, furthermore, having failed to create 'new tape' 'in specification', the event described below is the fourth test over a nine-month period at YamaMax.[3]

Tuesday: the 'Daily Production Meeting', meant to open at 9:00 a.m., begins formally at 9:20. Its members include all of the top French engineers, their immediate subordinates and foremen, representing every section engaged in the production process. The meeting is regularly conducted in French and is prefaced by a busy shaking of hands, greeting each member, as they enter the room, as this is ordinarily the first time during the day that they will have seen each other. Occasionally a Japanese manager attends. This morning Nagata-san – responsible for the first step (mixing) of the production process – enters late, at 9:25. Yesterday's production results and problems on various lines are reported (in French), discussed and plans for today's production are decided. This morning M. Marchalot, the general manager of production, attends. This is unusual as M. Marchalot usually simply receives reports and analysis of each section's activities. He announces to the French group that a decision will be taken by the end of the day concerning the schedule and plans for the new tape test.

Wednesday: M. Marchalot again attends the 9:00 a.m. 'Daily Production Meeting'. After the normal circulation of Tuesday's production figures, M. Marchalot shows the new tape test schedule to the French production team, including foremen. This is the first time the foremen have seen it, and its implications for worker scheduling are enormous. The meeting is followed directly, at 9:45, by a 'new tape' meeting, run by M. Marchalot. The majority of the French production managers simply keep their seats. The French foremen leave in order to return to the shopfloor, while perhaps stopping off for a cup of coffee en route. Nagata-san joins the 'new tape' meeting as he has been 'tasked' by his superior, Otake-san, to liaise between the Japanese and French engineers for the test. M. Marchalot opens the meeting saying, in French, 'This meeting will be in French'. His French colleagues respond briefly, and loudly, with gaffes in broken English or broken Japanese. M. Marchalot delivers the following lecture, typical of leaders in industrial settings.

> We feel cornered by the problems of 'new tape' and we want to be very focused for this next test. The test is *capital* [critical]. So I ask you to think about questions of quality from a global point of view. We need to concentrate ourselves. We are at a delicate point with our numbers, results and calibrations, but I have the feeling we are getting close to successfully understanding our technical problems. Each person will be responsible for *son terrain* [his area]. It is necessary that your area be identified exactly and detailed information be collected from it for support of the test. I do not mean you cannot help others, but I want to insist on this point of concentrating yourselves on your areas of responsibility.
>
> I want to point out that throughout this test, there is no one parameter to watch. We are starting to see that there are impacts on our quality coming from several directions. For this test we have to focus and discuss together so that we find a solution to those problems.
>
> Last thing. We will have the support of *Monsieur Honda-san* [sic], coming from Japan, who will focus on the details of the test.

The meeting breaks up without further comment.

As we know from earlier discussion, although Otake-san is the highest-ranking Japanese YamaMax, as 'adviser' he does not appear on the plant's organisational chart. He is, however, the most knowledgeable person at the factory regarding technical aspects of its machinery and processes. In his current position, he spends little time on daily production matters; his mission over the last year has been to get 'new tape' out of a test phase and into production. As the test approaches, Otake-san discards his tie and suit and dresses in a more informal Japanese style. He no longer shaves, and begins wearing Japanese sandals without socks, low-cut trousers pulled way down on his hips and a white sports shirt. Like a serious athlete, he seems to be gearing up for intensive work and enjoying the purposeful building of pressure.

According to the second-highest-ranked French engineer, M. Legrand, for the last two months responsibility for planning the new tape test has been taken by the, so-called, 'French team'. He had hoped that every manager who touches on production would involve themselves but claims that the process engineering department, i.e. the Japanese engineers, had decided that they needed a formal request from the French team for their participation. He tells me, 'The Japanese wanted to be invited to work with us, as though they were a group of consultants from the outside'. To M. Legrand, the long experience of the Japanese engineers, both in Japan and France, is essential both to the test and to getting 'new' production under way. There was no question of a division in his thinking. In any case, the French team did not invite the Japanese to join them in planning the test.

On Thursday, Nagata-san calls an extraordinary meeting with the French team to try to push through Otake-san's designs and ideas for the order of command during the test. The French team which, as described above, had been working on the design for two months, is uninterested in a new plan at this late stage, four days before the test begins. They largely pass over Nagata-san's suggestions.

On Friday, preparations for the test begin with the mixing of two batches of magnetic emulsion. One batch is mixed incorrectly. Otake-san's earlier comments to me concerning the lack of organisation of the French team seem to be coming true. Japanese and French managers at YamaMax put out a net of requests to the 'mother plant' in Japan, and a 'sister plant' in the US for a resupply of the wasted materials. If located, they would be shipped by air for the test. At the US plant, the materials are located on computer but cannot be physically located on site. It is decided in Japan that the expense of flying in the materials is prohibitive anyway. Though frustrating, it is agreed to go forward with a test that can only result in half the quantity of test videotape they had hoped for.

Honda-san arrives from the Japanese 'mother plant' late Friday night to assist with the test. He is 24 years old, and has worked at the 'mother plant' in Japan for six years. I find him at his temporary desk on Saturday morning (eight hours after he arrived in France) writing intensively in English with a pencil, his face near the page, using his eraser often. His work is entitled, in English, 'Mr O Honda's schedule for new tape August test'. Nearby rests a small, well-thumbed Japanese–English dictionary and a glossary of English physics and mathematics terms that he brought with him from Japan.

On the following Tuesday, from 6:30 a.m. all of the top French and Japanese engineers are on the production line preparing for the test. That evening, regular production is suspended and the machines are cleaned all night. On Wednesday at 9:30 a.m., about two hours later than originally planned, the test begins. Superheated mixed magnetic emulsion is to be applied mechanically to a 2 metre by 2 kilometre long sheet of plastic backing that unwinds from what looks like a giant paper towel roll (see Figures 3 and 4.) However, as the test begins and the plastic backing unwinds, it tears. The process begins again, and it tears again after lunch. Before they get started properly, they are already eight hours behind schedule. On the production line, in light blue, dust-proof 'bunny suits', M. Legrand looks harried and M. Marchalot's eyes are terribly bloodshot.

The office is empty nearly all day Wednesday except for the endemic background tapping of clerical staff, putting data into statistical computer programs, and Otake-san, who calmly reads a Japanese newspaper in his private office. He seems completely out of the action, and in a good mood even though he knows there has been a tear. After the second tear, he is piqued but allows the situation to unfold around him. Whenever a Japanese engineer comes back from the production line, he delivers to Otake-san a brief report, in Japanese, on current conditions 'on the line' with the test.

Nagata-san, responsible for liaising between the Japanese and the French, has been avoiding Otake-san all day (Wednesday). In the late afternoon he is huddled at a table in M. Legrand's office, not returning to his chair because, I sense, if he does so Otake-san will see him. Nagata-san and M. Legrand chat for 30 minutes, making a new plan of procedure to cope with the delays. Otake-san passes by M. Legrand's office shortly thereafter and very gruffly tells Nagata-san, in Japanese, to come to his office.

Later, at 6:15 p.m., Nagata-san and M. Legrand gather again. Other French managers, including the general manager of production, M. Marchalot, slowly join them to discuss the schedule between Wednesday evening and Thursday morning. At one point Otake-san pops his head in and tells Nagata-san, in broken English, that he has to have an answer about the schedule in ten minutes. The message is clearly intended for the consumption of the French engineers as well. The discussion continues, with M. Marchalot twice referring to Otake-san's request by pointing in the direction of Otake-san's office. The French engineers are outdoing each other with statements about their willingness to spend the entire night at the factory except, M. Marchalot suggests, for a two-hour break for dinner. They agree on a plan, and the discussion moves on to duty shifts and a rota of eating schedules for the evening through to morning.

After around ten minutes, Otake-san angrily bursts into the room. The atmosphere shifts utterly. Nagata-san curls up in his seat, physically avoiding Otake-san. Otake-san writes on the whiteboard three choices for the evening's schedule: they can work continuously until they complete the test, they can agree to stop at a specific time or they can cancel the entire test. He reminds them in broken English that they have not taken account in their schedule of the possibility of new mechanical breakdowns and he says, in English, 'What are we going to do then, just keep going?'. Otake-san diagrams a time chart, indicating that under current conditions, assuming nothing goes wrong, it will be impossible for them to finish coating before 2:00 or 3:00 a.m.

Confronted by Otake-san's technical and personal authority, M. Marchalot, the highest-ranking French manager, backtracks, insisting in English, 'I am not the expert here, and was going along with what I was told by Legrand and the other engineers'. M. Legrand refuses to take responsibility, and counter-attacks his superior, M. Marchalot, stating that there has been a lack of leadership. Otake-san speaks in Japanese for a while with Nagata-san, telling him he has taken no account of the safety of 'his' (Otake-san's) staff. Otake-san is particularly concerned about the two youngest members, in their twenties, Susumu-kun and the assistant from Japan, Honda-san. (Honda-san had in fact lost two fingers in an industrial accident in Japan three years earlier while working under Otake-san.) Towards the French managers he says, in English, 'What are you thinking about the workers? They must be getting tired now'. Challenging their resolve he says, 'I advise you to stop now and cancel test'. The French engineers are flustered, unsure what will happen next, but certain that Otake-san would not at this point be willing to cancel the test. They finally agree to complete the current phase of the test tonight, and resume the test Thursday morning after a proper rest. Otake-san asks how long they will need tomorrow to decide on a plan for the rest of the test. Then he almost immediately suggests that they call a meeting at 9:00 a.m. that would perhaps go on for two hours in order to 'find everyone's idea and opinions and build a consensus'. They agree to meet Thursday morning at 9:00 a.m. Otake-san returns to his office. The meeting breaks up with most of the French engineers departing for dinner.

Just after midnight, at 00:25 a.m., I am chatting with M. Marchalot, after his dinner, in his office. Otake-san enters. (Below is his verbatim monologue with M. Marchalot. Note that Japanese words are in italics, and that Otake-san is speaking in English with a Frenchman with limited English ability):

> Today problem is normal *da yoo* [emphasis]. Normal mean in my opinion next time very important. How to organise test? We need more discuss for example, more estimation. If this no good then next step, *ta da ta da* [a pause] then for example, if Legrand wants to run all the test he must plan ahead. For eight hours need to think through together. If they have opinion, think if they have good idea, then revise, revise, revise. Key point is always planning. If planning is good then some irregular is OK. For example we have two thickness [of tape] is wrong. In L type [tape] many trouble, why not change to T type, for example?

In L type many trouble, why not change to T type? Single task is no good. You, always multi-task. We don't need every person opinion, just key person opinion, three or four person. One of [a question of] style *nee* [isn't it]? We don't know which [style] is better or not. Today just one [style]. It's no good.

No means if we have no more paint or, huhn, [makes a questioning gesticulation with his arms] we cannot cover. If we have more paint [could we make] another tape? You have to estimate. Today is maximum two rolls. [They are behind.] Then how to catch up? How to use material we have [in order] to catch up, keep schedule? Inventory is minimised, that is problem for test. Normally we use them is not. [Normally they do not need to touch the inventory.]

I don't know if always you get test result good. Sometime shock impact. This is normal; sometime no good result, but always keep the original schedule. Three times test, but third test is no good, how to catch up, this is normal way for me, if always on schedule, easy. I don't know.

Please sleep. You, you, I switched very good. [It is good that I took over(?).] I don't discuss job matter. Always close [finish the day]. Now forget. Tomorrow ... how to cover. Please stay in your house. Forget is better. How to control is sometimes very difficult. Refresh is very important.

Otake-san leaves. M. Marchalot tells me, in French, 'I cannot understand this guy. Why is he not angry?'. While largely unintelligible to M. Marchalot this had been the warmest social exchange between the two in over a year, and just at the moment of M. Marchalot's demise with the new tape test. He muses, 'If Otake has all that knowledge and experience, why didn't he intervene earlier?'.

At 1:37 a.m. the remaining French engineers regroup in M. Marchalot's office to confirm the 9:00 a.m. start for the morning meeting. M. Legrand calls another French engineer, already asleep at home, to inform him of the morning meeting time. M. Marchalot repeats his earlier musing to his French colleagues, 'Why didn't Otake come to the meetings before?'. They have no answer.

By 2:00 a.m. both the French and Japanese engineers are preparing to go home. The atmosphere is friendly; everyone saying goodnight to each other, having *fait la guerre* (gone to war) together. As Nagata-san and Honda-san take off their Yama Corporation vests, Otake-san calls them and the other Japanese engineers into his office for a wrap-up meeting. Otake-san seems fresh and invigorated. Shortly afterwards, as the Japanese engineers move toward the coffee room for their final cigarettes, Otake-san shadow-boxes one French engineer who happens to be in the hallway and massages the shoulders of another. Apart from the occasional awkwardly offered handshake, this is the first time I have seen Otake-san physically touch anyone.

On Thursday, Otake-san takes full control of the 9:00 a.m. meeting and planning for the remaining three days of the new tape test. He takes his Japanese staff and the French engineers off the line at 11:15 p.m. that night and organises them for a 9:00 a.m. start on Friday. Again the Japanese gather in the coffee room for a final reassessment of Thursday's events. They are completely exhausted, they have not eaten since midday and all except Nagata-san and Otake-san inhale coffee and cigarettes at a high pace. As the meeting breaks up Otake-san provocatively, but perhaps not seriously, suggests they go out drinking in the nearby city, 15 miles away. His Japanese engineers do not respond. Around 30 minutes later, as Otake-san gets ready to leave, he says to me, '*Warui datte sekinin ni naru*' (When it gets bad, responsibility has to be taken).

Organising knowledge of organisations

In order that the importance of cross-cultural considerations to analysis of organisations may become clearly recognisable, in the theoretical discussion below I outline some of the parameters of formal organisation as it has been understood in academic discourse, how 'power' must be articulated in defining organisation, and offer an explanation of my understanding of Latour and Callon's theoretical vocabulary regarding 'actor–networks'. The ethnographic data will then be revisited analytically to encourage re-examination of the premises of these and other contemporary theories of organisation.

If we acknowledge organisations as central artefacts of modern society then we are bound to root our analysis of them in Weber. As key vessels reproductive of modernity, formal bureaucratic organisations, in both the public and private sectors and their related institutional contexts, were understood by Weber to entangle inevitably society in a 'iron cage' of its own making (Weber 1946: 196–244, 1947: 319–41; Bendix 1977 [1960]: 423–30; Giddens 1979: 146, 1984: 151–3). However, at the very least Weber's distressed analytic tone suggests we would, or should, toil against the dehumanising effects of our 'caged' condition. Though perhaps not Weber's emphasis, this might take various forms such as corresponding, but politically oppositional, formal organisations, for instance, unions, as well as forms that are not necessarily conscious but inevitably present in organisational life: day to day informal practices (Cullen and Howe 1991), including 'resistance' (Scott 1985). Thus, if 'modern man is man in organisations' (Blau and Scott 1962: ix), then the thoroughly messy foibles present among our activities in organisations – whether described as irrational hindrances (Mayo 1933, 1949; Roy 1952, 1954, 1959) or an integral part of work processes (Blau 1956, 1959, 1963; Wadel 1979) – point organisational analysis away from their characterisation as merely formal, mechanistic and functional. Whether we mean to or not, in every socialised context (including formal organisations) we appear to act unavoidably – that is, we act normally – in part in informal and, often, irrational ways.

Though we may intellectually accept this point, it appears that members of modern societies nonetheless project the cool rationality and functionality of our interactions with myriad organisations onto notions of activities within them. This pervasive viewpoint is rooted in both external perspectives, i.e. considering organisations from the outside, and, even more interestingly, internally generated perspectives which take as literal the explanations made by organisations of themselves. Such reifications – 'organisations speaking for themselves' – are remarkable for their very dissociation from our personally engaged and usually long-term experience of particular organisations, and are suggestive of the personal dynamics of organisational membership; that is, the personal effects of organisations as environments. Like other social settings, we perceive the formal organisations we know well as intimate, animated by personalities, gossip and innuendo, but tend to borrow vocabulary from the other end of the conceptual spectrum – rationally articulated and functionally achieving individual roles, organisational goals and 'mission statements' – to describe them. Indeed, the delinkage of what happens in the organisation – that is, how the organisation is known by its members – from the organisation's baldly explicit statements about what it 'should be' may assist in generating proliferations of 'dysfunctional', exaggerated, emotion-laden sentiments regarding internal organisational dynamics by its own members. The tension is further raised as such 'loaded'/emotional explanations are taboo. They are reserved for private talk away from the organisation or, within the organisation itself, ordinarily shared only with close and trusted (personal) colleagues of the same rank. This play or dissonance of taboo begins to explain why, beyond intimates, our cognitive and articulated models of organisations – even the ones where we are members – continue to be functional, clearly structured and, usually, mechanical. They resemble our ideas of how, as outsiders, we interact with, say, banks: explicit, determined, accurate, progressive, clean.

Another, related perception of organisations has been forwarded by Simon (1955). Drawing on Weber, he argues that the 'rationality' of actors is 'bounded'; that is, we are incapable of processing the degree of information required to act in our increasingly complicated and differentiated, i.e. modern, societies. Thus, we rely on organisations to assist us in this work. In turn, we impute to organisations precisely the character of machinery, understanding them as insulated and singular places that process our rational requirements. After all, what is the proper bureaucracy but a 'smoothly running' machine? A machine, I might add, that it is sealed off from the perspective of those outside of it. This way of imagining organisations might be termed progressive, or developmental, or modern, in the sense that organisations appear to compensate for human limitations: banks keep our money (safely) for us. Thus, as mentioned in the opening of this chapter, my informants wish that day to day their organisations could be made to 'run as smoothly' as their machines. Of course, they are aware – and rationally at that – that neither their machines nor their organisations 'run smoothly', but they do not organise their articulations of their organisations around that knowledge. If they did, they would generate alternative metaphors. Similarly, most analysts have misarticulated organisations, and so have reified their rationalised structures and functional patterns of action, i.e. administrative rules and procedures. While such structures and patterns are, of course, important artefacts of formal organisations – and also relatively simple to observe and, so, conduct research upon – they are merely an explicit version of what an organisation is meant to do, according to those at the top of the hierarchy. The work of leadership is to cut out, or direct, other voices, or versions of organising. The work of organisational analysis should include observing, but not colluding in this process.

In an internal process indelibly linked to hierarchy's predisposition to attract members' attentions upward and toward the organisation's centre, organisations' formalising processes and artefacts, such as organograms, make organisations feel external and inaccessible even to participating actors. This is especially so for those who hold little formal organisational power in the hierarchical schema. We might better understand such hierarchies as processes enacted *through* persons, rather than grids laid down upon them. As I will describe below, while such an approach does not neglect power originating in hierarchy, it allows for the articulation of the discretion of subordinates in responding to it. Meanwhile, looking outwards from the organisation, centralisation seems also to co-opt and incorporate events occurring at the organisation's periphery into its own structures, thus generating perceptions of organisations as entities that actively stabilise their environments.

The multiple perspectives on organisations I have forwarded as examples here – internal views of an organisation by its members, a view from the outside in, a view from the inside out – suggest just how powerful 'organisations' are in analytically constructing, or overdetermining, themselves for us as discrete entities. Remarkably, it is only relatively recently that organisational analysts have themselves proposed disentangling (or toppling) objectivised, stand-alone understandings of organisations from such reifications (for example, see Cooper 1992). The initial move, as above, has been a reflexive theorising of the processes orienting us – as organisational members, and as analysts – toward descriptions of organisations as formalised, rational, clean or as 'running smoothly'. If to make the point we might temporarily allow organisations to speak again, organisations may be accurately characterised (and self-referenced) as functional and objective in intent, and as such desiring to control both their internal and external environments. But, if we might put 'the organisation' on hold for a moment, more familiar ways of thinking of society tell us that the degree to which an organisation might capture its (internal or external) environment would vary tremendously depending on the context of the particular organisation under discussion, and could not in any case ever be absolute. We somehow allow organisations the authority to make statements about their actions which defy the logics of our own knowledge of society, as if they are split off from our understanding of how humans do things.

With this problem in mind, the so-called, 'new institutionalists' have correctly forwarded the view that organisations mirror the norms and values of society (Powell and DiMaggio 1991), even if their perspective lacks subtlety by analytically portraying 'societal norms' themselves in a conservative, unchanging and monolithic manner. In any case, rather than structurally isolated from its environment, as existing contra, or acting upon, the environment, or as reflecting the (external) norms of society, a more active analysis would see organisations acting *with* the environment of which it forms a part. Thus Serres (1982) criticises the notion of singularised, displaced, disconnected social 'spaces', such as our standard characterisations of organisations. He suggests that as persons move between many points (houses, streets, schools, workplaces, family, etc.), human action, and what it generates, is best understood 'not in spaces but between them' (Cooper 1992: 270). I take the theory here to mean that, especially in modern societies, on the one hand our participation in any particular setting – say, an organisation – is temporary, and so limited, while, on the other hand, we carry our knowledge of relations in each setting to every other setting, where it is recontextualised and does different work. Organisations might also be attractively understood, then – like 'the family' in Morgan's original configuration – as 'places' that co-animate the dichotomies by which we conceive of persons' lives; that is, as places 'both societal and individual, both institutional and personal, both public and private … at the same time' (Morgan 1985: 283, cited in Strathern 1992: 168). While, in theoretical terms, characterisations of human relations that depend on dichotomies might best be avoided, such approaches are instructive in extricating ourselves from the intellectual restraints heretofore pervasive in organisational analysis.

From the social constructionist position which I am encouraging here, then, there is no such thing as *an* organisation except as it is constituted through human agency, that is, through human relations and their ties to a broader environment. Organisations are sites that (temporarily) organise some aspects of complex, multi-sited, lives constituted of multiple relations, places and histories. A corporation, the machinery, paper, the activities within it, and the stock certificates representing it as property, are constituted of relations between persons. Emptied of those relations such artefacts are like the shell of an abandoned factory: lacking the active 'machinery' of meaning (except, perhaps, as cues for analysing what was, or imagining something about what could be.) They have no presence. I suggest focusing, then, on the verb form – 'organising' – in our descriptions and analyses of 'organisations' (Law 1994). This encourages a perspectival adjustment that places organisational activities (and responsibilities) firmly in the hands of the persons who create, occupy and use such places. This is a line of reasoning relatively familiar to general anthropology, and which coincides with a progressive understanding of organisational culture where culture, and the human relations so implied in its production, is treated not as a component of an organisation, but constitutive of organisation (Smircich 1983a, 1983b; Pettigrew 1979).

Organising power through networks of 'diffusion' and 'translation'

How would it be possible to develop analyses of organising that take account of such a perspective; an approach that would not allow organisations to hold reifications or statuses that in any way let them escape from a recognition of their constitution as socially constructed entities? If organisations are given meaning through the 'webs of significance' (Geertz 1973: 5) that we grant them, and that they mirror back upon us, then furthering the analogy to thinking of organisations as constituted of *networks* of relations may be fruitful. We commonly understand networks as long in duration, complex and, as we might be reminded by recalling our own networks, at play in particular ways in any particular context or moment, even if general patterns may be recognisable. In relation to formal organisations, 'network' would seem to encourage the idea of organising as something in continuous motion. Thus, networks sometimes come together in a form that can be called 'a formal organisation', and they come apart. Networks assist us, then, in analytically accounting for time and space.[4]

So far, so good. But what makes for the 'agreements' that get things like a building or a corporation constituted, or organised, or constructed? Some notion of power is required to understand how networks are controlled in the real world, say, in the case we are working on here, through the activities of members of a multinational corporation. Theory attached only to the image of networks suggests limitlessness, especially where we are concerned with processes of hybridity, i.e. the possibly-constant making of connections between things. We need to account for how relations are, often, quite precisely defined and controlled in the act of their constitution, including, of course, making organisations.[5] This is particularly important for examination of 'globalisation' which, as discussed in the opening of this study, suffers as a ubiquitous public concept ostensibly representative of our contemporary world. That is, as globalisation would seem to explain everything – it is limitless; identifiably everywhere; global – it assists in explaining very little.

Actor–network theory (ANT) has been helpful in pressing notions of power into the service of understanding phenomena that cut across common levels, or boundaries, of analysis. Although they do not emphasise or often cite Foucault, I implicitly read ANT in association with his complex thinking regarding power. For my interests ANT may also assist in breaking down the macro and micro distinctions which I suggest is required in order to make analytic, and practical, sense of 'globalisation'.

While, as I will expand upon below, much of Latour's work carves out extreme theoretical positions as a polemical and stylistic strategy – and as a problem of inattentive clarification of meaning in translations from French into English – his empirical focus is upon the organisation of knowledge and explicit bodies of information, i.e. the practices of science, broadly construed. The approach is highly applicable to multinational corporations, and in other contexts with which we are relatively familiar. That is, even if we do not work in science laboratories (Latour 1986, 1987, 1988; Latour and Woolgar 1979) or among transport engineers (Latour 1996), or follow natural scientists around as they conduct research in the Amazon (Latour 1999), through their presence in our contemporary environment we are aware perhaps of the habitus (Bourdieu 1984 [1979]: 172) of these subjects, as we may be aware of, or in any case are unsurprised by, state-sponsored advisers' interventions in the practices of European fishermen which engage Callon's interests (1986). While addressing similar theoretical territory, we can perhaps relate, then, more easily to writing about these topics than to Foucault's historical analysis of Bentham's panopticon (Foucault 1975). And like the laboratories described by Latour, YamaMax is proximate to us, and similarly, as it is a private corporation, at a remove from the general public's day to day view.

Building on the view that our existence stems from our exertions upon others, Callon (1986) and Latour (1986) argue that power is exercised through 'borrowing' the force of others.[6] This active approach to power paraphrases Foucault's notion that power is not possessed or owned as a latent capacity, but is the overall effect of a set of strategies that 'reduce discretion' among a 'network of agents'.[7] Callon (1986) understands this process as unfolding in the following way. An 'actor' becomes indispensable to others by putting itself between them and their other alternatives. Their discretion, or choice, so removed, they are 'enrolled' as 'passive agents', in effect forming a part of the 'actor'. The 'actor' is then claimed to 'mobilise' the 'force of passive agents' when they are engaged capably in 'speaking,' or acting, on behalf of the actor. When this occurs agents are understood as part of an 'actor–network'.

For both Callon and Latour the 'reduction of discretion' is a fundamental organising principle affecting both human and non-human agents. The scheme forces acknowledgment of the counter-intuitive agency of material objects by understanding 'agents' as 'anything/anyone that acts upon others' (Law 1986: 16). The false dichotomy between objects (nature) and persons (society) is, then, ANT's core critique of social science. The counter critique is that ANT analytically overemphasises objects and is, therefore, dehumanising (cf. Middleton and Brown 2005). It strikes me that this is a reaction to Latour's erudite but polemical style, which on occasion excitably wanders toward leaps of faith. In arguing against the common Western perspective in which society and nature are placed in a hierarchy that overwhelmingly favours the former, Latour and his collaborators forward the idea of 'symmetrical' relations between the two spheres. More persuasively and sensibly, what they seek is acknowledgement that neither stands analytically without the other: that nature and society are in a necessary package. Thus, an intensive focus on things, or documents, or machines is perfectly reasonable in unpacking the relations between 'society' and 'nature'.

Unfortunately, the forwarding of the role of objects in ANT has become sufficiently celebrated, and simplified, in recent years that it seems to have superseded analytically the role of persons. To my reading, even under ANT, inanimate objects only take on 'agency' as extensions of human relations. Twenty years ago, Latour put it this way: 'Every time a fact is verified and a machine runs, it means that the lab or shop conditions have been extended *in some way* ... Forgetting the extension of instruments when admiring the smooth running of facts and machines would be like admiring the road system, with all those fast trucks and cars, and overlooking civil engineering, the garages, the mechanics and the spare parts. Facts and machines have no inertia of their own' (1987: 250). It does not help that Latour mentions 'the mechanics' in the same throw-away phrase as 'spare parts' but in any case 'inertia', and much more, I argue, must be provided by persons. In practice Latour's achievement is that his emphasis upon and expansion of conceptions of 'agency' forcefully places human relations in the analytic forefront but *without the usual interpretative cost, negation, or devaluation of the relevance of objects, nor nature, in the world.*[8]

Whatever advocates of ANT might say – and they rather showily celebrate their ongoing discourses and disagreements – what I say is that material objects, machines, or organograms, are activities with others, i.e. they hold agency, because they were originally human products and continue to function as media between persons. This human intervention – producing the machine and, whether made conscious or not, the enormous chain of events allowing it – is reanimated and changed in the contingency of present use. In considering our relations to nature, then, a stone is only converted into a tool, i.e. given agency, through being grasped and considered. Once so shaped, it may continue to have agency similar to, but not the same as, its original use, or it may be used differently. In any case, it is inanimate, or returns to being so, if unused or untouched by us. Thus, in the case of our tripping over a random stone, it is temporarily animated through our relations with it, and made inanimate, or unrecognisable, once cursed upon and thrown out of our path of signification. *D'après* Derrida its 'trace' is not the thing itself but a memory that does other work for us.

In modern contexts such as the production of 'science' or, for our purposes, the organisation of industrial production, material forms, such as documents representing technical processes or organisational charts, or whatever is claimed as a fact, are 'technologies of simplification' that consolidate, clarify or make explicit – by making 'seeable' – community members' understandings of, say, an organisation, as an 'actor–network'. To my reading, this perspective grounds the symbolic value of artefacts such as facts or documents in their intended practical, rational function. The perspective is especially attractive to analysis of 'modern' contexts, then, where 'rationality is our rationalization' (Sahlins 1976: 72).[9]

Further, and related to our earlier critique of organisational 'formalisation' and 'centralisation', in conceiving of actor–networks Latour asks that we focus not on, say, an organisation as a thing, but on the processes whereby human agents commit themselves to models of an organisation (or models of society, or science). He proposes, for example, that social structure should not be defined by social scientists, but should be understood as 'performed' or, I would say, exposed, in the conflicts arising from the efforts of agents, i.e. social scientists, to define it. Whether or not one cares to accept 'performance' as an appropriate descriptive notion, Latour means us to understand that analysis of a society, or an organisation, a paradigm, or a fact, is given shape through competition over its versions: analysis is about the power to define: effectively, the granting of, often material, form to knowledge.

It is easiest to understand this process by focussing on particular case studies, which with Latour usually concerns the discovery and spread of scientific facts. To make a scientific fact prominent, so that it qualifies as 'truth', scientific proof is required, for instance through experimental reproducibility, authentification, verifiability, falsifiability, i.e. those processes that assist in obtaining the acquiescence of the 'fact' by influential persons. Although such facts are, thereby, constructed through agreement, they are not in any sense artificial. Facts represent action identified in the world but it is the social agreement regarding facts that grants them reality, or presence, or communicative effect in the world. As can be imagined, for natural scientists this perspective on their processes of knowledge creation has been controversial. While of course being subject to them, Latour constantly states, with amusement, that he does believe in the reality of, say, the 'law of gravity'. But like many working in the 'history of science', what is likely to interest him are the processes whereby – to generate an example – Newton, and others, created and propagated the 'idea of gravity'. A helpful way of thinking about this is to note that while we think of 'natural laws' as a complete set of facts, or an unassailable body, there remain an unlimited number of facts as yet undiscovered. And what in future will be discovered will depend on society. Looking back, for instance, we may have gotten there anyway but we rapidly extended our knowledge of atomic fission, atomic fusion, and atomic bombs because of the vicissitudes and compulsions of the Second World War. The 'reality check' of interests, then, is all important in establishing scientific facts.

In an organisational setting, this understanding of human agency in socially constructing reality (Berger and Luckman 1967), including the facts of science, or of organisations themselves, may be clarified by contrasting two notions of power. In the first, say, the traditional power model, commands are obeyed because they are understood as 'diffusing' outward – and usually downward, in a common structure of authority relationships – from a powerful source. In the second, Latour's preferred 'translation' model, commands are passed from agent to agent, each of whom, or which, is 'enrolled' to greater or lesser degrees by agreeing to the schemes of (more powerful) adjacent agents. Most simply, as above, an 'actor–network' is created when the goal of an agent is achieved through the acquiescence or agreement of a series of agents. Meanwhile the term 'translation' connotes activity – motion, or process, or travel – and it also, centrally, indicates the necessity of interpretation of meaning by each agent. This encourages an appreciation of the efficacy of each and every agent, for even 'passive agents' agree temporarily, and, in principle, 'for reasons of their own'. Power relations in organisations would, thus, be seen not merely as a top-down affair but, as mentioned previously, a process in which agents effectively retain for themselves a modicum of discretion – that is, power – even while, it must be added, perhaps deeply circumscribed in organisational settings by hierarchical authority, e.g. the position of an assembly line worker vis-à-vis the president of a corporation.

Accounting simultaneously for translations and for power has become a problem in the developing understanding of actor–network theory, which in generating its own 'seeability' is itself of course subject to the 'technologies of simplification' that it so evocatively advocates.[10] After all, in making simplifications, we gain a concrete perspective, at a particular moment in time, but may lose complexity, subtlety and perhaps depth, a point I will revisit when we return to discussion of YamaMax. As briefly outlined above, perhaps as a response by actor–network theorists to the perceived overdetermination of social agency in normal sociological analysis, actor–network *theory* has tended to underdetermine radically the issue of hierarchies of agents, or, as I would have it, the problem of positionality, by not much discussing it. ANT is of course attractive in that virtually everything is potentially in play: i.e. machines and objects are granted agency. It is nonetheless common sense that the specific codifications through which machines function, and so become agents, and without which they fail, make them far more passive in principle than any human being. Both men and machines may be 'passive agents' in the interests of more powerful actors in establishing networks, but persons necessarily retain volition. That is, being a medium alone between things, or having simple cause and effect, e.g. a step in a computer program, may be necessary to being an agent, but does not sufficiently account for power. Whereas much ANT writing is extremely theoretical, and usually thorough, it is as if accounting for power is taken for granted in the stories ANT tells about scientists in the lab and the history and proliferation of their discoveries, long distance communications, transport systems and engineers, soil specialists and entomologists, corporate technological development and government policy, and financial markets. In spite of granting agency broadly in terms of theory, it matters in studying these actor–networks that they are elite actor–networks focussing authoritatively upon the, seemingly, mechanical, perhaps hyperrationalised spheres of life within the societies in which they are constructed. Could the problem be that the overfamiliarity of ANT academics in studying aspects of their own, taken-for-granted, systems, i.e. the societies they live and work within, generates an analytic blind spot? (In the final chapter we will return to a similar problem among anthropologists in light of the influence of contemporary communications technology and the vicissitudes of 'anthropology at home'.)

In any case 'translation' between agents is not a new theoretical departure: the agency of all 'authors' involved is insisted upon in a basic, Hobbesian version of authority in power relations. This point was powerfully made by Callon and Latour in 1981, in their influential article, 'Unscrewing the big Leviathan'. While Hobbes has been quintessentially understood – simplified (?) – as generating a model 'totalitarian monster' in Leviathan, in Callon and Latour's view Hobbes' 'absolute sovereign is nothing other than the sum of the multitude's wishes ... [who] says nothing on his own authority ... without having been authorized by the multitude, whose spokesman, mask-bearer and amplifier he is ... He is the people itself in another state' (1981: 278). This reading of Hobbes, is a pure representation of the theoretical meaning of 'power in translation', and one which transcends democratic idealism. Thus, it is no surprise that Latour makes clear that Hobbes uses the term 'author' to describe members of the body politic, i.e. those who 'authorize' the sovereign.[11]

The idea of 'translation' generates a significant analytical gain because it causes a paradigmatic shifting of the subject of inquiry. That is, I believe we are accustomed to thinking about what those who *have* power do with *it*: i.e. at the extreme, the acts of the totalitarian monster. But what happens when we grant agency to, and take the perspective of, those who are traditionally treated as the victims of the possessors of power? When confronted, for example, with Scott's keen analyses of agency and efficacy – he calls it 'resistance' – among peasant populations (Scott 1985, see especially 289–350), the ground is shifted away from ownership of power – peasants *have* little power – and towards an analytical focus on *relations*. Power in agency should be seen to be constituted in social relations. As such, there is necessarily a hierarchy between agents which are things and agents who are people: the former does not arise, and cannot go on, without the latter. Now the quality of those relations are thoroughly contingent on the factors at play in a particular interchange. And it must be clarified again that supplying all agents with 'a modicum of discretion' is not meant to imply that agents interrelate with equality.

Unfortunately, in their same 1981 article, having elegantly represented the notion of translation via Hobbes' view 'that there is no difference between the actors which is inherent *in their nature* ... ', and iterating that '[W]e cannot distinguish between macro-actors ... and micro-actors on the basis of their dimensions, since they are all, we might say, the "same size" ... ', Callon and Latour go on to describe how macro-actors are built up from micro-actors, claiming that the 'aim ... [of] analysis ... [is] the construction of differences in size between micro- and macro-actors' (1981: 279). Reifying this micro–macro distinction is misguided (and has, thankfully, fallen off the map of analytic interests in ANT). Concern over size or scale leads to more confusion and analytic division than it does clarity in considering relations in the real world, i.e. for our purposes, the problem of understanding globalisation. Theoretically, 'translation' does the central work of drawing our analytic focus to the immediate process of 'association', or associating, between adjacent agents.[12] Our analysis then asks for discovery of a subsequent, or related, association and examination of its process of translation. The relative passivity, or influence, of one agent vis-à-vis another is the 'translation' of the hierarchy of power in the immediacy of the act of associating. With a series of translations/associations completed between agents, with its agents reliably speaking for it, an actor–network may be understood not to have established itself, but to have become established. Its size and scale are beside the point.

In my view, in formal organisations the combination of 'diffusion' and 'translation' can theoretically account for any action that moves beyond two or more agents. What is in the analytic foreground depends on perspective; the context of observation. That is, inside the boundaries of a single organisation, the centre, represented at the top of a formal hierarchy, very clearly 'diffuses' its interests to the periphery of that organisation. Meanwhile, a decision taken at the centre will have been multiply 'translated' – and so reinterpreted by the stamp of the interests of many agents – as it makes its way to the periphery, typically lower levels in the organisational hierarchy. Among individual members of an organisation, there is more leeway for formal discretion over interpretation among agents in close proximity to the centre than those at the periphery. In practice, however, they have the least interest in broadening interpretation as they effectively constitute the centre: after all, they have reached the centre because they are understood to 'speak reliably' for it or, as I would put it, they are its speakers. Those further from the centre are more likely to be interested in broadening interpretation, but must do so through informal means as they are formally more restricted from doing so, for instance, because they have less *author*ity as they are in subordinate hierarchical positions. Controlling the display of interests, and so the range of interpretation and action of agents, is the key work of hierarchy. 'Diffusion' and 'translation' are two useful tools, then, for understanding any organisation's multifaceted coin.

Turning this language towards the case study at the YamaMax, I propose that French staff are through their employment at least nominally 'enrolled' as 'passive agents', forming a part of the actor–network: in this case, the 'Japanese' Yama Corporation. And under actor–network theory the corporation would be understood to have succeeded in 'mobilising' the 'force of the passive agents' [French staff] when the agents are engaged capably in 'speaking', or acting, on behalf of the actor, thus, becoming part of its 'actor–network'. Are French staff part of the Yama Corporation's actor–network? With ethnographic data to hand, where shall we go to make analysis of such questions 'seeable' to us? How does our case study assist us in problematising received notions of organisational dynamics and encourage fresh analytic perspectives on relations within cross-cultural organisations, organisations that are increasingly proliferating due to globalisation?

Disorganising assumptions: reviewing cross-cultural relations

As we recall, for two months the French team had held weekly meetings during which they anticipated and organised the new tape test. Their effort is exemplary of attempts, typical of organisational life, to coax potential disorder and confusion into progressive/modern plans. In the process the new tape test was made 'seeable,' and therefore apparently rationalised and controllable, through its representations in schedules for the delivery of material goods, in activity plans and in organisational charts defining formal lines of authority. As I have earlier characterised Latour's position, however, social structures or organisations or designs should be understood as 'performed' by the conflicts arising from the efforts of actors to define it. In the case of this new tape test we have a radical 'performance of conflict' indeed.

Otake-san's efforts, through Nagata-san, to alter the new tape test *before it even began* suggest that he had reservations concerning the French team's capacity. During his many years in Yama Corporation's magnetic tape division Otake-san had been involved in well over fifty tests. Thus Otake-san and, by implication, his Japanese engineering colleagues held in their minds a version of how such an exercise ought to be planned and implemented. As the French team's plans had been made 'seeable' to him on sheets of paper and in the oral reports of his Japanese staff – who could discuss them with any of the French engineers or attend any 'French' meeting they chose to – Otake-san had a very clear notion of what the French team was organising. In the event, the French team's planning was displaced by Otake-san (and his Japanese colleagues), who increasingly took responsibility and authority over design and action when, at his discretion, it was deemed essential. Was this a spontaneous event? What allowed the Japanese to eventually define the parameters of the test? How would we understand these processes in terms of organisational power in 'diffusion' and power in 'translation'?

First, let me relate exactly how the power of 'diffusion' is processed through hierarchy at the tape division of the Yama Corporation. In this apparently technical, cut-and-dried characterisation, let us be reminded straight away that the communications that allow diffusion to work across hierarchy are negotiated relations or, in Latour's language, 'translations' between 'agents'. In these relations each actor theoretically sustains a modicum of discretion. And let us note that in order to move that theory forward into interpretation of actual events we always need to integrate thinking about the organising of power.

'Specifications', or agreed bands of technical variation, are based on equations of production that 'cost out' balances of efficiency and quality. These bands, or 'specs', are established by the 'mother plant' of the Yama Corporation in Japan, based on the assumption of a continuous desire for, in this case, a higher quality of videotape for a global market of clients. (Yama 'tape quality,' therefore, is continuously compared with the quality of competitors' videotape.) As at other Yama factories, during 'tests' members of YamaMax attempt to create sets of rules that align production methods – the mixture of men and machines – with the required boundaries of the 'specs'. Once production rules are established, as long as 'in spec' quality is sustained, French engineers at YamaMax are allowed de facto discretion, that is, leeway to carry forward the responsibilities of mass production. The social system they establish to make these arrangements between engineers, workers, information and machinery is YamaMax's organisational chart (see Figure 6). That organisational chart is reiterated and reinforced through the recordings of calibrations, measures and plans, in every piece of technical information that is made explicit or, in Latour's language, *seeable* at YamaMax.

An invisible organising 'chart' is, however, recognisable to all involved. It became more obvious during the test I have recounted but is, nonetheless, present more subtly throughout the day to day activities of YamaMax. It is made 'seeable' in texts of production in Japanese, some of which repeats and reorganises YamaMax's French information. Far more important than its explicit 'seeability', however, is its power over social relations at YamaMax as embodied in the Japanese themselves. Otake-san and the Japanese engineering team's de facto authority over the test was built into the relations of the French subsidiary's position within the larger framework of the Yama Corporation's worldwide marketing, production and technical facilities, and its enormous financial resources, which made possible the establishment of YamaMax in the first place. The Japanese team could, furthermore, draw on expertise beyond the specific organisational frame in which the test occurred. As described earlier, having produced videotape and run research and development exercises for the last twenty years, the 'mother plant' is an enormous resource to draw upon. This expertise appeared also in the form of young Honda-san, who visited the factory for the test. Apart from 'assistance' for the test he was charged with keeping his line managers at the 'mother plant' in Japan informed – in a real-time delay of around three hours – of events during the test as they unfolded in France. The 'mother plant' is the centre towards which the technical knowledge of YamaMax references itself. Otake-san and the group of Japanese on the ground in France thus embody a set of relationships within a huge Yama Corporation network which provided them access to a rich and important stock of resources, including information in Japanese, that the French team literally could not read nor, in Latour's paradigm, *see.* Conditions at YamaMax thus draw into question the analytic relevance of the 'seeability' of organisational features. At best, 'seeability' codifies social relations from a particular position. At YamaMax we have seen just how truncated and emptied of meaning such visions might become, for example, in YamaMax's organisational chart and the French engineer's plans. This is an example of what Strathern is referring to when she proposes that persons 'cut networks' by their social activities (1996).

The division between the French and the Japanese was thus further enacted within YamaMax through language use itself. The de facto control and isolation of this medium of exchange of technical expertise guaranteed Japanese authority over the rules of production. That they numbered eight, while there were over 400 French employees, further attests to the work of organisational 'diffusion', in this case mobilised through a different language and a different cultural identity as well as the usual prerogatives of hierarchy.

Let us stick for the moment, nonetheless, with Latour's metaphor of 'translation' in constituting relations, or action, between 'agents', for in its common sense meaning, translation begs us to draw further attention to the language (and culture) games at play in the analysis of organisation.

Cross-cultural efficacy and the exaggerations of language analysis

Theories of organisational behaviour overwhelmingly depend on the assumption of single-language use, usually expressed within a single-culture framework. I believe this is due to insufficient observation of persons in day to day social interactions; that is, these theories bypass assessment of actual practices of communication in organisations. Support for such a perspective is reinforced by the theories of language that underpin most philosophies and sociologies of communications – from the Greeks, to Wittgenstein, Austin and Derrida, through to social theorists such as Schutz, Habermas and Giddens – that are implicitly, and occasionally explicitly, used to support organisational theory. Ordinarily articulated as universals of communication, it seems that philosophers or theorists of society cannot get on with their work without the assumption of single-language use frameworks for society. This would be the case in Schutz' (1965) notions of 'intersubjectivity' which, important for our purposes, underpins ethnomethodology, Habermas' (1985) 'universal pragmatics', as well as Giddens' (1979, 1984) 'structuration' theory, which engage discussion from the level of individual psychology and motivation, through to group behaviour and, in some cases, their interactions with politics and the state. Now, in offering this criticism I am not suggesting that the work of these theorists is not extremely important nor, whether or not it is made explicit in their writing, am I suggesting that their work is not based on extremely astute observation of the vicissitudes of human behaviour. Rather, problems arise for our purposes at the mundane analysis of day to day communication. That is, while these theories are, effectively, treated as applied perspectives on human behaviour in organisations, they are extremely abstract, and, for the most part, entirely untestable hypotheses regarding social relations, broadly construed: discussions both about what they understand are relations between levels of social organisation and, important especially for activists such as Habermas, its potentialities.

The formal language sciences are, meanwhile, even further abstracted from the real world. I refer here to modelling in formal linguistics, i.e. semantics, studies of lexicon and syntax, generative grammars, etc., and Chomsky's theoretical linguistics, all of which assume universal or fixed structures of language. Chomsky (1964: 3, 1957, 1975) is explicit here: 'Linguistic theory is concerned primarily with an ideal speaker-listener, in a completely homogeneous speech-community, who knows its language perfectly'. While Chomsky's work is obviously an enormous achievement, formal and theoretical linguistics is philosophically and functionally distanced from actual social discourse. This is counterintuitive, for here language is recognised as a human production. Rather, these are theories about language without human beings.

In the meantime, how are we to get on in explaining observations of settings in which two or more language and cultural systems are simultaneously at work? We must look beyond the assumptions of single language understanding alone to begin to disentangle social relations where the knowledge of 'knowing subjects' is quite different from one to another. Acknowledgement of, and substantial work on, these problems has taken place under the broad label of sociolinguistics: which studies the place of language in social relations. For analysis of cross-cultural and cross-linguistic relations in organisations the approach seems enormously appealing in principle. Yet, as I discussed regarding my own field practices in Chapter 1, sociolinguistics, and other strains of linguistic study that take account of the context of language production, may be hamstrung by an empirical and methodological overemphasis on the details of language itself. In contrast, while the breadth and intent of socio-cultural anthropological methods may not be able to sustain an authentically holistic perspective, especially in studies of complex modern contexts, anthropology's effort to both be empirical detailed, i.e. to observe and analyse actual social activities and their products, and still articulate the forest in spite of the trees, remains perhaps its most important analytical, and communicative, goal. I will return to this once we have cursorily discussed sociolinguistics and what I take to be its precursor and core intellectual source: the analysis of 'speech acts'.

I begin by appreciating, and lightly critiquing, Austin's famous research on English language communications. In reflection on Hippolytus in the first chapter of his seminal work, *How to Do Things with Words*, Austin describes 'performative utterances' as not 'joking, for example, nor writing a poem' but as words 'spoken seriously' (1962: 9). In the second chapter he goes on to describe the conditions – the 'procedures' – through which the audience can be understood as upholding its receptive side of 'serious, performative utterances'. The remaining ten chapters of the book fine-tune the qualities of 'performatives' based on a close analysis of English verbs. Austin and those to follow him assume a 'natural language' of speakers operating with mutually recognisable comprehension of the rules of that one language. Apart from the implausibility of any two speakers of the same language actually holding perfectly compatible understandings of their shared language, it is of even less practical interest in deciphering what is going on in multi-language situations. In superimposing this scheme upon communications between the Japanese and the French at YamaMax, I witnessed 'serious utterances' in which much of the audience was largely incapable of linguistic 'reception'. Linguistically, they communicated, ordinarily in a third language (pidgin English), at the level of the problems discussed in Austin's second chapter, and they were not involved in the qualifying refinements described thereafter.

That said, Austin and the work it has inspired on 'speech acts' is vastly more valuable to developing an understanding of social relations – that I place at the heart of anthropology as well as analysis of organisations – than is work in theoretical and formal linguistics. What Austin and his interlocutors – Searle (1969), Bach and Harnish (1979), and others – have done is set the stage for elaborating how language, (social) context and knowledge intertwine. That is, as one moves through the chapters, Austin's elaborations of ever more complicated 'utterances' tell us about the assumptions of knowledge required in order to make proper responses and, effectively, to stay 'in the game' of English language communication. It demonstrates that there is more to language (and communication) than simply describing things; speech may be best understood as 'acts' which speakers carry out together, that is, socially, by virtue of using language. As such, it infers, even if it does not discuss, other communicative acts between persons that would arise along with the package of (proper) use of (a) language. Although I am perhaps being overly generous in projecting, backwards in time, the analytic possibilities of 'speech act' theory to the broader analysis of the social relations that are of interest to me,[13] Austin's work is a watershed in that it links language and communication by looking at what is at stake in the social relations involved in conversation.

Grice's very sophisticated work (1975, 1978, 1981), shows how each bit of information assists the interpreter in deciding what was actually meant by a speaker's utterance(s), including, of course, that the speaker may have meant to be evasive about his meaning. More recent work by Sperber and Wilson shifts the locus of enquiry even further into context or, as they put it, the 'relevance' of information (1986). While Sperber and Wilson explain at length that their specific definition of 'relevance' is not the vague one employed in general usage, they intentionally choose the term, and assume its common understanding, to evoke the direction of their efforts. A functional premise of their work that has attracted a great deal of attention is, what I would call, an efficiency, or cost–benefit, model whereby cognitive effort and effect are subconsciously brought into balance. That is, persons attempt to gain as much information as possible from the least effort. (We might be reminded here of the tremendously difficult work involved in persons 'communicating' in cross-linguistic conditions, such as at YamaMax.) The thrust of their research, in any case, proves with a great deal of specification that proper interpretation of 'signals' takes place in relation to a context that, theoretically, must be both linguistic and non-linguistic.

Along with other scholars, the important 'speech act' work sited briefly above is deployed in a rigorously logical and scientific manner which exposes what is relevant in particular language and communicative acts in particular 'speech communities'. These studies have been taken up broadly as 'evidence' for debates in philosophy, while Sperber and Wilson's cognitive interpretations of how meaning is established and, suggestively, the relevance of non-linguistic materials, has drawn the attention of social scientists, and anthropologists (Bloch 1998), more broadly. However, in empirical terms their arguments are already overloaded with language data, and these analysts do not engage substantively nor methodologically with the non-linguistic materials that, in principle, bear theoretical relevance to their claims.

Because its research target is broader and more complex, and so perhaps necessarily less theoretically sophisticated than the 'speech act' work described above, sociolinguistics explicitly assumes, and discusses, the relations of society and language; or, to my reading, society in language use. Methodologically it aligns itself, similarly, with intensive assessment of the technical details of conversational exchange, ordinarily transcriptions of (parts of) conversations. The materials making up these transcripts are manipulated by various means to produce data, or 'speech forms' (Labov 1972) that would identify patterns of usage of, for instance, a 'speech community' (Gumperz 1968). The interpretation of the data would thereby represent an explanation of how that community is constructed from the perspective of conversational practices; that is, how language use assists in maintaining 'attitudes' and 'values' reproductive of 'social norms' of membership (Labov 1972) or the parameters of 'community loyalty' (Milroy and Margrain 1980). This would, in turn, be linked to other attributes of the community under study, for instance, their status as immigrants, their class, gender, age, ethnicity (Fishman 1968, 1999), the associations of occupation with economic utility (Coulmas 1992; Tollefson 1993), identification with particular nations (Wardhaugh 1983), etc. In reference to the material at YamaMax, I have described at some length the social solidarity of the Japanese managers, and linked it to further affiliations with the Yama Corporation (and Japan more broadly). This solidarity gains expression, as it is made distinctive from the French at YamaMax, through Japanese language, as well as in a large number of other attributes of Japanese communications which I have detailed.

While a great deal of debate in sociolinguistics revolves around the technical efficacy of particular methodological tools, i.e. interview techniques, questionnaire design, survey sampling, multivariate analysis, etc., 'discourse analysis' can rightfully claim a highly interpretive and inclusive approach, familiar to the intent of anthropological analysis, in broadly taking on non-linguistic data. It seems to me that 'discourse analysis' is linguistics' response to the concerns of ethnopragmatics, or the ethnography of speaking (Duranti and Goodwin 1992). Hymes (1974), helpfully, generated an acronym to account for broader context in assessment of speech events. That is, SPEAKING, i.e. Situation (setting, scene), Participants (addressor and addressee), Ends (goals and outcomes), Act sequence (message form and speech content), Key (tone, manner), Norms (norms of interpretation and interaction), and Genres (text types), based, I would argue, in Malinowski's (1935) early insistence on establishing the context of situations surrounding the consideration of 'utterances', which was further elaborated in linguistics by Firth (1956) and, later, and more technically, by Halliday (1985).[14] Whether discourse analysis succeeds in its ambitions of accounting for the breadth of subject matter suggested by Hymes is questionable. It is no surprise, in any case, that in attempting to do so while maintaining a link with the rigorous methods of linguistics, it has been forced into detailed and complex analysis of short periods of social interchange. Discourse analysis distinguishes itself, nonetheless, by its methodological and theoretical sophistication, and interpretive intent.

Since attention to the distinctive linguistic characteristics of any community is implicitly built up analytically by comparing it with those of other communities, unsurprisingly a great deal of work in sociolinguistics assesses what happens explicitly when two communities, or, practically speaking, members of two communities, come into contact with one another. Obviously this would be of specific interest to our case study of YamaMax. Although neither the Japanese nor the French were competent speakers of each other's languages, when in contact with one another they could be seen as combining aspects of both 'pidgin' and a form of 'code switching.' Pidgins are languages, different from those used day to day in speech communities, that assist in communicating – usually in a limited fashion – with another speech community in order to accomplish a specific task, such as transacting business. Code switching, on the other hand, focuses on the skills of individuals, and assumes higher fluency in two languages than would be suggested by using a pidgin. Each code, or language, does a different kind of work for the user. Blom and Gumperz' (1972) early example of code switching was a study of rural Norwegians buying stamps across a post office counter in their village. A local dialect was used to exchange greetings and make inquiries regarding family members, while standard Norwegian was used for the business transaction, i.e. buying stamps.

At YamaMax it seems to me that (limited) English is a pidgin for the Japanese and the French, deployed in relatively formalised contexts like meetings and, it should be acknowledged, as the formal written language of YamaMax's paperwork. Meanwhile, among YamaMax's highly experienced French and Japanese engineers, who I studied closely, communication regarding the organisation's core rational tasks – in this case, production – was accomplished via the technical, quantitative 'language(s)' of engineering. This was available both in complex, computer driven analyses yielding printable, and downloadable, numerical accounts of speed and outputs, graphs, and the like, as well as in immediate, informal, 'back of an envelope' technical schema. Hand signals were often used around active machinery, where discussion was ruled out by noise, to 'describe' problems and 'decide' on next steps. In addition, and aligning with the perspective forwarded in this study granting agency to machinery as extensions of social relations, simply 'reading' calibrations, or numbers, off a machine is a form of communication with others.[15] The French and Japanese engineers were, respectively, then, fluent in their – mutually incommensurate – local language, and fluent in the – shared – languages of engineering, while they could manage limited communication in a third language, English. They did not share fluency in any two spoken (formal) languages, however. But if, for the moment, we were to consider engineering knowledge of the French and Japanese engineers a 'language', would 'engineering language' at YamaMax be properly considered in sociolinguistic vocabulary as a – very fluent – pidgin for communications regarding their work? Or would its use be a 'code switch' even if they shared no fluency in any other language? Perhaps with the exception of discourse analysis, sociolinguistics focuses, literally, on language in use, and usually in conversation. So a claim of the kind above – expressing technical engineering knowledge as 'language' available for a 'pidgin' or 'code switching' – would be quite unorthodox. Thus, as discussed, while many linguistic theories move toward a theoretical appreciation of context, in practice the subject that they explicitly claim to link society and language in communication is language itself.

As an anthropologist, I take the empirical 'experience' of fieldwork as the discipline's most important methodological asset. Therefore, I appreciate the seriousness with which sociolinguistics operates as a data-driven empirical science, and the high quality of debate regarding substantive output of particular research methodologies, which must be ever improving. These very strengths, however, would seem to naturally drive its research into ever more technical fine-tuning of the details while perhaps losing sight of the larger contextual picture. One can further appreciate, in practical terms, that assessment of cross-linguistic situations would become exponentially more complex in methodological terms, even if computer technology might be expanding the possibilities of assessing more variables. It is for this reason that in Chapter 1, in description of my own fieldwork techniques, I suggested that in its practical obsession with detail, conversation analysis, for example, did not deliver on the promise laid out by the originators of ethnomethodology (Garfinkel 1967; Schutz 1965). Thus, although the language sciences now acknowledge the importance of context to communicative acts, 'context' seems not to be revealed in forms that feel approachable in human terms.

Again, I raise the question: when it seems in general that most analysts of communications cannot get on with their work without the assumption of single-language use frameworks or, even more detached from the real world, assumptions about universals of communication, how are we to get on in explaining observations of settings in which two or more language and cultural systems are simultaneously at work? We must look beyond the assumptions of single-language understanding alone to begin to disentangle social relations where the knowledge of 'knowing subjects' is quite different from one to another.

Construction methods for understanding communicative contingency

We have theories to hand that recognise the kinds of problems and creative potentialities that arise in such cross-cultural/cross-linguistic communications, some of them forwarded by sociolinguistic study of multi-language situations. As detailed in Chapter 1, I would like to recall here as well that the notion of 'hybridity', while much of its discussion is caught up with postmodern hyperbole, may valuably serve us. As forwarded by Bahktin, and as I have also understood it in its most common-sense meaning, 'hybridity' is explicit in its attention to the effects of mixing and negotiation. Although much of Bahktin's use of hybridity specifically addresses *language* change through such mixtures, it can be equally and powerfully applied to other forms of relating socially,[16] including general organisational studies, as is apparent in my analysis of organising at YamaMax. And as I have suggested, 'hybridity' as a concept can be subsumed under the principles of contingency, which I have cited as the foundation of 'social constructionism'.

The problem, rather, is methodological: how to move such theory out onto the street, as it were, in order to push it along in ways applicable at a sensible, recognisable, interpersonal scale of social relations. As discussed above, sociolinguistics certainly provides detail, but is so densely engaged with language alone that is seems emptied of the social contexts it claims to expose. Socio-cultural anthropology, meanwhile, is in principle well disposed to do this kind of work – and to provide observation and interpretation of a wide range of cases – while anthropologists themselves obviously seem to be well positioned to deploy their own, personal knowledge of cross-cultural dynamics. However, while I acknowledge the person-centred work in anthropology on the dynamics of language use by Hymes (1964, 1971, 1974), Gellner (1968), Ardener (1971), Gumperz and Hymes

(1972), Pride and Holmes (1972), Goody (1978), Grillo (1989), McDonald (1989) and Morrow and Hensel (1992), it seems to me that so far little work has surfaced that combines an appreciation of the issues raised in cross-cultural dynamics with the implicit theoretical concerns of 'contingency' and 'constructionism' at heart.

In anthropology, there is a great deal of discussion about globalisation – as we have seen, an important mixer of cultures, things, ideas and words – but little detailed analysis of what persons are doing day to day that might have to do with globalisation, i.e. accounts of globalisation's hybridising effects. Noting that over one-half of the world's population is bilingual, that bilingualism is present in nearly every nation-state (Grosjean 1982: vii), that linguistic diversity is increasing dramatically in waves of immigration into North America, Europe and Japan – which drive the political economy of globalisation – attention to language use in this dynamic contemporary context is obviously important. However, the tensions between apparent homogenisations, that come with mass consumption, and diversity, or hybridity, occurring in day to day contacts between persons (and also made possible by global technological trends) suggest that analytic attention to language alone is insufficient. Thus, it seems to me that anthropological methodologies have much to offer the general repositioning of theories of communications across languages and cultures by, at the very least, closely exposing variations in forms of communication in hybrid contexts. As I have argued in this study, an important arena for beginning this kind of work is ethnographic analysis of the varied forms that communicative acts take in specific organisational settings; settings in which different 'knowing subjects' who may not know much about each other are engaged, under considerable pressure, in substantive social exchanges that are important to them as persons.

A specific example of how this type of analysis has unfolded in my own work is examination of meetings. In all organisations meetings are exhibitions of expertise and hierarchy, but in cross-cultural contexts members are likely to be conscious of the display of other means of communication as well. This is encouraged by unfamiliar language use. For example, meetings at YamaMax are generally formally conducted in English, which, as we know, no one in the subsidiary, French or Japanese, speaks or understands well. Since, as we have seen, none of the French speak any Japanese beyond the most basic level of greetings and, nearly without exception, the Japanese are only slightly more advanced users of French, communication in these meetings is explicitly divided, or compartmentalised, when either French or Japanese is spoken or, as often occurs, when both are spoken at the same time. An extraordinary linguistic dynamic is thus 'normal' in such meetings: stilted, often non-comprehensible English is combined with segments of 'native' language use during which linguistic meaning is virtually isolated from the 'non-natives', or 'others' present. Many of the meetings I attended – such as those during the test – were conducted in order to clarify technical problems; and here engineers are assisted toward understanding by cues such as timbre of expression, dress and eye-to-eye contact. These are all 'languages', if we are to carry forward the metaphor, that along with, as described above, mathematics and technical graphical representations were made all-the-more important by difficulties in the (cross-) linguistic medium. It seems that in cross-cultural social contexts non-linguistic features of communication become exaggerated – or at least take on greater importance as the attention of the participants is drawn to them – because communication is already linguistically unsteady. These exaggerations are important and interesting, and may provide guidance to analysis of the construction of cross-cultural social relations.

Whether or not we should make it analytically apparent in our written work, I would further argue that anthropologists may be especially attuned to noticing both linguistic *and* non-linguistic means of communication.[17] As a practical matter, anthropologists' attention to non-linguistic media while in the field may be an artefact of limitations in our own foreign language skills. This may be especially so at the beginning of a long-term fieldwork experience, when we are grasping for 'their' meanings; or perhaps grasping to explain to ourselves what we are up to, day to day. That said, many of my subjects at YamaMax were also highly attentive to the non-linguistic behaviour of their cross-cultural counterparts; and those who were attentive had a firmer understanding of, and could ultimately communicate better with, 'them'. Thus, at YamaMax, where discussion of how to solve a problem or the communication of decisions already taken was often the formal justification for a meeting in the first place, body language and emotional style, along with the technical apparatuses of engineering, were quite evidently critical means of circulating information and persuasion.

Of course this general situation is not altogether unlike meetings we have all experienced in organisations with which we are familiar; that is, in 'our' organisations. Decision-making is rarely cut and dried. The endemic meeting 'discussion', which for Westerners may provide the moral antidote to the formal, de facto inequities of organisational hierarchy, is an opening for exchanges of linguistic and non-linguistic kinds in which suasion and personality are given considerable play, often in ways with which we are unlikely to be conscious, and which are perhaps, thereby, especially potent.[18]

Finally, then, in spite of belabouring the importance of cross-linguistic/cross-cultural phenomena throughout this study, I am not claiming that Japanese–French meetings, or what has been uncovered here about cross-cultural organisations, are analytically distinctive from what occurs in all organisations, or more generally throughout social relations. With globalisation there will be more cross-linguistic/cross-cultural organisations in future: they will become the norm. But what close analysis of social processes on the ground day to day at YamaMax makes clear is how identifying 'difference' works as an organising tool of persons as builders of their understanding of their worlds. In the course of any day, we are not unlikely to organise our understanding of situations in which we find ourselves based, among our huge and evolving range of discerning activities, on 'superficial' perceptions of differences in such variable forms as accents suggesting class, region, nationality, management or labour/academic staff or student; the apprehension of differences in technical knowledge and education, rank, gender, sexual orientation, skin colour or ethnicity in one 'national' culture; differences of age, taste, fashion, personality as well as those differences ascribed by the organising power of hierarchy.

Organising difference is of course also the process underpinning language use (and language learning) that allows most directly for the sharing of (linguistic) community. However, we need not, and indeed should not, confine the premises of social relations to the premises of the exigencies of 'shared language' as mainstream organisational analysis, including actor–network theory, has done. Our understanding of organisations is necessarily complicated, and made more interesting, when confronted with the linguistic and cultural divides that are increasingly common features of our contemporary, hybridised social landscape. When persons make organisations, they expose, rather more clearly than we might otherwise be aware, the creative power of organising difference, constructed through both social conflict and social continuity.

Diffusing translations

How might our ethnographic data be mobilised analytically to encourage re-examination of the premises of theories of communication and organising which I have forwarded in this chapter? The new tape test at YamaMax was not understood by its participating 'agents', including the use of expertise built into machinery, as an exercise in 'speech acts', 'social relations' or 'power', 'diffusion' or 'translation'; those are our analytic preferences. It cost the company over £500,000 due to lost production and the use of special materials. The tape test was articulated at YamaMax in the language of 'market expansion', one of the central and most explicit texts of 'corporate survival'. Thus, during the test, the intervention of Otake-san and his Japanese staff came as a relief to some of the French engineers. They were aware of the stakes and the costs involved in YamaMax's capacity to learn to produce a new and more technically exacting tape. If in the end they needed help from the Japanese, so be it. For other French engineers, the intervention by the Japanese induced rage, tempered by exhaustion. In any case, the test's ultimate failure caused disappointment for all of them. The French team's months of planning and making things 'seeable', and, thereby, apparently acceptable, was reduced, at best, to a training exercise that even the exertions of the bona fide Japanese experts could not salvage.

In considering the parameters of actor–network theory, I take it as a matter of course that all employees ('agents') of YamaMax are at least marginally 'enrolled' as 'a part of the actor' – engaged in the activities of the factory – through their status as employed by the Yama Corporation. The substance of an actor–network, however, depends on the 'mobilisation' of its agents; that is, the 'reliably' of members of the network to 'speak' for it. As discussed earlier, the theoretical dynamism of actor–network theory depends on the granting of agency to all engaged in 'translating', or organising and interpreting the flow of information. The model is appealing because even peripheral members of organisations are understood as 'actors' who retain a certain degree of discretion and authority – and so power, volition and knowledge – over their 'networked' acts. We would expect, then, that because of their position in the YamaMax hierarchy that the top French engineers would have considerable leeway over interpretation of the wishes of more central authorities that they produce videotape 'in spec'. Indeed they do, where day to day, systematised, 'in spec', mass production is concerned. But, as demonstrated in the new tape test, during the organisation's more central and dynamic task of creating new forms of production, while the French engineers can be formally seen as mobilised to gather and spread information, their discretion was clearly truncated by a cross-cultural divide. As a result the '*agreed* set of relations between persons' that generates an organisation, or in this case an overseas subsidiary, was also truncated. The organisation was made formal and so literally 'seeable', but is merely a shadow of the larger, unknown and largely unseen organisation of which it forms a minor part. Conditions at YamaMax thus draw into question the analytic relevance of the 'seeability' of organisational features. As I have suggested earlier, at best 'seeability' codifies social relations from a particular position at a particular time. At YamaMax we have seen just how peripheral, or emptied of meaning, such visions might become, for example in YamaMax's organisational chart and the French engineer's plans.

This formation was embodied in the French engineers' dependence on their Japanese colleagues, whose attentions and interests were in turn largely focussed away from them and onto relations with central authorities in Japan. At significant organisational moments, such as the new tape test, it is evident that Japanese engineers in France were unwilling to 'enrol' the French engineers to 'speak for the actor', that is, in this case, to design organisational action within the firm. These French team members remained in the highest positions on YamaMax's organisational chart, above some 400 other Frenchmen, but during the new tape test they experienced 'the centre' reaching into them, altering their discretion, marginalising them, cutting them out of the network (Strathern 1996) of industrial design and prowess, and making explicit their position on the periphery of the Yama Corporation. Their efficacy, thereby, largely removed, the French engineers could not be substantively claimed as part of the Japanese firm's 'actor–network.'

In actor–network theory there is analytic space to account for conflict or redirection of information or understanding via agents' own 'translations'. However the 'boundary-less' idea of a network nonetheless suggests theoretically that it will spread inexorably. Our observations of YamaMax show how networks are controlled in organisational settings, and demonstrate that we need a pervasive theory of power working hand in hand with the expansive drives of translation and association. I have suggested, at a minimum, a combination of the notions of 'translation' and 'diffusion' in understanding the accomplishments of organising.

Notes

1 A thoroughgoing analysis of even so-called 'utopian' communities would reveal their own underlying correspondence with modern organisational forms, if for no more complicated reason than their self-conscious refusal and redesign of those forms.

2 The term 'strain' is prominent in Law's writings, i.e. he understands modern patterns of ordering to 'strain' to reach an impossible goal of mind–matter dualism. Again, to quote him (1994: 138), '[M]odernity more or less successfully (though partially and precariously) generates and performs a series of ... divisions. It works itself, for example, some way towards creating the effects that we call "mind", or "organisation", or "decisionmaking" [*sic*] or "management" or "consciousness"'. While Law's thinking is important I nonetheless find that he bounces methodologically between highly abstract quasi-philosophical statements, such as those above, and straightforward descriptions of mundane – not trivial – day to day activities in organisations, without accounting sufficiently for the analytical frames of reference through which they could be linked conceptually.

3 In an attempt to animate the evolving tensions of the event at hand, in the following detailed ethnographic account I purposely retain the flavour of my field notes: the explicit use of language, a sense of body language, physical places and the passage of time. Most of the characters in this episode were introduced in the previous chapter.

4 One would not deny, say, that a building as a physical object may represent 'an organisation'. One should recognise, however, that the power that allows it to be known in that way – a building's representational *gravitas* – arises from the organising of the network that 'takes place' there, and not vice versa. The building is but an artefact of organising which, furthermore, may in practice take place elsewhere. Indeed, an 'historic building,' empty except of historical artefacts, continues to do the work of organising *gravitas* only if so determined by persons who continue to admire and make claims in the present concerning the (earlier) work that the 'historic building' represents.

5 Strathern identifies a theoretical problem with 'network', and by implication perhaps, actor–network theory, in its apparent 'auto-limitlessness; that is, [network as] a concept which works indigenously as a metaphor for the endless extension and intermeshing of phenomena' (1996: 522). I concur with her proposal that persons, indeed, 'cut' networks by their social activities, as we do analytically in pausing to name and, so, consider any particular hybrid. (See Chapter 1, p. 21 on this point.)

6 I should point out here that neither Latour and Callon, who are major actor–network theorists, identifies himself with postmodernity. This may be deduced from the title of one of Latour's books, *Nous n'avons jamais été modernes* ('We

Have Never Been Modern') (1991), a work that, among other things, savages the methodological underpinnings of the postmodern turn.

7 I am paraphrasing Law's explanation of Foucault's analytical intent here (1986: 11–12, 16). ANT, admittedly, puts less specific emphasis on the 'productive' aspects of power, which Foucault emphasises, in favour of a more traditional political understanding of processes whereby paths to authority are carved out. (See also, Foucault 1980: 133.)

8 I examined briefly in the conclusion of Chapter 3 the literal anthropomorphising of machinery in a Japanese factory in Japan, where I observed a maintenance engineer describing to a machine the operations he was performing upon it. I take this as an extension of the paradigm described here, if an extreme one.

9 It should be noted that while it could be helpfully applied in any context to my knowledge there have been no 'ethnographic studies', however broadly defined, using actor–network theory at traditional anthropological fieldwork sites, i.e. in those less 'developed' settings, sometimes referred to as 'simpler' societies.

10 For instance, a recent edited volume called *Actor–Network Theory and Organizing*, while potentially very interesting for my purposes, seems to suffer from an effort at overclarifying and (over)simplifying the accomplishments of ANT. Here actor–network theory can be construed as traditional organisational analysis – the standalone 'diffusion' of interests – dressed up in new language. Given what I have argued about the value of collapsing macro–micro levels of analysis that, as Latour (2005) has again lately argued, have effectively crippled 'social' science, I was naturally ill-disposed to Czarniawska and Hernes' (2005) opening, editors' chapter, 'Constructing macro actors according to ANT'.

11 The 'paradox' is that Hobbes' 'social contract' – the reorganisation for the greater good of the otherwise dog-eat-dog world – is understood as a one-off, and is unidimensional, i.e. it only concerns relations of formal political power. This creates the monster, for having once decided to acquiesce to the sovereign, subjects are locked into acquiescence. While this is a powerful tool for explaining totalitarianism, it is a radical oversimplification of day to day activity, including the world of formal politics and governance.

12 In ANT 'association' has been used interchangeably with, but less prevalently than, 'translation'. While it does not generate as much analytic purchase, it nonetheless rather parsimoniously and directly grounds explanation of relations between agents which, I take it, is the core issue in actor–network theory. As will be seen I choose to use them not interchangeably but in combination: effectively with 'association' in relation to structure, and 'translation' to process.

13 In my view this is taken up in 'pragmatics' and 'relevance theory' which space does not allow me to elaborate upon here.

14 I was not aware of Hymes' SPEAKING paradigm while conducting fieldwork, but have found that my notes regarding, say, meetings at YamaMax for the most part take direct account of his suggested categories.

15 It should be noted here that in claiming 'communication' I am not making a claim as to quality of those communications. Human communication through work with machinery must be practically regarded as far less rich than interpersonal contact as it is likely to be more specific, or confined. Meanwhile, I have gone to some length in the ethnographic descriptions in this chapter to elaborate how the Japanese cut out communications and the spread of knowledge with their French colleagues by mobilising their Japanese 'speech community' when together which, importantly, in combination with their engineering languages, allowed them exclusive access to vast stores of information and know-how in Japan, or among Japanese members of their corporation.

16 As, indeed, Bahktin has done regarding carnival (1984).

17 Body 'language' and physical demeanor, for instance, are obviously essential media of human relations, and they have drawn anthropologists' analytic interests. See, for example, Bateson and Mead 1942; and Hendry and Watson 2001.

18 The successful organisational leader, in the Western context, would seem to be someone who can mobilise all of these attributes so that members 'feel' that the decision taken – even if they disagree on detail – is 'correct'.

5   Mobilising architectures of timing and spacing

Ethnographies of locations, histories of social relations

All recent history in mythological in that, by selective use of documentary evidence, it converts what we do not know about the past into a charter for what we imagine we know about the present.

(Leach 1984: 1)

Introduction

We understand face-to-face interpersonal contacts as contexts where life, work and human relations are acutely and actively negotiated. Physical spaces are ordinarily taken to be mere vessels that formally structure and contain such human action. However the apparent solidity, or exaggerated durability, of such 'structures' are projections of our own and our subjects' desires to stabilise our environments. These perceptions are convenient, but fully artificial, artefacts of our work of sense-making. The plasticity of physical spaces, and therefore their relation to time, is more durable than, but it is not different in principle from, the plasticity of face-to-face interaction. By no means am I trying to imply by this plasticity that physical spaces are thereby false, ephemeral or unreal. On the contrary, I hope to describe them as fully effective, evolving productions, made meaningful as they *take place* through social relations.

In this chapter, I examine this claim through analysis of the shifting architecture of physical and social relations among members of YamaMax. Specifically, I take one large office area and demonstrate how it is used over several years as an organising tool of social relations. The point is simple but important: arenas we take to structure human action are themselves revealing of socially active negotiations over an extended time frame. Making such matters visible hones our appreciation of human volition over the expansion and compression of perceptions of, and authority over, space and, as we shall see, time.

The central 'data' of the chapter – a spatial diagram and a time chart identifying seven stages, or 'steps', in the life of the office – were generated by a group of French engineer informants. Significant for our purposes, all of the events recorded occurred before the eighteen-month period during which I conducted ethnographic fieldwork at YamaMax. However, the explicit production of the French engineers' data was prompted by our discussions, as were stories and further elaborations concerning changes in the use of the office space over time. The joint analytic process articulated here, therefore, throws up questions regarding memory, participation, cultural and intellectual background, language, research design and the uses of knowledge.

Along with presenting these data and their elaboration as a joint research project, I interpret these French engineers' transformations of forms of sensitive 'scientific' knowledge – of design and calibrations in the production of consumer goods – into data regarding spatial timings of negotiations of social relations. Their new, and delicate, social codifications – motivated, it is argued, by a gradual decline in their relative hierarchical authority in the workplace – compels thinking about who is an ethnographer, who an informant, and what constitutes and validates data and interpretation. The question as to the relevance of actual presence among events is of especial interest at present, when anthropologists and historians are focussing some attention on what power acute attention to the remains of the past – the traditional domain of historians – and what power acute attention to the present – the traditional methodological arena of anthropologists – may offer the other in analysis and interpretation of the human enterprise. Based in an appreciation of Sorokin and Merton's (1937) work in elaborating 'social-time', I am concerned here, then, with questioning representations, i.e. social science stories (see Czarniawska 1997; Watson 2000); based in the ethnographer's sharing of 'coeval ... intersubjective Time ... [with the] Other' (Fabian 1983: 148), social-spatial constructions in organising (Yeung 1998); and, therefore, general problems of research strategy regarding organisations (Latour 1999; Lee and Hassard 1999).

After this introduction, the chapter is divided into five further sections. In the first, I briefly relocate the office area under study within the physical layout and in the context of the work of the factory itself. I then identify how the site's analysts, in this case the group of French engineers/informants, came to YamaMax in the first place, and the kinds of work they performed there day to day. The second, and central, section of the paper presents the spatial diagram and time chart – the 'data' – and examines organisational shifts apparent during each of the 'steps', or codified time segments. The last three sections interpret the motivations behind the French engineers' interest in and, later, production of the data, and reflect upon the analytic outcomes of what became a joint research project.

Making social relations: taking place, in time

While sociologically compact and rich, factories are not characteristically pleasant locations in which to conduct ethnographic fieldwork. One of the benefits of working within them, however, as suggested in my descriptions in Chapter 2 of production at YamaMax, is that one is constantly reminded through all of the senses of their very physicality. Parts of enormous machines whir loudly, visually blurred by their high rpms (revolutions per minute), while cellophane exudes noxious odours as it is heated into place around boxes of, in this case, videotapes. Here relations between persons are visibly negotiated through the medium of machines. This seems especially apparent, perhaps, as YamaMax is in the business of mass production. If an assembly line slows, the impact shows immediately on production rates; a technician is soon brought to task by his head engineer and the matter is likely to be discussed inches away from machinery that would immediately mangle a misplaced hand. Meanwhile, away from the 'line', the number and technical quality of 'goods produced' are pored over in quantitative graphs and numerical columns by production engineers; but 'final product' can be identified immediately as boxes of videotapes on wooden pallets, plastic-wrapped for shipment.

At YamaMax the decision to expand the factory for start-to-finish production of videotape had been taken in Japan in 1989. It was an investment of very large scale; initially between £30–£40 million. The design of the expanded factory into TP3, which I introduced in Chapter 2, was held in consultation with a major Japanese construction firm to which several French construction firms were subcontracted. Setting up the machinery for the technically demanding work of the early stages of magnetic tape production required new, and more highly qualified engineers. Following up advertisements for employment in several French engineering publications, from early 1990 a specially selected and highly skilled group of French engineers (my informants in this chapter) was hired by YamaMax from various engineering jobs throughout France. They had varied educational backgrounds – from, at the extremes, a postgraduate degree in aeronautics, to a vocational school leaver – but all were in their mid to late thirties and had substantial engineering experience. Although none of them had any previous experience of working at Japanese firms or in doing business at any level with the Japanese, they began working intensively, apparently pleasurably, and for extremely long hours with a group of Japanese Yama Corporation engineers: a Japanese 'start-up' team assigned solely to the task of overseeing the installation of new machinery and getting production up and running. The shell and floor space of TP3 were completed by mid-1991, when staff and workers could move in and, so, start-to-finish production of magnetic tapes could begin at YamaMax. From then, whereas the Japanese 'start-up' team dispersed back to various Yama jobs in Japan and elsewhere, the French 'start-up' team took up other engineering posts at YamaMax.

As mentioned in Chapter 2, because of the large scale of TP3's tape production machinery only one section of 'floor space' in TP3 is currently divided into three floors. Our interests focus here on the middle floor where the engineers, managers and staff overseeing the work of TP3 have their desks, computers, telephones and fax machines; their office lives. I kept a desk in the open-plan area of TP3 – nearby the French engineer informants (as well as two Japanese engineers) – from which I could follow all of the comings-and-goings of the entire office area. While of course observing the French engineers at work at their desks, on the shopfloor and its various robotic control rooms, I also had many opportunities during breaks, over lunch, and indeed, during working hours, to discuss YamaMax and its evolution with them. They assisted me with explanation of the factory's technical tasks, past and present, and were interested in my queries about their experience of the firm's socio-technical dynamics. It was eventually determined that headway into this topic could be gained by drawing a time map outlining various phases in the office evolution, to be used in combination with a blueprint of the TP3 office space. (In the final section of this chapter, I will account in detail for the process of coming up with this analytic tool.) This space was divided into 14 'areas' (see Figure 7). Four of these are within a large, central open space with windows to the outside of TP3 along one entire side. This central space serves both as offices and hallways between each of the other ten areas of various sizes, each with floor-to-ceiling walls and a door opening onto the central space. Two of these ten areas (6 and 10) have a windowed wall facing the outside.[1] A further chart by my informants (see Figure 8) outlined a longitudinal series of seven 'steps', within six of which they described to me various aspects of the office's organisational sociology and, so, personal (personnel) dramas.

I will not burden the reader with their complete record of office movement in TP3 for the entire 1991 through to mid-1996 period. Rather, I will elaborate upon notable situations that were highlighted by my French engineer informants, who were present throughout the period (as well as, obviously, throughout my fieldwork). I add some of their specific comments in inverted commas and italics translated from the French. I embellish their observations and interpretations with my own impressions which I discussed with the French engineers. These interpretations briefly describe the situation from my position of expertise regarding the Japanese.

'Data'

With Figure 7 and 8 to hand, then, the TP3 office space was initially occupied as period 'Init x' (May 1991–June 1992) – in the following way:

(Only in the case of this first period do I indicate the occupants of all fourteen 'areas', while persons designated in *italics* below are mentioned in the brief discussion to follow.)

(Number of personnel at the end of period 'Init' are 7 Japanese and 18 French, i.e. 25 persons.)

Room:
1: French production manager
2: *French engineering manager*

3: French chemical laboratory manager
4: *French utility manager*
5: meeting room
6: meeting room
7: Quality assurance (QA) office: 1 French, 1 Japanese
8: Planning office: 1 French, 1 Japanese
9: *Japanese plant manager* (carpeted room)
10: *Japanese plant manager's meeting room* (carpeted and windowed)
11: *Japanese (female) secretary*
12: *Utility group: 1 Japanese, 4 French*
13: *Engineering group: 2 Japanese, 5 French*
14: Miscellaneous: Office temps and French (female) secretary

There are three matters of interest here. First, in Japan the Japanese are accustomed to working together at blocks of perhaps six or eight desks that face one another, where all phone conversations and in-person interactions of colleagues can be overheard and, indeed, commented upon. In effect, over time through this arrangement knowledge pertaining to 'work' (and a good deal of personal information) becomes communal knowledge. The two Japanese managers in area 13 and the one area 12 re-enacted this familiar arrangement in the foreign environment of France. The Japanese are, thus, sharing space with the second hierarchical tier of French engineers; my informants for this chapter. (It might be noted that the hierarchical authority of the Japanese engineers in areas 12 and 13 vis-à-vis their French colleagues is formally ambiguous, as the Japanese are recognised on the organisational chart simply as 'advisers'.)

Second, those single French managers in hierarchical positions higher than their French colleagues in 13 and 12 have their own, private offices (in areas 2 and 4), thus reflecting their expectations about office space and, thereby, authority.

Third, the Japanese plant manager, who is the highest-ranked Japanese at YamaMax, is the only Japanese with a private office (9). He keeps the carpeted and windowed room next to him (10) – the most pleasant room in the TP3 office – as his private meeting room. Most meetings here are with his Japanese staff. However, occasionally there are meetings in room 10 with Japanese guests, who are likely to be impressed by this space, in which formal Japanese seating arrangements would be recreated. These arrangements are such that the highest ranking person sits furthest from the door with his back to either artwork and/or a flower arrangement, or an impressive exterior view, so that others, looking at him, will associate him with these aesthetic splendours. Here the Japanese plant manager at Yama-Max has literally re-enacted space arrangements, including the placement of his secretary (in area 11), as they would be found in Japan only among highest ranking private sector and public sector managers. Notably, this Japanese plant manager is unlikely ever to have the possibility of an office in

Japan in which an arrangement of this sort could be organised. His overseas posting is an opportunity to – temporarily – expand the spatial horizons of his office and his commensurate sense of authority.[2]

'Step2' (May 1992–December 1992):
(Number of personnel at the end of period 'Step 2' are 7 Japanese and 18 French, i.e. 25.)

Areas 13 and 2. The work of the French engineering manager in area 2 is not up to the expectations of the Japanese, so one of the Japanese 'advisers' in area 13 moves into the French engineering manager's office. This is obviously highly intrusive from the French perspective. My French informants (in area 13), ranked lower than their French colleague in area 2, indicate that '*the Japanese managers say that, "He is joining the French manager for better support", in fact it is for close control*'.

Areas 12 and 4. The French utility manager in area 4 has a conflict with his Japanese counterpart (who sits in area 12). The Frenchman is eventually sacked. According to my French informants, '*He is given a "window promotion"* [stated in English], *staying in room 4; thus, in the "environment", but has been stripped of authority until his departure five months later*'. (I have no details on the conflict between the Japanese and French utility manager.) Interestingly, the description by my informants (in 1997), seven years after they had begun work with the Japanese, of the French utility manager's '*window promotion*' is a direct translation into English of a Japanese concept. A '*window promotion*' is a typical Japanese managerial phrase used to describe someone who has been deemed useless to the organisation but, under the lifetime employment system, cannot be removed until retirement. He is now merely near the window (to look out of?); in any case, irrelevant to organisational action. I expect that the French manager was not sacked outright because such a radical move would not be found in the workplace repertoire of Japanese managers at first-tier Japanese corporations like Yama, especially in the early 1990s.

Area 9. A new Japanese plant manager comes from Japan, replacing the previous Japanese plant manager who had overseen the set-up of TP3.

'Step3' (January 1993–December 1993)
(Number of personnel at the end of period 'Step 3' are 6 Japanese and 16 French, i.e. 22.)

Area 12. The Japanese utility manager returns to Japan, thus reducing their number by one.

Areas 2,13 and 8. The beleaguered French engineering manager and his Japanese engineering manager – who share area 2 – move to (larger) area 8. The Japanese engineering manager in area 13 joins them in 8. The consolidation of all engineering managers (two Japanese, and one French) in 8, with the return to Japan of the Japanese utility manager, means that no Japanese is sitting in an open space office. The open-blocked-desks arrangement, 'natural' to the

Japanese, and recreated at the outset of their work in France, has been a failed experiment in the cross-cultural negotiation of the spacing of social relations.

'Step4' (November 1993–December 1994)

(Number of personnel at the end of period 'Step 4' are 1 American, 4 Japanese and 16 French, i.e. 21.)

Areas 9 and 10. The Japanese plant manager is replaced by a US plant manager. The American comes from a 'sister' Yama plant in the US, which is already doing complete start-to-finish production of magnetic tape. The US plant manager makes area 10, with a window, his office; area 9 becomes his meeting room.

Areas 8 and 4. The French engineering manager in area 8 is, according to my informants, '*kicked out*' of engineering to a '*special project*'. He joins the French utility manager who is on a '*window promotion*' in room 4. The French engineering manager is fired three months later by the American plant manager and is given two weeks to depart.

Area 1. The French production manager is fired by the US plant manager. He is given three hours to depart.

Area 11. The Japanese (female) secretary returns to Japan, and is replaced by a French (female) secretary.

A period of radical change in the TP3 office that is recalled during my fieldwork at YamaMax by all French staff who were present during the period as dramatic and exhausting. Note that at this point the original work of setting up the machinery has been long completed and the goal is to stabilise production. The posting of the second Japanese plant manager in France, who took over from the Japanese plant manager who had been overseeing set-up, is brief: less than two years. This suggests he has not been successful. Indeed, production has been well behind schedule and the company is generating significant operational losses. These losses are covered financially by 'Japan' – which understands them as part and parcel of YamaMax's 'learning period' – but it is apparently accompanied in Japan by considerable unease. Using a US Yama plant manager as a replacement suggests that the Japanese directors in Japan, frustrated with the progress of YamaMax, decide to let Yama foreigners (French and American) work with each other, i.e. they collapse the French and Americans into one category – 'foreign' – external to the Japanese. I would suggest that 'Japan' is feeling 'out of its depth' at handling YamaMax after having just invested tens of millions of pounds to build up a – technologically speaking – cutting-edge factory.

The US plant manager obviously has no qualms or feels any restraint in shaking things up on the personnel level: he fires both a French engineering manager and a French production manager. Judging from conversations with French members of YamaMax during my fieldwork the American had a reputation for constantly coming up with interesting ideas but not stabilising them in practice by providing the guidance to see them through. The French found this management style very disconcerting. Whereas vis-à-vis the French, the Japanese are often indirect, or obtuse, about what should be done, the American provides constantly shifting directions. Stylistically he expects (perhaps as among many US managers?) his subordinates to debate his ideas with him, while the French, very reticent to challenge openly hierarchical authority and, perhaps also, concerned about language barriers, are made uncomfortable and are unable to engage him in this manner. In addition, note that the American's spatial aesthetic of authority is more privately driven – he takes the 'best' office (area 10) as his own – than that of his Japanese predecessors, who prioritised the visual and physical impression-management of their relatively infrequent Japanese guests.

'Step5' (December 1994–September 1995):
(Number of personnel at the end of period 'Step 5' are 3 Japanese, 14 French, i.e. 17.)

Area 10. The US plant manager is replaced by a Japanese plant manager, Otake-san, who had visited the plant in April 1994, and again in May 1994, with a three-man Japanese 'recovery' team, sent from Japan as YamaMax is running a huge loss.

Area 3. The production planning function leaves TP3 when the French planning manager quits and the Japanese planning manager returns to Japan (and is not replaced). Area 3 is left vacant.

Area 8. One of two Japanese engineering managers in area 8 returns to Japan, and is not replaced. He is said to have been 'broken' by Otake-san. Now area 8 is the office of a single Japanese manager who oversees 'quality assessment' (QA).

In my interview with Otake-san (in 1997), recounted in Chapter 3, he related that the US plant manager felt threatened by him and his Japanese recovery team's visits; feeling that Otake-san was after his job. Indeed, while the American was put in 'to turn the factory around', the experimental nature of the move is evident: he was in France just over one year when most overseas postings are for at least three years. According to my French informants, Otake-san's impact on the TP3 office and general activities throughout the factory are increasingly sensed. Overall, in anticipation of Step 6, we can note a general thinning down in terms of personnel and general responsibilities of the TP3 office. Otake-san keeps area 10 as his office.

'Step 6' (July 1995–June 1996):
(Number of personnel at the end of period 'Step 6' are 7 Japanese, 12 French, i.e. 19.)

Areas 9 and 10. M. Marchalot, a production manager, is made plant manager, formally replacing Otake-san in this role. Otake-san formally becomes an 'adviser'. M. Marchalot's office is area 9, right next to Otake-san in area 10, and in fact there is a door directly between areas 9 and 10.

Areas 13 to 12. A new French engineering manager arrives from another Yama factory in France – which does not produce magnetic tape – and is joined in open area 12 by four French engineering staff members (my informants), who have moved from area 13.

Areas 11 to 8 to 11. A new Japanese team, of Otake-san's choice, of three young Japanese engineers arrives from Japan in February 1996. While Otake-san stays in area 10, he places all four (three new and one remaining) TP3 Japanese engineers in open area 11. He then moves them all into closed office area 8, then moves the three new Japanese engineers back to open area 11. The remaining engineer, who handles QA, returns to his original office in area 7.

In keeping with public corporate ideology regarding 'localisation' – and, after all, neither the Japanese nor the experiment with the American succeeded in 'turning the factory around' – the decision is taken to formally make a Frenchman plant manager. Otake-san, who takes dictatorial control over the organisation of TP3 office space, puts him into connected office 9, next to his. Meeting tables remain in Otake-san's large office 10 with his desk. This is the first chance in his career for Otake-san to have his own office, and he keeps it for himself.

With the arrival of a new Japanese team, Otake-san – frenetically – rearranges their desks over the course of four months. He is awkward cross-culturally, and apparently wants distance from the French and an all-Japanese space close by him: thus, the construction of a barrier between himself and the French by placing all four Japanese engineers in area 11. In ambivalence he moves them to 8 and then returns three of them – the newest members – back again to area 11.

Creating researchers

Redesigning the social architecture in the fourteen areas of the TP3 office space was a continuously available, organisationally powerful, rationalised tool at YamaMax. Of course, it is the longitudinal data that make this appear obvious, for during any one period the 'movement' has largely evaporated. Only when spread across longer periods of time, punctuated by several sets of observations, does the rapidity, indeed the intensity, of organisational, cum social, cum physical changes in the social occupation of office space become apparent, especially when compared with 'normal' transitions in the use of office areas in most 'domestic' Japanese, French, US or British organisations. This is a 'nervous system' (Taussig, 1992): hotly contested and politically fraught.

This data and the narrative stories attached to them could be extended and deepened in order to generate full analyses of cross-cultural as well as general organisational dynamics, as we have seen in the previous chapters. Here let me focus on the processes, structures and meanings attached to the creation of the 'data'. While we are by now familiar with ideas that appreciate technologies, machinery and data as media between persons, as socially constituted, and/or as 'agents' (Law 1986: 16) animated by social relations, as outlined in the previous chapter in their work engineers treat technologies, machinery and data 'naturally'; that is, as common sense objective forms for achieving rational goals. Why, then, was some of the data generated by these French engineers made explicitly social?

As mentioned earlier, these French engineers were the specially selected and highly skilled team hired in 1990 to work intensively with the group of Japanese engineers who came to YamaMax solely for the installation and the start up of a new set of machines at TP3. The Japanese TP3 'start-up' team was there for about a year and, their task complete, disbanded back to Japan or on to other start-ups in other countries – of which there were many in the late 1980s and early 1990s. With YamaMax's line expanded for complete start-to-finish production, an expanded version of mass production – and its attendant search for predictability, consistency of output, cost-cutting, automaticity, internal organisational stability and normalisation – resurfaced as its core focus. With the structures of manufacturing processes defined and, thus, the parameters of product 'specs' accounted for, younger, less highly skilled and lower paid French staff from the less technically demanding downstream segments of the factory production line, i.e. TP2, as well as from other factories in France, came onto TP3's new and more technically demanding line. They quickly gained experience and were rapidly promoted. Meanwhile, the disbanded Japanese 'start-up' team, with whom my French engineer/informants claimed to share considerable mutual respect, was replaced many times over by the normal cycle of Japanese engineers circulating on three to five year assignments, as well as a steady stream of short term Japanese 'advisers'. None of these 'new' Japanese engineers knew the French engineers, or about their earlier, and important, work with the Japanese 'start-up' team.

With the 'start-up' completed, among the new tasks of two of my French engineer/informants was redesign, improvement and technical linkage of particular machines at TP3. They worked in close contact with two other of their party who focussed on maintenance. Another dedicated himself to parts procurement. Another – the former aeronautics engineer – worked side by side with a series of Japanese engineers on process engineering of the delicate and dangerous first stage of production: the chemical mixing of magnetic paste. This latter work, however, was so critical to the entire production chain that the Japanese engineers effectively controlled it. Thus, while the French engineers were formally labelled, and defined themselves, to themselves, in technical 'adviser' or 'consultant' roles – and to an extent this was accurate – they gradually became marginal players in TP3 activities: technically, socially and, so, organisationally. Their declining position with regard to top-priority, core production tasks was also demonstrated in their stagnant progress up the hierarchical ranks and, so, the relatively slow pace of their salary rises. They were, it appears, growing obsolete.

For these French engineers this is apparently a story about psychologically balancing the common rational, and often harsh, justifications of formal organisation. That is, as a form of compensation the French engineers' early days of respectability with the high-powered Japanese 'start-up' team were glorified, made nostalgic. In time the French engineers came to exaggerate the distinction between their superior capacity to *create* the methods or machineries of production and the limited capacity of rising 'Fordist' (Gramsci 1971: 277–320; cf. Kenney and Florida 1993: 8–10) staff who could only *oversee* (or 'do') production in TP3: many of whom, as above, came to TP3 from the less technically demanding downstream segments of the factory production line. Over the years it appears that my French engineer/informants did not push themselves onto the production 'line' – into YamaMax's core rational space – and they did not make the – admittedly, counterintuitive – move of understanding that, while mundane on the surface, the maintenance of consistency (as mass production's central requirement) is an extremely challenging and complicated process; subtle and, possibly, analytically interesting.[3] Effectively, having become outsiders, the French engineers were bitter over their declining authority at YamaMax.

'Coeval' analysis

The tradition of key informants as outsiders to their own society is a strong one in anthropology (Rabinow 1977), but that is the sort of problem ordinarily realised, reflected upon, and, occasionally, theorised, in retrospect; after fieldwork is complete. (It should also be noted that while I highlight a particular set of French engineers in this chapter, as we have seen I had other informants among both the French and the Japanese at YamaMax who were '*right* in the middle' of YamaMax's core activities.) When I arrived at YamaMax, five years after the start-up was complete, comparatively speaking my French engineer/informants had time on their hands, and they were prepared to talk about (their understanding of) YamaMax. After all, while most of the other members of YamaMax were (typically) reticent in my first months at YamaMax, what tangible threat did my growing understanding of YamaMax pose to these French engineers' already-dismantled authority in the organisation? Their difficult situation had already been pressed by them into the service of irony-charged observation – and low-level, coalition-sustaining discussion between them – of organisational and technical changes over which they had decreasing control. Because these discussions were socially construed and unusually elaborate – especially for engineers – I picked up on them quickly. (Indeed, after a while I was somewhat concerned not to become overly identified with their camp, as it were.) So, while through my observations of organisational dynamics at YamaMax I could eventually confirm the French engineers' marginality, I did not witness the organisational history of YamaMax as they laid it out to me. I was entirely green when my fieldwork began at the end of 'step 6'.[4]

All sorts of questions about 'timings' and 'spacing' and 'data' and 'research' are at stake here. In *Time and the Other*, Fabian raises the problem of translating shared experience with subjects – what he calls 'coeval' time, articulated in the idealised form of 'shared speech' during fieldwork – into 'allochronic', distanced, artificial, quasi-scientific texts for a professional audience (1983). Effectively anticipating anthropology's 'crisis of representation' (Geertz 1988; cf. Tyler 1986), to my reading Fabian makes an early argument for avoiding obsessiveness over literary 'intertextuality' in our writing (and reading) about society. Rather than killing themselves off, authors are encouraged towards responsibility to their shared experience with others, while recognising, of course, that the difference between experience and its representation will never disappear (see also, Lejeune 1989.) I share Fabian's concerns over accounting for this difference. Here, let me make explicit my experience of accidentally falling upon a partial resolution to some of these problems through reflection on conducting research with these French engineers and so, further examine representation of timing and spacing in research practice.

There are (at least) three researched perspectives available here. First, my 'prospective' experience of the organising of YamaMax, including by the French engineers, engaged through day to day participant–observation; second, a 'retrospective' story about the past I did not experience but was in the heads and speech of the French engineers, and engaged through 'speech' in interviews, or listening to them talk together about the past (Czarniowska 1997:65); and, third, a co-produced research project, or dialogic embellishment, or generation of a hybrid, third language (Bakhtin 1981; Brown 1989), combining their stories, our discussions, and a joint experience encouraging the elaboration of a researched story. Let me examine, further, how our research proceeded over time, in order to also suggest that (the tool of) bracketing research into three categories of field practice, as I have just done, if analytically instructive, makes artificial what actually happened.

The French engineers and I naturally began our discussions with an interrogation of the present in which I could at least literally see things, even if I had no idea 'what was going on'. Their responses to, 'Who's who in the office?', were, as I have discussed earlier, unusually rich. Although their explanations – in combination with my evolving observations of, and discussions with other people, as well as coming to grips with organisational charts, job descriptions, machinery and other artefacts – brought on the confused information-overload typical of the early stages of fieldwork, 'the present' gradually took its place for me at YamaMax. And perhaps better appreciation of the present's fullness suggested accounting for its past, a subject about which the French engineers were in principle, as we have seen, very accommodating, even insistent. How would we get at it, however; and did I really want to go there?

I had already established that organisational charts were a flimsy approximation of organisational dynamics at YamaMax, to say nothing of misrepresenting actual communication patterns among members of YamaMax as they occurred both within and outside the organisation. This was made evident, further, by no one at YamaMax, apparently, paying any attention to organisational charts because they were produced and replaced with such rapidity: as ANT advocates would put it, they had limited 'durability'. (Over the eighteen months that I followed and collected artefacts 'in use' at YamaMax, there were seven different organisational charts representing the engineering section of TP3 alone.) Since my initial queries with the French engineers about social relations at YamaMax concerned the most obvious, observable thing – 'Who is it sitting over there, and what do they do?' – and this had stimulated substantive reflection by the French engineers – about 'Who used to be there, and why?' – it was somehow determined that our discussions would be initially organised by the unchanging walls of the office space or, effectively, the layout of identical desks which, apparently due to their surplus, remained for the most part *in situ* over the years. (Especially in the central open-plan office (areas 11, 12, 13 and 14), once it was determined where someone would move to, they simply brought the contents of their desks, their computer, and their chair to another desk.)

Practically speaking, I recognised that this fully contained, or 'canned', history would of necessity require thickening through a long series of discussions between us. While that would be interesting, frankly it was not the top priority of my research: I was, rather, focussed on the details of social relations, lived day to day in the present. Thus, although from time to time we discussed the past, and I took notes, the information somehow did not organise itself: perhaps there was too much density to the detail for me to see how it might hang together. Furthermore, though we kept going with our history project, I was unsure what would emerge from it beyond overarching statements about a cross-cultural enterprise that would be, in any case, relatively thin compared to my participant–observations. In retrospect this ambivalence is indicative of a transition in my understanding of YamaMax. The rational/technical framing of our interchanges via an acute awareness of the presence of walls and desks – stable and obvious to the fresh observer – seemed 'canned', or 'tinny', because these physical attributes were evaporated, or displaced, as my knowledge of 'office space' was, over time, increasingly reproduced as 'social space' (Lefebvre 1991).

One Monday the former aeronautics engineer – my key informant among the French engineers – and who was perhaps, also, frustrated by our research, showed up with the blueprint of the TP3 office with numbered office spaces, the time chart of the seven 'steps', and a set of handwritten comments on each step (but the seventh, when I was there): an entire time-and-motion toolbox (see Figure 7 and 8). He had apparently spent the entire weekend putting it together at home. While the blueprint was already present in our heads, as it was ever-present before our eyes, I was impressed with its work in combination with the time chart in bringing order to our discussions. Allow me to elaborate this point.

In their day to day work, I had watched engineers producing and discussing data that reported on engineering processes – the temperature of polished rollers compressing plastic backing film and magnetic paste, the frequency of breakdowns on particular machines under particular conditions, etc. – which became records that assisted in organising plans (Latour and Woolgar 1979; Latour 1986, 1987, 1988; Callon 1986). It was apparent that these engineers were keenly aware of the implications to analysis of the qualities and interactions making up data and calculations in the apparatus of material production. However, although I could read their data, and see its linkage to actions, I could not comprehend, and so fully appreciate, the organising properties of their formulae: what was gained or lost in any particular, usually mathematical, form of data production. This was the case, that is, until an operation of this kind was translated through the raw material of social relations, about which I had many other sources of knowledge with which to triangulate their forms. In their seven-stepped time chart the French engineers importantly called for each step to overlap at the margins as an expression of their sense of the analytical tension between providing demarcations to 'fix' observations and the 'continuousness' of flux in office, cum social, cum architectural, arrangements. This was an explicit, visible representation of the tension between social change and continuity. Indeed, had I decided to divide the historical material by 'steps' over time, I probably would have strictly annualised them for clarity's sake. (I was implicitly – if meaninglessly – doing so by simply recording dates.) Their form for organising the time-and-motion model of office social architecture – softening the edges of those very demarcations in order to account for the rise and fall of tension in physically reorganising social relations – was very satisfying, and accurate.

With these tools to hand, we shared a 'coeval' medium to speak through (Fabian 1983) and, so, quickly increased the quantity of detail while also enhancing the quality of our reflections. Based in what they recounted about the organisational episodes, they were interested in my views of how work at YamaMax, and living in France, may have been perceived among YamaMax's series of Japanese managers and engineers; as well as those back in Japan with whom the Japanese at YamaMax were in close and deliberate contact. In our research project, or dialogue and negotiation of technical and social languages, we continued to embellish the steps and, ever more interestingly, the tensions of overlaps in the spacing of social timing and social relations.

In retrospect this seems, perhaps, a 'natural' process of research stimulated through the combination of observation and reflection. However, the low probability of having made this research may be best appreciated by way of contrast with other YamaMax engineers' accounts of the past. In the field, and chock full of an ethical stance vis-à-vis my host community, I of course never considered asking the opinion of the more successful, rising French engineers, or indeed the Japanese, of my French engineer/ informants' time-and-motion diagram of TP3's office space. To do so would have risked sharply undermining our mutual trust. However, as I was learning a great deal about YamaMax's past, when I did press other engineers to reflect on it, they would often mention transitions due to changes in top leadership at YamaMax, or suggest that further detail could be acquired though a review of old organisational charts. That said, they had discarded their own old charts: as each was superseded by whatever rarely consulted organisational chart represented the present. They guessed, however, that old organisational charts were held on record somewhere at YamaMax. They were, in short, dismissive of such queries about the past. Many of these other engineers also, eventually, became good informants, and I am confident of what they would have felt about their colleagues' time-and-motion diagram. They would have been briefly amused, but seen the production of such diagrams as a waste of time, an analysis fully irrelevant to the present and future: YamaMax's rational timing and spacing.

Reaching conclusions

Questions remain as to the quality of my French engineer/informants' anxiously acquired social knowledge articulated in their time-and-motion data. What are the implications of the fact that it was produced because of their alienation from their authority over the types of knowledge that their organisation explicitly rewarded? What was the use for them of transforming forms of engineering knowledge into explicit interest and interpretation of other sorts of knowledge?

In coming to terms with these questions we might ask how it was made and used differently from knowledge generated for the academy. In anthropology a central approach to articulating the comparative method – which, I believe, is at least implicit in all sound scholarly practice – lies in combining the positional realities of visitations for distinct periods of time – 'in the field, sharing time and speech' – with professional obligations to stand apart from, but represent, the subjects they have studied with – 'at home'. This is articulated in anthropology through an explicit focus on the idea of 'the other' as a methodological tool. However, scholars in all fields to a greater or lesser degree cope with a similar form of methodological conundrum by, simply, doing analysis: which, though hardly as cut and dried as this in practice, I take to be what occurs in the gap between data–field materials and text–representations, whether or not this difference is articulated in terms of representational aesthetics, physical distance, or both. The French engineer/informants however, unlike scholars, were unintentionally made into observers and analysts of that environment that so poignantly affected them – their own – while continuing formally *in situ* as organisational 'members'. Once made organisationally marginal they were good at explaining their organisation to themselves. After all, they had exact 'native' knowledge of it. (Indeed, how could they not?) My temporary interventions, as an outsider, or 'other' to them, encouraged a (temporary) formal representation of their spacings and timings in the form of the time-and-motion chart. (Otherwise they were only 'in speech' with each other about their situation.) It is no wonder, then, that they were quite clear about the meaning of the Japanese term '*window promotion*'. Perhaps not unlike ethnography, they knew that observing action – even if live and unpredictable – was like participating through glass: they could see it, but were not meant to touch it.

The French engineers' process of generating new kinds of knowledge was made possible, necessary and, presumably aided by our joint research, increasingly poignant *because* their colleagues had gradually *taken their social 'place' 'right* in the middle' of YamaMax's core goal of mass production. This is suggested by a key artefact of their time-and-motion chart. Apart from one move of the entire group between areas 12 and 13 – which elicited no comment in our discussions – the French engineer/informants themselves never appear as actors, or 'agents', in any of the stories of the seven steps in the office area of TP3. In their 'data', they represent themselves as non-artefacts. Even though, unlike scholars, their work was continuously present at YamaMax, they analysed themselves into the position of pure, completely objective, scientific observers, as if invisible, and having no effect on the subjects of their studies: their colleagues at YamaMax. Unlike scholars, who strive for the success represented in grants and research time for going away and coming back and productively writing, the French engineers' own organisation oversocialised them away from, and so decontextualised them socially and, effectively, physically away from their organisation's rationalised, and powerful, 'scientific' formations. As they increasingly became 'distanced' members, the organisation delivered time to them for reflection and, so, the motivation for calibrating their distressed self-perceptions. At the end of the day, their research project – circulating stories about others in their own organisation – served to provide encouragement of their in-group identity formation, as it was a means of improvising with me upon 'coeval time and speech'. Of course our sharing of time and speech ended when I left the field. How the group communicated after my departure I do not know. I suspect, however, that as before my arrival, rather than charts and timings, they relied, again, upon their own time and speech.

In this chapter I have examined the experiences of a group of French engineers for assistance with organising ideas about timing and spacing in research. These informants developed an enriched view of the past – a codification of the use of desks and offices as social space – which represented their declining organisational status over time, and was used by them to understand their present circumstances. Our joint research – engaging the physical/linear/chronological/progressive conception of time in use, as deployed in their formal work – has appreciated the flexibility – indeed, the social construction – of rational conceptions of time (Orlikowski 1992) as a tool of the socio-spatial timing. I suspect I would have missed this point, however, if we had not been able to make explicit the conversion and co-production of technical forms and social knowledge (Grint and Woolgar 1997). The French engineers literally connected the dots in front of me, and those dots overlap at the margins of categories. Thus, their model preserves tension between continuity of practices – articulated through specific, representational stories of designated periods – and periods of change – where stories could not yet be articulated. While the collective situation of the French engineers was perhaps unorthodox, especially among relatively highly ranked persons in organisational settings, who would, nonetheless, be 'expert' (Bauman 1987, 1993; Beck 1992; Wynne 1996; Berglund 1998; Lee and Hassard 1999) – an anthropologist or the engineers – in sensitively expanding our understanding of timing and spacing in a factory, albeit in this unusual case, concerning social relations?

Notes

1 In addition there are four areas on the left side of the layout, also opening onto the central space. Two are large meeting rooms (named Arc de Triomphe and Tour Eiffel), one a room with a highly efficient copy machine and a fax machine divided off from a space holding supplies and files, and the last a small office where two technicians track production processes on computers. These areas are irrelevant to the current discussion.
2 While foreign postings are certainly challenging and strenuous for Japanese managers (and their families), it should also be recognised how the return to Japan into cramped offices (and homes), where superiors stand heavily and numerously on managers' shoulders, is a cause for substantial reverse culture shock in terms of relative individual volition and decision-making opportunities enjoyed while abroad.
3 I, too, as a social analyst, and accustomed to focussing explicitly on the exigencies of 'change', have had to back my way over some years into an appreciation of this point.
4 Even though the 'data' did not exist until over a year later, from this point, represented on the time-and-motion chart as 'from then', it was presumed by my French engineer/informants that I was able to map and tell stories of the social space of the office without their assistance.

Part III

Incorporating cultures: local reductions, global repercussions

6 Circulating others among Japanese managers
Perceiving difference, explaining to ourselves

Introduction

A Japanese manager of a Japanese multinational corporation experiences 'globalisation' at many levels during his typical five-year posting at a subsidiary abroad. As suggested in Chapter 2, with his compatriots at home he has been subjected to the rising profile of 'globalisation' in the public media. Interpreted as a matter of corporate ideology it might also appear as news in semi-private, in-house media, both as synopses of the chief executive officer's thinking on the corporation's global future, as well as data in articles on its extensive projects abroad. At corporate ceremonies at a French subsidiary it might appear in a speech by a visiting corporate '*biggy*' (a high-level executive) from Japan – delivered in English translation to 130 French employees on the day shift, and their eight Japanese colleagues – to commemorate production of the ten millionth videocassette. These, then, are examples of globalisation as rhetoric in two separate but, of course, complementary arenas: public and corporate.

Meanwhile, his *shigoto* (work) – the primary day to day engagements of a Japanese manager at a subsidiary abroad such as YamaMax – is thoroughly caught up in cross-cultural interchanges that supply some of the local social contents – the actual social processes – of the rhetorical vessels called 'globalisation' or, often, in Japan, 'internationalisation'. These activities are seldom explored or acknowledged in official texts. For example, a Japanese manager might engage in analysing why an assembly line is working inefficiently. He must communicate his findings in a *mélange* of English, French and Japanese, by drawings on available sheets of paper and by the physical handling of industrial machinery: the varied media in which communication in the setting of an overseas subsidiary precariously and creatively floats. For example, he is at first surprised to find the office empty of French manager colleagues for 1.5 hours at midday when he finished his lunch in fifteen minutes, but over several months learns to appreciate the slow midday meal he takes once a week. For example, when he can pull himself together after a 70-hour work week, he studies French at 8:30 a.m. on Saturdays.

Working the intersubjective social whole

Members of 'communities' are ordinarily capable of describing the communities in which they participate as unified in certain contexts, while in other contexts they are uneven or in flux. From an academic perspective, then, they are 'contested' both in practice and in theory (Stewart 1996). As a result anthropological doubt has, it seems correctly, been cast on the accuracy and analytic incisiveness to be gained from representing, or 'essentialising', any community we study as a social or cultural whole. Indeed, a major point of critique within recent ethnography has focussed on problematising the boundaries implied by theorising cultures as unadulterated by external interaction (Tsing 1994); a point that was ethnographically and theoretically articulated by Leach in 1954 (1977 [1954]).

Under the professional guidance of anthropology, like every other space of social interaction I also understand the large and successful Japanese corporations that I study as contested locations in both social and physical senses. Such is not the vision of Japanese *salaryman* of their own organised community, however. For instance, they understand the descriptions of their work of cross-cultural communication – such as the examples forwarded at the start of this chapter – to be underpinned, or preceded, by their authority over action and analysis at overseas subsidiaries. In turn, as was explored in Chapter 4 and will be further examined here, they control the subsequent representation of these organisational activities. Thus, although in the organisational charts of overseas subsidiaries Japanese managers may appear as marginal 'advisers', their authority is *realised*. By this I mean not merely legal 49 per cent, 51 per cent or 100 per cent Japanese ownership of an overseas firm; I mean de facto ownership of, and power over, the means of *production* in a broad sense.

On the ground in subsidiaries abroad, the medium of this 'ownership' and authority is not only the functional reach of quantifiable technical know-how and financial resources. These are combined with a series of psychologically dense and reinforcing descriptions of Japanese managers' work and their organisation that link their techniques and their products with themselves. Remuneration enhances commitment, but the motivations of Japanese managers are deeply rooted in the particular visions they hold of their activities within the corporation. A range of icons focus their attentions. These may include notions as broad, and rich, as 'their' firm's 'Japanese-ness', or an appreciation of their firm as the 'best among Japanese firms' and/or 'the most internationalised among Japanese firms'. Such abstractions are linked with specifics such as personal identification with the particular products upon which they labour in the course of their careers. Japanese managers are likely to be involved in the development of specific work practices surrounding the design, manufacture and/or distribution of these products. Indeed, I will show that techniques of production, products, careers, the corporation and time itself are all fetish objects of Japanese members of large, Japanese firms such as Yama. As a result, such corporations profit from their members' creative maintenance of a unifying image of the corporation as a seamless social whole, and circulate this image though various interdependent strategies. Their members' 'corporate culture' holds organisational value – it generates activity at their organisation – because it is made personal. They are indeed physically, cognitively and, perhaps most importantly, emotionally incorporated into the corporation.

Let me explore the prospects for this interpretation by forwarding both the background to such circulations, in Japan, and how, in turn, these circulations are articulated in the experience of Japanese managers working with non-Japanese persons abroad. We will thereby be examining some critical parameters of the experience of globalisation among Japanese members of such firms.

Idealised Japanese manufacturing

To understand how such regenerative practices as Japanese managers' incorporation into their organisation are sustained, we may begin by considering the social characteristics observed at large-scale manufacturing firms at home in Japan as an 'ideal type' (Leach 1977 [1954]: ix–xii, 4, 7–8, 284–6). Important among these social characteristics is long-term commitment by employees to the firm as much more than a 'workplace' in the Western sense. Indeed a firm such as Yama is a totalising environment, permeating the identity – in both the private and public spheres – of employees *and,* to a significant degree, their families. (Thus the inclusion, in the vignettes opening Chapter 2, of the concerns of a Japanese engineer's wife in my descriptions of 'the Japanese corporation'.)

In day to day work the overlapping of areas of responsibility engages members in the tasks of their colleagues, who are prepared to offer assistance and advice if needed.[1] This process also helps to defuse interpersonal competition through mutual dependence. Mechanisms have, meanwhile, been put in place to cope with the filtering, and altering, of information as it passes between persons; a significant issue in hierarchical organisations, made especially so where accurate information is required for day to day competency. For example, while flows of quantifiable technical detail may be less difficult, the viewpoint of workers concerning work practices is preserved through encouraging suggestions, which are written out and deposited at a specified location on the shopfloor. These are assessed by managers, often at considerable hierarchical distance from the shopfloor and, where deemed appropriate, rewarded and operationalised. The system ideally devolves authority – over a limited sphere of activities – down to lower levels than would be the case in a traditional Western manufacturing model. Thus workers, who are generally highly trained both at school and at the company itself, appear to have a high degree of autonomy over their specific tasks while at the same time pushing a great deal of information about those tasks into the organisational system.

Although structurally more difficult, communications across organisational functions is greatly facilitated by the structure of careers. Upon hiring, a male, full-time employee can reasonably expect to work at a firm such as Yama for at least thirty years.[2] The firm encourages and expects the development of a broad set of skills and experiences in many aspects of corporate operations. Thus there is no job risk in becoming a relative novice at several points in a career. Meanwhile, as he moves within the firm between different positions and with increasing hierarchical (formal) authority, his personal network widens and so his (informal) authority. Such a manager may be genuinely capable of appreciating the concerns of lower level employees. It may be a particular artefact of the tremendous economic growth of postwar Japan, but it matters that at present many upper-level managers in major Japanese firms joined the firm in their late teens or early twenties as assembly line workers, at a time when hands-on, craft skills were central to the ethos of industrial labour. Thus, there is no romantic attribution in my several observations of a Japanese factory president in a foreign subsidiary spending time on the shopfloor touching, with his eyes closed, the exterior body (the *skin*) of newly manufactured automobiles with his fingertips in search of flaws. For the last twenty-five years this is one way he has known the quality of his work and the success of his organisation.

The potential organisational dynamism of the Japanese manufacturing model can be appreciated conceptually by contrasting it with 'Fordism', which is associated with traditional Western manufacturing and has by now become the *bête noire* of industrial organisation (Gramsci 1971: 277–320; cf. Kenney and Florida 1993: 8–10). Under Fordism a worker is said to have been 'atomised'. That is, he is defined as an input (like a machine or a raw material) to mass production, repetitively performing a simple and specified task without knowledge of the relationship of his work to either the product produced or, perhaps, to the overall organisation itself. Fordism is claimed to recreate management–labour divisions by continuously reiterating the distinctions between managers, who design and decide – 'think' – while labour only operationalises – 'do'. The diminution of the value, or potentiality, of the human factor in 'labour' made Fordism noxious to many (even non-Marxist) analysts of industrial organisation at the end of twentieth century, and perhaps to some industrialists.

In any case by the mid-1970s many Western industries were not 'working' well and were recognised as organisationally cumbersome. In short, they were losing money. As outlined in Chapters 1 and 2, Western consumer goods industries, in particular, declined one after another in the face of Japanese competition, followed by automobiles; a situation that might have been anticipated by the earlier decline of US and British motorcycle firms.[3] Interest in the Japanese model by Western industry has therefore been a multifaceted affair influenced both by competition and general attitudes in Western societies. In industrial circles the 'Japanese manufacturing model' is by now a well-travelled set of general ideas which – often renamed in non-Japanese contexts – have become normative among manufacturers worldwide.[4] This broad acknowledgement of the strengths of the Japanese model among industrialists – as well as in business studies, as described in Chapter 1 – has reinforced the confidence of Japanese managers, especially at firms with strong manufacturing traditions such as Yama. The Japanese media, meanwhile, is an important source of instruction in these matters as it generates a vast array of publications targeting an avid audience of Japanese business managers and engineers.

This model is of course most powerfully articulated within the organisational systems, practices and histories of the Japanese firms to which Japanese managers are attached. However, the sociality and institutional/organisational structures underlying 'work' at large Japanese manufacturing firms have been effective throughout domestic manufacturing in postwar Japan. Thus, while most work in Japan has not taken place in large firms (such as Yama), they have been the prime articulators of this model, which is widely understood and, to a greater or lesser extent, pursued in most Japanese formal organisations, especially so in the private sector.

Why this might be so requires an historical analysis beyond our current analytical goals. Briefly, however, the context is the following. The broadly recognised domestic heroes of Japan's impressive recovery from the devastations of the Second World War are a triad of workers, corporate manager *salaryman* and government 'mandarins' leading them.[5] The will of the Japanese at the close of the war and over the decades to follow in facing up economically and organisationally to the radical domestic wartime and immediate postwar situation should never be underestimated. Indeed, the historic reach of the postwar response as a culture (or, perhaps, cult) of work has been poignantly described as follows: ' . . . the so-called economic miracle . . . allowed the manic overcoming of war's trauma through the displacement of memories in the routine of overwork' (Ivy 1995: 15). To my thinking, this was driven by the complex interrelations of the triad suggested above. It should be noted, however, that the Japanese had a well-established industrial labour tradition, similarly tightly aligned with state interest, stretching back fifty years before the war, to draw upon in the postwar rebuilding process. This has been very thoroughly documented in the work of Gordon (1985, 1998a), while Tsutsui (1998) has traced Japan's development and exchanges of manufacturing knowledge, especially with the US, throughout the twentieth century. Meanwhile in Vlastos' (1998) edited volume, broadly applying Hobsbaum and Ranger's (1983) notion of 'invented tradition' to the Japanese context, Gordon (1998b) exposes the possibilities available to 'Japanese-style labour management' relations in light of a deep well of, fully manipulable, 'tradition'. This eventually led to 'a consensus about the elements of a modernized Japanese style of "cooperative labor–capital relations"' in the postwar period (Gordon 1998b: 36). Matanle (2003) assists in clarifying Hobsbaum and Ranger's intent with regard to Japanese tradition and the experience of industrial practice when he states: '[A]lthough managerial, union, and government leaders actively and purposively incorporated traditional structures into their construction of the modern Japanese corporation in the interests of furthering Japan's modernization project, many rank and file employees certainly internalized a genuine belief that their corporation was, and perhaps is, a traditional structure incorporating an authentically Japanese traditional ideology' (2003: 21).

It should be noted that at present the proportion of industrial labour among employed persons in Japan is substantially reduced from postwar highs, while government officials have since the late 1990s, and for virtually the first time in the history of modern Japan, come under intense public scrutiny and suspicion. While not untainted, and perhaps not exciting, I would argue that among the Japanese postwar heroic triad outlined above the remaining role model providing a recognisable bridge to the future, and a positive link with the past, are private sector *salaryman*. In spite of newspaper reportage to the contrary, the empirical evidence is in the continuous attraction of such positions for young university graduates. Less obviously observable, but nonetheless logical, it is my view that in the recent post-bubble period of economic difficulty in Japan and, indeed, currently – during which there are fewer new jobs among large private sector firms in Japan, and the subsequent generation of underemployment among new graduates – the security provided by such firms draws them more deeply into the imagination of the Japanese and intensifies the longing for the careers this type of firm continues to provide.

In any case, while articulated in compacted form here – and recognising that the boundaries of models are intrinsically soft and dependent on contextual factors – Japanese industrial managers at Yama actively engage with and maintain a fairly stable 'Japanese manufacturing model'. It is based on their long-term knowledge-building regarding the technical information supporting the production of specific products, gained through hands-on experience within a particular, but multifaceted, organisation. This entire process is rooted, furthermore, as above, in a fertile historical, political–economic and ideological context in Japan. The currently fashionable term for describing such a phenomenon would be to stress the 'embeddedness' of the model in the work practices of Japanese managers (Granovetter 1981). Having established some specific, and partially technical, features of the model, then, what follows is an interpretation of how these features circulate as processes that reiterate and reinforce the Japanese corporation.

Circulating the fetishes of production

Members of corporations such as Yama have recognised that in the contemporary contexts of advanced industrialised economies, 'products' are synonymous with image. A Rolls-Royce, for example, is understood to ride comfortably, well before one slips inside and smells the leather seats. Or, stated somewhat more analytically, as any advertising executive will tell you, consumption of product and consumption of image are, if not literally the same act, deeply linked.[6] Advertising agencies, and the theories they deploy, understand the integration of producer image and product consumption as a problem of generating 'value added' through brand name (Davidson 1992). While accurate, this perspective is limited to the parameters of advertising agencies' activities and their intersection with producers' marketing departments. Practically speaking, this is a matter of positioning information relative to audience: consumers interact with the corporation's final products and its 'public' image, literally, outside the firm.[7] It is no magic particular to successful consumer electronics firms that from the outside a company such as Yama appears as a unitary 'solid'; as seamless. This process is aided by the symbolic 'prop' of consumers' physical interactions with high-quality, seamless products. However, nearly all organisations, including companies, governments or university departments, are imagined as seamless when we are external to them. It is only once we work in them, gain knowledge of them, that we know that all organisations are mottled, socially contested and, if slow, fluid. The issue at stake here is that different organisations, operating in different contexts, treat the boundaries of such information differently.

Although knowledge of organisational flux is generally held exclusively by its own members, i.e. not displayed outside the organisation, it is of especial interest that at large, Japanese firms such as Yama any *potential* crack in the façade of corporate seamlessness is understood to entail great risk. Producers, especially manufacturing firms, believe that a failed product exposes cracks to a degree that no amount of advertising can authentically seal. Thus while large industrial organisations such as Yama thrive through creative tensions between its various specialisms – from obtaining raw materials through to postcode-based marketing of products – all of its members acknowledge the priority of seamless products, efficiently produced. So let us slip *production,* producers and, so, companies back into recent analytical preoccupations with the *consumption* of products (cf. Miller 1987; Douglas and Isherwood 1979; Baudrillard 1981) or, in the context of such theories, recognise in the processes of production a form of self-consumption. The maths of this fresh paradigm triangulate as follows: product = image; image = company; company = product. These are not literal equivalents but, to link in Fabian's (1983) notion, forwarded in the last chapter, of 'shared time', they might be understood as 'coeval', or cooperative. The corporation's circulation and reproduction as an object/

product – like the objects/products it produces – is thus mobilised by the members of the firm to not only be seamless on the surface, and so when consumed – that is, when circulated and viewed from the outside – but also seamless when produced: when circulated and viewed (and so, metaphorically, consumed) within. How would these circulations work?

Within Japanese corporations such as Yama the maths of product/ image/ company are operationalised by Japanese managers and engineers through relentless internal campaigns to increase the product 'quality' upon which the future of the corporation is claimed to depend. However the mass production systems – within which objects are made – also require increasing rates of efficiency in order to make profit; a reckoning that turns time itself into a fetish object.[8] Thus, the external image of the corporation's seamlessness is generated largely through products, while the internal image of seamlessness is generated through the efficiency of production. That is, the structural tension created by corporate engineers' necessary desire for seamless products (or *output*) can only be resolved through attempts at perfecting (or making seamless) the efficiencies of *internal* techniques and systems of production.

This analysis exposes the 'essentialising' – the creation of the 'socio-technical whole' – of the corporation by its members (as well as its external public) not as sourced in any specific act, but as a set of circulating relations that are centripetal in effecting the corporation. Thus, I understand any number of objects and activities in the corporation – products, advertisements, techniques, time (efficiency), careers, etc. – as 'fetishes' in that each symbolises the seamlessness of the total corporation to itself. Fetishes, however, are ordinarily evoked as objects symbolic of something not present; that is, representing something missing that is desirable.[9] My use of the term is thus unorthodox in that each of these fetish objects, techniques and systems is both symbolically endowed and an active, fully operationalised aspect of the corporation as well. Each object, technique and system is powerful in that it constitutes the corporation both functionally and symbolically, and so doubly focusses the attention of its members. Or, somewhat less mathematically, the symbolic value of corporate objects, techniques and systems is enhanced through the 'rational' preoccupations of its users in their practical functionality.

Let us reacknowledge production, then, and understand it in relation to its linkage to these firms' enormous investments of financial and social *capital,* in the sense deployed by Bourdieu (1977), in a circulating package of 'our' 'Japanese'– 'efficient methods'–'quality products'. Through such complex social/technical/organisational investments in products, the firm and its members gain 'distinction' (Bourdieu 1984) both within and outside the firm. As analysts of consumption are aware, like the *kula* ring, the value of the sale of a Yama product is not only within its functional use by the new owner, 'but with [the resultant] legitimacy in his or her respective community' (Moeran 1996: 94; cf. Malinowski 1922: 89–99). This is, of course, also (if not primarily) a reflection of Yama's legitimacy and an extension of the reach of its brand name. For those who can make the claim to personal membership in Yama this reflection is multi-angled and especially bright.

Such forms of circulation operate also among the 'network' of firms related to Yama.[10] A major Japanese 'high-street' bank supplies the financing, and so oils mutually-reinforcing corporate relations often called, in Japan, horizontal *keiretsu*. A particularly satisfying articulation of this system, however, is that of suppliers (Sako 1992), often tightly integrated in financial and technological, or know-how, terms with a major corporation in vertical *keiretsu*. Here, unlike *kula* rings, auctions, or sales of objects to the public, what are transacted are not final products but partially completed objects, that are made whole as they are integrated into seamless products by the corporation. A supplier's relations to the larger firm confers it with legitimacy; it captures, as it extends, a *part*icipation in its aura.

For managers at model firms such as Yama this rigorously personalised and extensively organised 'complex' raises particular problems concerning articulation of form outside of 'home' context. Japanese managers expect the high density and high quality of social/technical/organisational flows they have experienced domestically in Japan when they are posted to subsidiaries abroad. In returning to one of the vignettes that opened Chapter 2, however, recall that a Chinese supplier was willing to sell plastic cassettes to YamaMax at a far lower cost than would YamaMax's traditional Japanese suppliers. The Chinese firm's price was actually at, or below, its production cost. Nonetheless, in making the financial sacrifice the Chinese firm could establish a relation – a reflected distinction – with Yama upon which it could trade in future, and profit. It is significant, of course, that this relation was established at the periphery of Yama, at YamaMax in France. None of Yama's video production factories in Japan purchased videocassette cases from this Chinese firm; all were purchased, at higher price, from Japanese suppliers, as they had been for many years. Recall that YamaMax's French *directeur général* waited for some time for 'Tokyo's' approval of relations with the new Chinese supplier. What was Yama 'Tokyo' thinking as its YamaMax 'French' colleague waited? We are drawn toward a discussion that could make use of the notions of 'centre and periphery' – and the power relations so implied – as it has been articulated to describe state interactions under imperialism, and in international relations theory generally (Wallerstein 1979). However, in this case, this apparently macro, i.e. international relations-like analytical framework is collapsed, or carried, in a single organisation, in the particular microcosm of a single decision, albeit at a multinational corporation. Of course, such decisions are how 'international relations' work day to day as well, in spite of their apparent 'large scale'.

Let us begin to address the 'global–local' problem in analysis of the multinationalisation of Japanese corporations by, first, appreciating general structural issues – the external environment – experienced by all multinational corporations attempting production abroad. This shall be followed by an analysis of the success of the Yama Corporation in transferring its model of production as it operates on the shopfloor – a key basis of its seamlessness – to YamaMax, its subsidiary in France.

Managerial technology transfer and the hybrid foreign shopfloor

In principle all multinational corporations attempt to fulfil their goal of profit-seeking based on similar sets of external constraints and opportunities in each particular foreign environment. At a high level in the corporation 'strategic' decisions on foreign direct investment are taken which may allow multinationals to, among other possibilities: benefit from lower labour costs abroad, avoid restrictions on foreign trade by setting up production within trade-restricted countries, capture local expertise and information, gain tax relief through transfer pricing, sell their locally produced goods in local or regional markets or reverse-import cheaper products to their home markets. It is not necessary in the current context that the reader understand these 'strategic' possibilities. It is important however to recognise that once foreign investments are made multinationals manufacturing abroad face one fundamental problem: how are they to overlay the varied environments in which they manufacture with a grid of training and tools that develops and maintains local skills so that largely identical goods are produced for their (generally worldwide) sales market? Thus, for example, at two Japanese videotape factories, in Mexico and France, assuming machinery is similar the same basic skills must be learned by Mexican and French employees so that a standardised product can be assembled and sold throughout the globe.

The core technical problem in foreign manufacturing, then, is how to pull standardised output out of varied local environments. Engineers may switch or alter machines to cope more easily with varied local worker capabilities, but over the long run this provides relatively marginal flexibility. Ultimately, manufacturers must successfully make managerial technology transfers so that output is standardised and machines are used as efficiently as possible. While the terminology may suggest mechanical precision, 'managerial technology transfer' concerns the processes of learning about the interplay of technical information and the social arrangements surrounding industrial production. Whether or not planned, managerial technology transfer will in practice reflect the local environment – local organisational culture, the skills background of local staff, locally available hardware, etc. – as local conditions intersect with know-how brought to the overseas subsidiary by the multinational corporation's machines, personnel and organisational network.

In practice overseas production depends on the boundaries of the subsidiary being broadly permeable to its host, foreign environment, with which it must sustain a complex range of technical, financial and social interactions that underpin the physical production of goods. The contents of these interactions are as various and divergent as the many different global settings within which Japanese multinational subsidiaries are found. Thus while final product is largely the same throughout the world, it is produced differently within the particular social frames of each factory setting. In subsidiaries abroad Japanese managers cannot and do not reproduce Japan, nor the 'Japanese corporation' as it exists in Japan. As we have discussed, what they produce is a hybrid corporation.

Practically speaking, what are the implications to Japanese firms, at a social and organisational level, of 'hybrid' conditions produced by processes of 'economic' globalisation? We might begin to sort out this aspect of globalisation by asking: how successful is the Yama Corporation in transferring its model of production to YamaMax?

Techniques of the shopfloor

Specific activities associated with 'Japanese production' may be most conveniently observed on the shopfloor itself. Often cited by industrial specialists and academics as 'representative', shopfloor activities may provide a guide to measure the progress of a factory toward an ideal state of 'Japanese manufacturing'.[11] Allow me to preface this discussion, however, with some reservations. First, what follows are not dense ethnographic descriptions of each category of working practices. Indeed if I were to ethnographically describe production processes I would highlight interactions, not categorical divisions, across practices as they unfold day to day. These are, rather, consolidations of my own ethnographic observations deployed along categories that *Japanese managers* use to dissect some of the very complex operations making up their 'manufacturing management model'. The anthropological perspective within which I work begs me to link them, and at times I do this, but these are – essentially – *their* categories. Second, in noting that some external, especially Western, analysts have simplistically 'found', for instance, that the use of similar uniforms suggests that members of Japanese factories are unaware of hierarchical divisions, we are reminded that considerable methodological and conceptual care must be taken in studying social relations in industry.[12] Third, going to the shopfloor for examples in no way privileges them as the most significant activities in a factory setting. Indeed, most of my ethnographic description of social activity in this study concerns the relevance of communication patterns at considerable hierarchical distance from the shopfloor to both shopfloor activities and to the broader processes and ethos of YamaMax's organisational setting. As markers to ground our discussion, however, here let me explain simply and non-technically some common Japanese shopfloor techniques and see to what extent conditions observed at YamaMax in France match the model derived from the domestic context in Japan.[13]

Quality control circles

In industrial production 'quality control' has a wide breadth of potential meanings. The activity most closely tied with quality control in Japan is *QC circles*. These are small group activities in which, typically, assembly line workers share ideas about how to solve minor problems on their lines. Ideas are tested by gathering data from the line that can be analysed using simple statistical measures. 'Circles' are based on the intuitive logic that a worker who is thinking, while he is doing, can make valuable suggestions regarding how work can be conducted more productively. As such, QC circles constitute perhaps the best known operationalisation of non-Fordist manufacturing concepts. In the process of participating in circles, workers are assumed to become more interested in their jobs, more engaged with the work of their colleagues and more highly committed to the company. While there are of course variations in Japan, QC circles tend to meet regularly once or twice a week near the shopfloor, after work, for 30–40 minutes.[14] Workers are not paid for their participation.

At YamaMax in France, when QC circles were conducted it was under overtime pay conditions. They were eventually dropped altogether when two Japanese managers who had been keen on them were transferred back to Japan. While equally concerned about 'quality', their Japanese replacements were less interested in QC circles per se. QC circles passed into the history of techniques at the factory, remembered fondly by a few French engineers who were no longer encouraged to carry on with it.

Job rotation and on-the-job training

Through job rotation an employee of a large firm, who is likely to spend his entire working career in that firm, will change tasks and learn new skills such that he will eventually have worked on a number of lines or task areas. As described earlier, over the course of his career, broad, hands-on knowledge of the factory will make him a more competent manager as he rises through the corporate hierarchy. In my view job rotation goes hand in hand conceptually with on-the-job training (OJT), thus forming a system in which workers in Japan are given responsibility for quickly learning new tasks on a functioning line (where mistakes immediately affect output) under the tutelage, typically, of a group of experienced co-workers. Awareness of the effect on all line members of a worker's failure to quickly learn new tasks is deliberately used to motivate new line members.[15] In job rotation we are describing organisational risk taking: over the short-run mistakes can be made, but over the long run fewer mistakes will be made because learning under real-time, real-world conditions is learning at its most dynamic.[16] This is a matter of organisational style – typical of large Japanese firms like Yama, with stable, long term and well-educated employees – that has made 'Japanese production' unique in a global context.

Japanese-style job rotation and training among shopfloor workers at YamaMax in France was complicated by concerns suggesting organisation-wide ambivalence towards its practical requirements. French workers were hesitant to change tasks. On the one hand they did not want to separate themselves from the social relationships they had established with their co-workers on their shifts and they felt it might indicate that they were judged incompetent in their current jobs. However they were also interested in promotion and salary increases, which were partially linked to breadth of experience across technical task areas. Japanese managers, meanwhile, on the one hand voiced the importance of rotation but were, day to day, satis-fied with the arrangement that held shopfloor labour in place as it generated stability on the production line and did not require that they retrain workers for new tasks. Thus, while Japanese managers could mobilise the organisa-tional leverage to enforce rotation, this was a lower priority than sustaining day to day production. In terms of practices across hierarchy, the Japanese engineers directly engaged with the technical concerns of production were linked to shopfloor personnel issues through three ranks of French engi-neers and technicians. Personnel decisions, including those concerning rotation, fell in fact to French engineers in discussion with French techni-cians and shopfloor foremen, all of whose career progressions were more tightly linked to sustaining production than rotating labour.[17]

Meanwhile, the calculation by Japanese managers on how intensively to rotate French engineers was based essentially on whether it was best to spread out limited engineering manpower by frequent rotation or keep good engineers focussed on tasks they could manage consistently. The latter option was viewed as safer, and overwhelmingly prevailed. In fact, the organisational movement of engineers at YamaMax was not a matter of 'rotation' in the sense of training, but the result of higher level machinations by both Japanese and French managers in putting engineers into coopera-tive working relations with particular managers. There was considerable jockeying involved in this process: some French engineers were thought to be difficult, or lazy, and it was a matter of organisational 'power plays' as to which sections, and which high level managers, would be forced to work with them. Over time, as would be expected, those managers who had the power to draw competent and agreeable engineers into their sections enjoyed exponential organisational successes at the expense of their bureaucratically weaker colleagues. (Recall the social dynamics in the con-text of hierarchical relations between Japanese engineers/managers and their French colleagues explored in detail in Chapter 3.)

Meanwhile, on-the-job training was rare at YamaMax, especially on the more technically demanding and dangerous machinery. Engineers were careful to ease new workers onto lines so that mistakes could be tightly controlled. The 'best choice' for training, as the Japanese saw it, were two-week sessions at the 'mother plant' in Japan. These opportunities, however, were offered only on occasion and only down to the level of foreman. While interesting, French participants recalled to me that because of language barriers and time constraints on hosts in Japan relatively little technical knowledge was in fact gained. Except where very specific technical issues were at stake the French understood training in Japan clearly, and accurately, as a reward for the development of a positive personal linkage with a Japanese engineer at YamaMax. Though it was left unstated, the Japanese found the priority of human relations implied in such decisions perfectly acceptable. As a result, the bulk of technical training took place in France in classrooms at YamaMax. Many technical manuals had been translated into English and, after the initial stage during which machinery was first put in place, French engineers conducted most of the training in small groups. After some time an individual technician or worker would move into the role of observing others at work, and he would gradually be offered tasks in an apprenticeship model. This package of training schemes was explained to me by Japanese engineers as a response to high demand for output, as opposed to the 'best choice' for training.

Overall, the use of Japanese shopfloor methods in France was quite limited. Since no product could be released from YamaMax at below standard quality, intense production pressures, in combination with human and physical resources on the ground, produced a set of shopfloor manufacturing methods at YamaMax very much at odds with the Japanese ideal. Meanwhile, as was amply demonstrated in earlier chapters, the production system at YamaMax is managed from above, with decisions controlled tightly by a centralised cadre of managers and engineers oriented to a top-down flow of information. From the evidence here it appears that this large-scale Japanese manufacturing multinational in France reproduced the atomisation of labour and strong centralisation of decision-making authority – the 'Fordism' – that the company had learned to avoid in postwar industrialisation in Japan.

Circulating others

As described in our discussion of managerial technology transfer, the Yama Corporation produces consumer electronic products in a wide range of 'developing' and 'developed' countries besides Japan. In these places, unlike their Japanese colleagues, local employees have diverse educational backgrounds unfamiliar to the Japanese, varied work experiences before joining the firm, and speak little or no Japanese language. As a result of this and a multitude of other environmental factors, in foreign settings Yama manufactures differently, but it manufactures to exacting standards, largely identical products sold throughout the world. How, then, do Yama's Japanese managers who work in foreign settings cope with information about Yama work processes which, as I have demonstrated, diverge substantially from those at home in Japan? How would the matter of de facto variation in what might be called 'the sociology of Japanese production' affect the production of seamlessness that I argue is sought, within and without, at large Japanese corporations such as Yama?

In Chapter 4 I described, i.e. during the 'production test,' some of the social processes through which conceptual control of (future) production – if not, as we know, day to day control over the details of standardised mass production itself – is sustained among Japanese managers at YamaMax. These processes are practically based on cultural affiliations among Japanese managers/engineers: including communication based in common claims to ethnicity and language, elaborated through deep-seated experience at Yama based on assumptions about long-term commitments to the firm. We have seen that while under normal conditions of mass production Japanese control is hidden behind local organisational charts, formal lines of hierarchical authority, previously determined specifications, and hands-on contact by French employees, during special events such as the production test power over industrial technique can be rapidly brought to bear on the ground at YamaMax. Among the cultural affinities making these practical mobilisations of power possible are linkages with the centre of the firm, back in Japan: such as records of past practice, which influence ideas and exchanges of information, and literal embodiments in personnel, i.e. Honda-san's presence.

Meanwhile, the Japanese corporation's requirement of efficiently produced, high-quality, standardised, 'global' products would seem to be 'ideologically'[18] carried forward by its Japanese managers by packing variations inherent in any particular industrial context into an equation of 'men and machines'.[19] While men and machines are not, of course, literally equivalent, they are bound together as variables in the equations of industrial technique. Particular contexts or unique dispositions – such as those prevalent in an overseas setting, like those described in my discussion of the production test – are evoked as quantities *within* a variable; they do not shift the relations between the variables in the equation itself. This symbolic manipulation lays down an 'organizing' (Law 1994) grid to cope with the different persons, contexts and machines making up the social, organisational and technical variations of any particular environment.[20] The outcome is the following. Even if the actual means of production are theoretically different in every organisational context, and clearly, identifiably and specifically different in 'foreign' industrial environments from those appearing in Japan, the 'means of production' as they are made to appear in Japan are the 'equations of men and machines' that are understood by Japanese managers and engineers, including those operating abroad, to be the authentic story of how their work is done.

How might we clarify the practical tolerance of this internal contradiction – the cognitive dissonance – between means *in fact,* observed while abroad, and means *in mind?* After all, this combination is upheld by Japanese managers and engineers: persons who, like scientists (Latour 1987), understand rationality and tightly observed calibration as the *sine qua non* of their professional activity and professional/personal identity. It seems that for Japanese managers and engineers 'technical' variations experienced while working abroad are treated psychologically as a component of their sojourn away from the corporate and life practices in which they are embedded in Japan. And I choose this word 'sojourn' with precision to convey the understanding of a – usually five year – overseas posting as temporary and peripheral to what are understood as the set of practices that have been, effectively, purified by taking place 'at home'.[21] I should clarify that at the technical level of industrial production this differs from managers with experience of foreign settings at most non-Japanese multinational corporations, lest it be imagined that such descriptions characterise 'the multinational corporation' or manufacturing industries generally.[22]

Now, I have been told by some Japanese managers that they themselves have benefitted from exploring, and learning from, differences observed and participated in while abroad. More rarely but, nonetheless, on occasion it has also been suggested to me by Japanese managers that their corporation might benefit from further examining these practical variations. However, organised space 'at home' is not made available to do so. In effect, Japanese managers returning from abroad are organisationally, that is, implicitly, instructed at headquarters and at factories in Japan that variations are aberrations. 'Hybridity', in whatever setting, is thus trivialised as particular, and unique, phenomena. That is, hybridity is precisely contextualised: identified, and, so, located as foreign, and so marginalised and dismissed as operationally irrelevant – of little 'value' – to the larger organisation.

Among Japanese managers, while careers are enhanced by a 'sojourn' abroad, foreign 'experience' of manufacturing is erased. This is the seamless whole at work: through local, Japanese operational contexts in factories and administrative centres built up of the social relations of the firm and the entire communications-rich package of assumptions and relatedness constructing them. This process is furthermore supported by the multiplicity and high complexity of 'the' home organisation, made up in the case of the Yama Corporation of over 100 formal organisations, in which the authority vested in hierarchy mirrors appropriate versions of itself that is actively enhanced through the denial of other versions of activity that are actually, as we have seen, practiced within it, if abroad. Organisational power controls the generation and spread – and so the circulation – of stories about what occurs in foreign contexts, and so invests the personal fictions upheld by Japanese managers. Institutionalised acts of forgetting account for Japanese managers' displacements of observed facts.

The pervasive fictions of seamlessness

I have suggested that at large, Japanese corporations, readily-observed, variable information gathered while 'abroad' is apparently disposed of when Japanese managers return home. Why should corporate disposal of this knowledge *need* to occur in order for Japanese managers to continue to do their work? The means of suppressing information arising from 'different' environments are the circulations of the corporation that generate its seamless product/image/organisation. This is articulated consciously as manufacturing (and accounting) techniques, such as those I have described in detail. It is also present in less conscious but nonetheless active features of corporate regeneration, all of which are deployed abroad as a functional consequence of Japanese managers' postings as a part of Japanese corporate investment in foreign manufacturing. As long as the manager is reproductive of, or living inside, his unified vision it evidently makes little difference if day to day practices of work and life are inconsistent with how they are made to appear. For him, the unified vision of himself and the thoroughly seamless corporate social whole are successfully linked.

One might call a Japanese corporation such as Yama a 'total institution' in the sense deployed in Goffman's analyses of prisons and asylums (1961). However our described organisational configuration is far more powerful as the 'gates' are locked by the apparent 'choices' of 'free' 'individuals'. That is, Goffman's 'total institutions' are constructed upon the tension between controllers and their occupants: between various forms of keeper and society's prisoners or those deemed mentally unstable. Similarly, Marx's 'occupants' are labour; controlled, in effect, by higher classes of owner-managers. The large Japanese corporation, as an organisation that strives to generate a social whole which approaches its own 'ideal type', may be construed as a contemporary 'iron cage', to be sure. But, unlike its organisational predecessors (prisons, asylums and nineteenth-century factories), especially among its core Japanese 'occupants', the large Japanese corporation is not a site of human misery, a source of disenchantment or class struggle. Rather, it is a pervasive fiction in which core controllers and core occupants are collapsed into each other as 'owners' capable of organising, through acts of forgetting, 'coeval' representations across time, space and difference.

Notes

1 The following descriptions are based on my own participant–observation at Japanese firms, discussion with personnel at such firms, and the previously cited 'classics' on the topic: Cole 1971; Dore 1973; Rohlen 1974; Clark 1979; Abegglan and Stalk 1985. I fully acknowledge the distinctions between these large firms and the diverse set of small and medium size Japanese firms that are appropriately forwarded to undermine generalised claims about 'Japanese enterprise'. For example it is important to recognise that at its peak fewer than one-third of Japanese employees were beneficiaries of the 'lifetime employment' that is understood as typical of Japanese firms. As for their forms of 'internationalisation', small and medium size Japanese firms have had related but different, and thoroughly interesting, histories abroad, which will not be discussed in this study.

2 In spite of current media reports, this situation has not fundamentally changed at Japan's large firms. Rather than an alteration in the structure of careers, the

number of entrants has been reduced as have the number of employees who could normally expect to extend their careers at such firms beyond formal 'retirement', at age 55.

3 In spite of the fact that since Japan's 'bubble' burst in the mid-1990s the Western public's – media driven – view is that the Japanese economy, its firms and techniques are weak, Japan remains the world's second-largest economy, with Japanese firms remaining dominant in consumer electronics and leaders in the automotive industries. It is true that Japanese firms have not kept pace with the dynamism of 'Silicon Valley', though they lead in digital telephony. However, the actually proportion of 'hi-tech' industries in the total economies of both the US and Japan is far smaller than the enormous media attention to it would suggest: less than 10 per cent in both cases.

4 In US manufacturing we should note, for example, that while in the 1970s and early 1980s the recalcitrance of the US automotive industry to adopt new techniques was well publicised, the computer industry has never lagged in adopting, or reinventing, techniques that might improve productivity. Many of these techniques closely correspond with Japanese manufacturing models. See Cole (1989) for discussion of the spread of 'learning models' in manufacturing, many of them inspired by the Japanese.

5 While the notional consolidation of this 'triad' is, to my knowledge, my own invention, these three subjects – and their various institutions – have been the central interests of social scientists of Japan in the postwar period. The literature is enormous on these topics, but among the most significant works are: Johnson (1982); the three-volume series, *The Political Economy of Japan* (Yamamura and Yasuba 1987); Inoguchi and Okimoto (1988); Kumon and Rosovsky (1992); and Gordon (1993).

6 In the context of Japan these notions are elaborated with ethnographic precision by Moeran (1996).

7 Though not of their foremost concern, consumers also believe that activities within a corporation's factories across the globe are as consistent as are the corporation's products.

8 Concerning industrial preoccupations with time reckoning, and their impact on modern consciousness, see Thompson 1967.

9 See Freud 1955 [1927], and Zizek 1991. Both are discussed with reference to Japan in Ivy 1995.

10 In studies of Japan the 'network' has become a major explanatory vehicle to cope with the differences between Japanese business (and international) relations and the more contractually based systems of Western business relations (especially in the US) which have traditionally provided the bulk of empirical evidence guiding analysis. See, for instance, 'Japan's corporate networks' (Imai 1992); *Network Power: Japan and Asia* (Katzenstein and Shiraishi 1997); and 'The business strategies of Japanese production networks in Asia' (Tachiki 1999). (In none of these cases is the idea of network explicitly related to Japanese phenomena in reference to 'actor–network theory', which I discussed in Chapter 4.)

11 The evolution of the literature on Japanese management is long in the public domain, as discussed in Chapter 1, and even longer in management consultant reports. Interest in Japanese techniques by UK manufacturers from the 1980s onwards is a good, local, example. A thorough academic response to this interest is reflected in Oliver and Wilkinson's (1992), *The Japanization of British Industry.*

12 Simplistic analyses of observations such as the one I refer to here appear more often in 'quick and dirty' consultant reports for corporate clients than in the public, academic domain. As discussed in Chapter 1, this was especially the case in the 1980s when Japanese techniques, i.e. 'knowledge-creation', was an

influential industrial fad, especially among US manufacturers, that generated an army of consulting 'experts'.

13 We should recognise that in Japan the use of these techniques varies considerably. At the Yama Corporation, and other large Japanese firms I have studied, they are used extensively on the shopfloor in Japan and are taken very seriously in the lore of their 'corporate cultures'.

14 Not every factory in Japan uses QC circles, nor is every worker in a plant that is using them likely to be in a circle. Participation depends on a number of contextual factors including the importance attached to the activity at any particular time by upper management (in a factory and in the corporation as a whole) and the interest of foremen in getting the activity off the ground.

15 For a somewhat frightening account – by a journalist posing as a temporary worker – of the assembly line at a Toyota automobile factory in Japan, see Kamata (1982).

16 Anthropologists will appreciate this as a central tenet of their field research methodology.

17 The situation on the consumer electronics shopfloor of YamaMax, in France, reflects substantively similar concerns by Japanese management with outputs, and so profit, in Japanese consumer electronics firms in Malaysia as described by Ong (1987), especially her chapter 7. As such, Ong's analytic emphasis on 'gender hierarchy' strikes me as overplayed. Gender was not a potent medium through which these, similar, processes unfolded at YamaMax. Thus the manipulation of female labour she witnessed in Malaysia strikes me as an epiphenomenon of the capitalistic orientation directing any or all available means of production, broadly construed, towards profit-making.

18 As Giddens (1984: 25–6) points out: 'The reification of social relations, or the discursive "naturalization" of the historically contingent circumstances and products of human action, is one of the main dimensions of ideology in social life'.

19 While seemingly spared corruption through the holism implied by its appreciation of the human aspects engaged in production, even QC circles may be understood in these mechanistic terms: their intent and purpose – their 'output' – is the focussing of the creativity of human minds upon production.

20 Allow me to acknowledge here that it only requires an adjustment in the fineness of one's theoretical net to recognise that, while I have proposed a 'Japanese' model that is forcefully essentialised by its own practitioners, variations occur in practices in any particular context due to the conditions of circumstances and persons; including factories of the same Japanese corporation, producing the same products in Japan itself. That stated as a matter of theoretical fact, analytic purchase on the subject of cross-cultural social relations can be fruitfully gained only by forwarding the relevance of degrees of difference from other circumstances. I am positing here that – although a vast number of variables may be made present in an anthropologist's perspective on social relations within any community – in an intimately mixed or hybrid community such as YamaMax, cross-cultural social relations are an explicitly observable problem among my subjects. It pervades – that is, explains – much while it is also articulated by its own practitioners, i.e. by members of YamaMax.

21 The retrospective treatment of work experienced abroad as a personal 'sojourn' may relate to an often observed projection, in the face of contrary evidence readily available to Japanese managers, that local work practices at subsidiaries abroad will, in future, come to match practices in Japan.

22 My own knowledge of Western and Japanese multinationals at various locations around the world, as well as considering the literature forwarded, say, by Westney (1999), strongly suggests that Japanese managers are far more aggressive in forwarding their solutions to problems at all levels of overseas operations

than are expatriate managers at Western multinationals. Although the situation naturally varies depending on particular conditions and the skills of local engineers at particular factories, in Western firms expatriate engineers made themselves available to assist their local colleagues who were in the end responsible for their production lines in what we might call an 'arm's-length' model of management. This matter is explored in detail in Sedgwick (1999).

7   *Postscript*

Circulating others among anthropologists: perceiving similarity, examining ourselves

Anthropology and the work of representational aesthetics

As a means of comparison and reflection on institutionalised power, in this final chapter I discuss anthropologists' experience of fieldwork with others, and, more importantly, their subsequent representation of this work. Along with theory, my discussion engages the practical effects of the day to day use of communications technologies and its role in altering perceptions of timing and spacing and, importantly for anthropology, modes of participation with, and representations of, others. Apart from suggesting that analytic erasures risk arising through mishandling notions of difference, this chapter treats problems of method in anthropology as a proxy to re-engage ideas regarding 'globalisation' which always, it seems, is caught up in the effects of the use of contemporary technology.

Among anthropologists 'at home' in the academy a central currency of transactions over reputation, career and social relations concern representations of 'field experience'. That efforts to address this core aspect of our work seem at times 'stripped out' – by administration and heavy teaching loads – itself acknowledges the power of the organisational configurations we share with other members of our departments, the academy and with modern organisational life more generally. This is not unlike members of Japanese corporations, and it is also nothing new: anthropologists' most highly valued form of storytelling is restrained and at times made secondary to the tasks of careers as organisational participants. Nonetheless, we explicitly state and, if successful, i.e. get published, we demonstrate our intent: to relate the field to our audiences as best we can. Indeed, recent anthropological obsessions with forms of representation acknowledge the importance we attach to this process.[1]

In spite of hierarchical and other relations of power present in every human effort, anthropologists, especially those who have conducted research in foreign settings, appreciate that compromises are made by all involved in the work of creating understanding across cross-cultural boundaries. In describing their fieldwork these efforts might be said by anthropologists to be based on cooperation that may generate a quasi, if momentary, egalitarianism of communicative discourse. In Chapter 5 I raised, but here wish to elaborate further upon, Fabian's concern with the 'contradiction' between the 'strategies and devices' of anthropological writing and, of particular interest here, 'fieldwork [as] a form of communicative interaction with an Other, one that must be carried out coevally, on the basis of shared intersubjective Time and intersocietal contemporaneity of experience' (1983: 148).

By 'writing' Fabian refers to the history of analytic modes in anthropology and their linkage to academic presentation. He argues that these processes sterilise or objectify the experience during field research of 'cotemporality of producer and product, speaker and listener, Self and Other' exemplified, he believes, in 'speaking' (1983: 164). Unfortunately Fabian's analysis suggests that speech is somehow a pristine, automatic, unadulterated and uncontested mode of communication when, in spite of the relevance of presence and immediacy to speech, it is not credible to maintain that any communicative act is unmediated; 'as if language (spoken or otherwise) does not always imply deferral, difference, and miscommunication' (Ivy 1995: 17; see also Derrida 1976, 1982). His emphasis on the purity of speech may thus unwittingly isolate other artefacts from proper anthropological inquiry while it implies – presumably unintentionally – that the only communities justifying our research are primitive or illiterate: those famed, in anthropology, for generating oral records. Nonetheless, his key point – that there is an 'epistemological sore' between fieldwork 'research ... experience' and 'writing ... [and] ... science' – is well taken (1983: 33). So well taken, in fact, that this problem has been normalised in anthropology. Nonetheless, the outcomes of providing succour to the 'sore' remain heatedly contested.

Clifford and Marcus' widely read *Writing Culture* aggravated the 'sore' by shedding light on the politics of ethnography's discursive practices (1986). This exposure was fully appropriate. However, I expect I am not the first anthropologist to have thought that Clifford's criticism may have been more generous, and perhaps more subtle, had he conducted fieldwork and written an ethnography himself before he embarked on problematising the processes entailed therein. On a more general level Said's *Orientalism*, if focused on area studies, offered an early critique of the colonial, and neo-colonial, shortcomings and pitfalls of Western academic perspectives on non-Westerners, including the work of anthropologists (1978). These two canonical works indeed set the political economic and literary vocabulary for a veritable growth industry of self-reflection on anthropological practices.

Fabian's concern with the division between anthropologists' field experiences and professional academic discourses is additionally, and possibly more fundamentally, impacted by attention to the epistemology of effects accompanying our intersubjective interactions with others. Indeed I have used the word 'work' to describe cross-cultural communication because of the effort required in the sifting of its vicissitudes by anthropologists (or anyone participating in cross-cultural activities, including, for instance,

French and Japanese members of YamaMax). With the best of intentions, it must be said, from the late 1980s many anthropologists have made considered efforts to address the challenges of both new theoretical opportunities, much of it stimulating, and criticism from within and without, much of it justified. The reaction to this so-called 'crisis of representation' (Marcus 1986) has (perhaps often) been defensive where privately felt, and certainly erratic where publicly written.[2] Especially in certain sectors of North American anthropology, a dominant response to the transpersonal, and suggestively political, aspects of interactions during fieldwork has been a 'reflexive' concern with the self; that is, the written, and so explicit, deployment of the anthropologist's experience as field subject.[3]

Meanwhile, the highly theorised 'linguistic turn', for example, Derrida, *et al.*, has assisted students of humanity in appreciating the dialectics of all aspects of communications, if not existence itself. However, this effort is unlikely to satisfy practical anthropological concerns with temporal and other distanciations from the persons with whom we study. While oral records – and any other event for that matter – may of course be construed as 'text', the methods employed in textual analyses, rooted as they are in formal deconstructions of writing and problems of audience (in reading), have, if anything, 'reinforced allochronic tendencies in anthropological discourse' (Fabian 1983: 148). Another related response – the 'literary turn' among anthropologists, as I shall call it – may in principle hold considerable promise. However, while laying claim to a new 'aesthetics' or 'poetics' it is hamstrung by the fact that most anthropologists remain untrained in creative writing.[4]

A good example of this 'literary' genre is Stewart's, *A Space on the Side of the Road: Cultural Poetics in an 'Other' America* (1996). I find particularly compelling her portrayal of her fieldwork arena as a 'nervous system' in which, following Taussig (1992), 'the very image of "system" itself slips out of the grasp of all those quick assumptions that associate it with things like order, unity, (ancient, timeless) tradition, coherence, and singularity' (20). However, I have some reservations about the larger goals of the project she espouses. In far more detail than I have suggested above, Stewart examines some of the 'correctives' and 'myriad critiques' of anthropological representation. Indeed in one tour-de-force paragraph on the 'new ethnography' she covers historical, contestational, transnational, hybrid, inventive, imagined, ironic, feminist, subaltern, postcolonial, minority, discourse-centred, signified, performative, dialogic, reflexive, deconstructive, poetic and political approaches, in no fewer than 307 citations (25–6). One may wonder in such a productive critical context if a discussion of anthropological orthodoxy is not perhaps moot. Indeed the 'immanent critique' within new ethnography might be better understood as the new orthodoxy. In Stewart's hands it seeks to 'displace the premature urge to classify, code, contextualize, and name long enough to imagine something of the texture and density of spaces of desire that proliferate in Othered places' through 'using cultural critique ... to open up ... passionately ambiguous space to fashion emergent insights that culture is dialogic, hybrid, contested, situated, and imagined into techniques of imagining and re-presenting the complex interpretive moves that constitute a cultural real' (26). The style remains excessive in Stewart's ethnographic descriptions, and it is at times very successful. However, more than the stylistic or theoretical means, the ends are of concern. Indeed, especially when grounded in the dialectical approach that Stewart presents, one must be sceptical of the goal of imagining what might 'constitute *a* cultural real' (my italics), as well as its claims regarding a freshly envisioned 'cultural politics'.[5]

In any case, as we have been aware for some time, it must be concluded that the anthropological experience of the field is unavoidably re-formed when it is recalled – or, as Fabian might prefer it, re-'told' – elsewhere.[6] Be that as it may, our efforts to find more creative means of representation in effect acknowledge that – soiled as they are by our own presence – anthropologists seek to articulate, and so celebrate, those experiences shared – positive and negative – with persons and communities in the field by presenting those persons and communities to our audiences in forms that will generate as powerful an understanding of them as we are capable. Anthropologists are likely professionally, and as a matter of experience, temperament, style and politics, to endorse a cooperative or egalitarian ideal for both their own cross-cultural communications in the field and its (unfortunately, but necessarily) subsequent representation. Such, in any case, has been my understanding of the ideal.

Going inside, losing touch

The experience of 'traditional' fieldwork in distant climes among 'primitive', 'simpler' persons was different to that of an overseas posting of a Japanese manager in that it could not in any way be contrived to match, and possibly be erased by, a local, 'home' version of experience. Difference was perhaps too great to be ignored or, rather, professionally, 'difference' was celebrated, if not exaggerated, for the purposes of presentation and theorising, grounded, at least implicitly, in comparative method. The 'crisis of representation', however, suggests something more distressed than the standard compulsion toward critique of past practices that structures inter-generational competition and stimulates intellectual growth in a subject area. What has been the problem?

As described in Chapter 1, acknowledgement of the social 'construction' of identity, kinship, organisation, the state, economic relations and the like – even if not necessarily articulated in this particular language – appropriately undermines the apparent factuality of comfortably functional structures that have appeared to stabilise social life. In an intellectual environment that has brought such new analytic opportunities and targets to hand, the focus of social science and the humanities was bound to focus with some resolution upon our societies, our modes of generating academic discipline(s), and ourselves. In hindsight, for anthropology it was perhaps inevitable that to some extent a (so-called, 'reflexive') rethink of key methodological categories – fieldwork–homework, us–them, subject–object, 'the other', and so on – would occur. And it was inevitable that deep, if perhaps necessary, scarring would accompany that operation, for anthropology had most powerfully, and unambivalently, constructed its disciplinary identity upon the observation and articulation of difference, either in implicit comparative contrasts between our own (read Western) and 'other' societies, or in the explicit, large-scale and often hierarchical comparative schemes characteristic of Victorian anthropology (Stocking 1987).

However, the reception of constructionist notions as a broadly 'trendy', popular, ostensibly intellectual, discourse has perhaps created what might be called 'word-based angst', in which the inevitable mix between professional and lay contexts in the usage of words may generate slippage, excess and, possibly, disillusionment among those trained in Western intellectual traditions. Social 'constructions' – including also 'imaginings', 'collective fantasies', the 'ethereal' and their evasive textual brethren – are not to be taken as 'social facts'; they are to be taken to connote processes by which what-are-understood-by-persons-as-social-facts are sustained. These are operations at a high level of abstraction; they are intellectual exercises (generating an unfortunate plethora of jargon), albeit powerful and often convincing. It was never implied by post-structuralists, nor anyone deploying ideas about the active 'constructions' underlying and creating social relations, that a society's institutions, organisations or 'society' itself did not have quite real and powerful effects, day to day, *as* inventions. On the contrary, the core post-structuralist argument, as I understand it, is that action in the real world is *motivated* through imagination. In turn, if political activism were of interest, or understood as an imperative of raised consciousness, in becoming aware of the fact, and power, of imagining, one may become less susceptible to forces that seek to control one's imagination.[7]

The motivational gestalt implied here is no different from that claimed by Freudian psychotherapy, though the critical target may have shifted scale from families to the state or, perhaps, by the time we have integrated Foucault into our discussions, the state embodied in the family, or, for those familiar with Japanese history, the state *as* family. Indeed, it is not surprising that in the current Western intellectual environment, notable for its self-consciousness, Freudianism has enjoyed a resurgence of interest among social analysts.[8] This direction of analysis is made doubly personal: it links stories about how we think of our society – or how we imagine that others think of their society – to our ways of imagining our own psychology – or how we imagine others to understand themselves. What was external, for instance stable democratic states (within which, incidentally, most 'published' theorists live) become – and in fact are only possible because they have been – internalised, or embodied. Foucault, after all, is shifting the ground under France's '*société, fraternité, égalité*' when he links historical analyses of the genesis of (Western) regimes of incarceration with modern self-surveillance of our own bodies and thoughts: the pan-societal controls of 'democratic' regimes (1975). And Derrida's '*différance*' (1967, 1973 [1967], 1976) theorises, or 'deconstructs', Westerners' own language use in the context of our own intellectual traditions: the modes of organising our thoughts and language extending back to the Greeks (Derrida 1967). No wonder this intellectual work feels disorienting; we do not often turn our acts of (quasi-) objective analysis upon ourselves. Movements beyond the imperatives of empiricism are unusual, fascinating and disconcerting analytical moments.[9]

It is in turning toward, or upon, ourselves analytically, however, that (individual's) problems crop up that resonate with anxieties about globalisation. For instance, widely circulating 'evidence' of culturally homogenising, global influences, such as the 'McDonald's-isation' or 'CocaCola-isation' of consumables (of 'popular culture'), may suggest that local production of material culture, culture itself, and thereby the stability and uniqueness – that is, the boundaries – of cultures are under threat. By logical extension, the popularisation and, so, homogenisation of persons' experiences may cause alarm: as we consume alike, we become more alike, and less differentiated from one another. To such perceptions may be added theories suggesting that the belief that persons ever 'had' individuality was nothing more than a bourgeois capitalist myth (Jameson 1985: 115). So decentred, deconstruction's textually oriented 'death of the subject' may be seen to have killed off the *relevance* of individuals as well.

In the context of Westerners' obsessions with (their own) psychology (Sennett 1977, 1980, 1998; Lasch 1978), however, the logic is more likely to work in the opposite direction. That is, once destabilised, Western persons are more likely to opt for personal exaggeration rather than self-diminution, at least where the *display* of individuality is concerned. Individualism requires differentiation, categorical recognition of others' forms of individuality (in order to support one's own form(s)) and, so, acknowledgment of a world of individuals. Thus as cultures may seem to disappear by becoming homogeneous or less distinctive, the individual may become *over*valued, recognisable as the only self-apparent category. Strathern suggests that what may arise from the postmodern image of the 'death of the individual' is 'hyper-individualism' (1992: 150). Here the 'Individual' is relieved of its former theoretical task 'as a connecting hinge' between 'Society' and 'Nature.' 'Society' and 'Nature' become but tools for the (transient) whims of hyper-individuality rather than prerequisites for grounding the idea of the individual. Such untethering of the individual may encourage idiosyncratic private behaviour that is, in turn, (ironically) 'cancelled' by pastiche: 'the imitation of unique style' (Strathern 1992: 150). It might be suggested, then, that with 'Society' apparently made irrelevant, shattered by homogeneous but individualised cultures (with the assistance of globalisation?), the possibilities and promise of social coalition become less achievable and less apparently relevant. Making less difference outside of ourselves, cynicism creeps into (by some interpretations) the 'modernist' agenda for responsible engagement in social change which, in the Western context, is the theoretical premise of democracy (Habermas 1971; cf. Taylor 1987 [1979]). To expand the list of anxious excesses: the creation of 'nostalgia' may be understood to treat the past as a receptacle for 'desires' – perhaps for a more stable and real (less constructed?) social environment – that, along with 'retro' and 'pastiche' – markers apparently now residing at the centre, rather than periphery, of postmodern 'cultural productions' – reflect the impossibility of authenticity in a skimmed present. Meanwhile, perhaps at the other – and possibly mirrored – extreme of the intellectual spectrum, the resurgence of fundamentalist religious beliefs appear as a compensatory hydraulics for apparent meaninglessness, where structures of society, and their relationship to God, have been undermined by decadence.[10]

We might recognise in these self-conscious exaggerations re-rehearsed, contemporary versions of modernity's social *anomie*. As such, it may be overstating the case to lay them at the feet of an intellectual encounter with the 'social construction of reality' (Berger and Luckman 1967). After all, the comparative method, which at times explicitly (and always implicitly) underpins anthropology, has for well over a century provided sound evidence of tremendous variation in the things we do that make us human; and, thus, a sound means of generating a theory of social constructionism. We might better recognise contemporary *anomie* and constructionism as products, and producers, of our present conceptual environment – including postmodern fascinations – and call this contemporary existential encounter a network of unease about the present with which the 'lifeworld' (Bourdieu 1977) of anthropologists is deeply engaged.

Experiencing social theory: technologically speaking

Allow me to ground this theory regarding excesses of self-perception, and the possible attractions to it by 'new' ethnographers, in the context of day to day activities undertaken by anthropologists. Anthropologists and their peers are familiar with the increasing rate of boundary-crossing movements of persons and objects throughout the twentieth century. Since the 1990s, however, ever higher rates of such movements have been accompanied by tremendous expansion in the proliferation of communications technology. This has dramatically increased access to, and commensurately increased production of, information (Castells 1996, 1997, 1998), while it has also, perhaps, aided the reorganisation of our implicit understandings of the quality of social relations, and knowledge itself, as contingent and, as such, constructed through complex relationships. Now, of course, before 'the Net' contingency was broadly theorised in the humanities through 'intertextuality'

(Ricoeur 1974) and 'deconstruction' in literary studies (Derrida 1976; cf. Rabinow and Sullivan 1987 [1979]: 23–4), especially in the Yale-sourced 'lit crit' movement (Culler 1982), as it was previously in philosophy (Rorty 1967, 1979). Contingency has thus spilled over to students of society, as both philosophy and literary criticism at times generate concepts of interest to us.

At the end of the day, however, it is not that anthropologists are less astute thinkers than philosophers, it is that, rightly, anthropologists are, or they should be, observers *before* theorists. It is perhaps not a coincidence that the *technology* that allows for (at least 'imaginings' of) 'virtual communities' corresponds with the contemporary rise in acceptance of, as well as excesses of, the theoretical construction of society and politics, possible flexible selfhoods and, at its extreme extension, fully (intellectually) constructed 'cyborgs' against which we humans necessarily measure ourselves since we created them by writing of them (Haraway 1985, 1989; Strathern 1991: 23–30).

Whether or not we choose to engage conceptually with cyborgs, however, it seems nonetheless that the explosion of accessibility to computer-based, communications technology in the hands, and day to day use, of social scientists, their colleagues, their students and, evidently, the 'masses' in 'advanced' societies, may have made vivid a new model for rethinking the contingencies and the nature of boundaries understood to underpin the conditions of communicative acts. Relations that were previously understood as outside or physically distant can nearly continuously, nearly in 'real time', reach and affect us: we hold technologically readily available, and pervasive, representations of connectedness beyond the local. As such, we bring the global to ourselves, in an apparent space and time compression, which may suggest that intersubjectivity can be experienced under new means. We now have to hand a technologically-enabling, 'transformative' (Strathern 1992: 135–6), and – exactly as it should be – an *almost* physical means of modelling the categorical plasticity we have intellectually constructed about the 'nation,' 'organisations' of all types, 'community', 'family', 'sexuality', the 'self', and so on.[11] I suggest that this sentiment is enhanced by these forms', and thus our, dependency on technology: the 'prosthetics' (Haraway 1985: 97) that allow such (intellectual) 'extensions' (Strathern 1991: 31).

Thus, while anthropologists may not require mass movements to draw our analytical attention, it may be important to our contemporary theories that we are subjected to the pervasiveness of the technologies of 'Net'-related phenomena. However, if our understanding is so subject to our experience, it further suggests that we work from the inside (ourselves) out in our construction and understanding of analytical problems. Indeed, we always have done so,[12] but at present some anthropologists would seem to be particularly vulnerable to falling into nets of their own making, from which anthropology may have trouble extracting itself.

Going global, or staying at home and losing the other

The implications of such intellectual currents upon the practice of anthropology may be the following. Perhaps as lay persons, anthropologists we are currently hurtled (if not herded) into processes which collapse time and space in unfamiliar ways; ways that, as lay persons *and* as professional anthropologists, are likely to be understood by us as effects relating to globalisation. As described above, daily use of high-technology communication tools is obviously implicated here, as is the routinisation of (our own) global displacements that are extreme by any historic standard. As a result, it would seem that in all our boundary-crossing, mixing and hybridity creation, our professional deployment of 'difference' may have become less well-managed as an analytic tool. That is, we may easily believe that we share far more experience and information than ever before with persons who might be – or have been – construed as other. As we – physically and electronically – go to them easily, and the other is easily drawn in among us *in situ* 'at home', we may all become homogenised. On the other hand the other may be – with equivalent analytic outcome – brought 'home' by inversions of homogeneity – that is, exaggerations of individuality and the dismantling of persons from society – that, furthermore, require no physical displacement for the development of analytic purchase: 'postmodernist' perceptions that difference is everywhere; between each person and at every scale with which we might choose to think. Either way, such perceptions are encouraged by, or may be generative of, a tendency to turn inward: demonstrated by the elevation of self-reference – the exhaustive 'critique' of anthropology as a form of self-consciousness – to high status.

Methodologically, these conditions might furthermore assist in explaining away any problems with fieldwork undertaken *in* our 'home' locations. The by-now largely uncritical acceptance of 'anthropology at home' suggests at the very least that no particular analytic advantage would arise from the personal displacement of 'going away' to the field.[13] That it has become ubiquitous suggests perhaps an intellectual denial of the problem of subjects–objects, us–them, and even, perhaps, time itself.[14] That is, Fabian's problem with allochronism between the field and its representations is solved if we would seem to be sharing speech, experience and time with our others as with ourselves. Of course, the other also risks erasure by such professional co-evality, and our reflections on our own conditions.[15]

In the context of the organisational fields explored in this book this intellectual scenario suggests the following question. Is it possible that processes linked to globalisation may be insidiously doing the kind of work on some areas of anthropology that Japanese multinational corporations perform explicitly on the foreign experiences of their Japanese members? What I am suggesting is that two entirely different treatments of others may come to a similar outcome. Specifically, whereas Japanese managers, in circulating their firms for themselves, erase others by denying them (or intellectually and emotionally throwing them away) 'at home,' anthropologists may erase others by overly integrating them, forgetting others through a projection of their sameness to us. Through entirely different means, then, the same ends risk, unfortunately, being achieved.

As keen observers, anthropologists may be susceptible to over-identification with the processes engaged in the use of contemporary communications technology, which would seem to detach social relations from the presence of familiar time and place: those very contexts in the field about which anthropology lays claim to a powerful methodology. This may conflate with a, more obvious, and more significant, tendency to misinterpret 'constructions of reality' suggested by, but not present in, contemporary post-structural models, which imply unrestrained flexibility in general and, in an environment that is already overtly self-conscious, the tendency to relegate 'the constructed' society as secondary to the, fully flexible, individual. Let us reflect, then, finally, on the ends – the emptiness – enacted by misconstruing the constitutional power of persons *in social relations*: means by which Japanese management may totalise itself in the face of difference and means by which anthropology may lose track of the analytic efficacy of difference – deployed through the notion of the other – by finding it everywhere.

Notes

1 In an incisive paper querying ethnographic processes, Wardle (n.d.: 2) asks, 'Do we construe the purpose of reflexivity as one of improving our representations or do we consider the purpose of ethnography to be a demonstration of reflexivity?'.

2 An exception here are the astute reflections on fieldwork, writing and sharing the products of research with 'subjects', in this case policy-makers, in Mosse 2006.

3 In the literature on Japanese workplaces Kondo's thorough and interesting analysis – focusing on women in a small-scale Japanese enterprise – is, in my judgment, distracted by prolific reflections on her experience in Japan as a Japanese-American (1990).

In the general anthropological literature Marcus and Fischer's *Anthropology as Cultural Critique: An Experimental Moment in the Human Sciences* (1986) is often cited as setting the groundwork for a reflexive anthropology. However, as Ivy points out, '[t]he authors recognise a number of different modalities in accomplishing politically, aesthetically, and theoretically moving anthropological works; the genre often known as "reflexive" ethnography is only one of the possibilities they discuss' (1995: 27, n. 58). I believe, nonetheless, that in practice an orientation to the 'self-reflexive' has been the ordinary response to the critique I have described.

As for the 'political', there has been considerable mobility in the term's use in anthropological discourse. There are differences between the radicalism of the civil rights and Vietnam-inspired era – represented in anthropology most cogently in Hymes' 1969 edited volume, *Reinventing Anthropology* – and 'politics' from the 1980s onwards that has generally carried more personalised, private, local and 'lifestyle' connotations, no doubt informed by concern with the environment, sexual orientation and, though far more varied and complex, feminist perspectives. Perhaps as a matter of generational politics within the academy – a denial and/or erasure of positions articulated by activist elders – many 'radical' anthropologists from the 1980s onwards seem to have lost interest in the Marxian perspective to which they might otherwise ascribe at the level of practice: 'For Marx, theory should not relate to the world merely at the level of abstract philosophy, but should be engaged in its transformation' (Miller 1987: 35).

4 I find myself perennially amused by the comment of an observer of anthropology who despairs of ethnographic writing: 'How, one asks constantly, could such interesting people doing such interesting things produce such dull books?' (Pratt 1986: 33). Personally, I feel that many novelists and essayists convey with far more lucidity and success than do anthropologists the 'sense' of a place and local persons' understanding of it, as well as the particularities of the author's position vis-à-vis persons and places. However, these writers rarely explicitly and systematically theorise their observations. Under the current 'critique', anthropology's traditional stylistic exercise of splitting description and theory has come under implicit and explicit critical scrutiny. This suggests future 'ethnographies' of the radical style advocated by some 'new' ethnographers – 'roaming from one texted genre to another – romantic, realist, historical, fantastic, sociological, surreal' (Stewart 1996: 210) – or, my preference, 'ethnographies' more typical of novels, that work across dialogue, description and theory, sometimes smoothly, others jarringly, but always with maximum communicative intent for the widest possible audience.

5 Again quoting from Stewart: 'The "new ethnography" that I try to imagine here would take a cue from the tactile, imaginary, nervous, and contested mode of critique of the subjects we study not in order to decide what these interpretive modes "mean" in the end but to deploy them in a cultural politics' (1996: 25). Elaborately articulated, but what would deployment of this 'cultural politics ... cue[d] from the ... mode of critique of [our] subjects' amount to? The possibility that anthropologists' forms of representation should represent the end in itself is surely too facile – too cloyingly (self-) referential to the intellectual community that reads such texts – to constitute a cultural *politics*. Anthropologists may have only recently quit imagining themselves through the pretense of 'model builder (and model world citizen)' 'capable of self-discipline and distanced, discriminating judgment' who 'fixed "culture" as an object of analysis that was whole, bounded, and discrete' (Stewart 1996: 25). However, throughout most of the twentieth century, most anthropologists have nonetheless attempted to be keen but non-judgemental observers; participated, where allowed by subjects, in *their* modes of experience; bore, through trying to communicate, 'other' subjectivities in different (for instance, in our professional 'home') contexts; and have at times been activists on our fieldwork subjects' behalf where they unfortunately have less political power. One is prepared to dismiss parts, or all, of 'past' practice if a compelling alternative is on offer.

My discussion suggests that the only consensus in sociocultural anthropology that has survived the 'crisis of representation' mobilised in the 'new ethnography' is that we straddle a line – an interesting one at that – between *humanities* and social *science*. But the underlying question remains regarding the 'cultural politics' around which the 'new' ethnography embellishes its theory. Is the deployment of 'cultural politics' meant to be anything beyond re-examining past forms of representation by substituting a (new and apparently purer) ambivalence toward theoretical claims, while it forwards ambiguity regarding the modalities of informants, anthropologists, and their occasionally joined activities?

6 This major anthropological theme is also acknowledged by Stewart (1996: 210), who cites Trinh (1991: 162).

7 Constructionists may or may not be interested in the explicit political implications of their retheorising of the institutionalisation of social structures, nor in its psychological aspects. They may also use different words from imagination and

the like to relate this work: the 'fluidity' of social institutions, for instance, seems to grant institutions more history and gravity in day to day life than does understanding them as 'ethereal' or 'imagined'. The point of analytic correspondence, however, is that in deploying the notion of 'construction' we are reminded of human volition in creating and *sustaining* all social institutions. Constructionism seeks to fundamentally question and undermine an understanding of social structures as predetermined in their presence and, thereby, solid, unchanging and, thus, 'by nature', conservative.

8 As applied by analysts of Japan, see Ivy (1995) and Allison (1994).

9 As the Chinese saying goes, 'May you live in interesting times'. This process, however, also tends to wax indulgent. For instance, while perhaps misunderstanding Fukuyama's (1992) reference to Hegelian historicism, since the Renaissance closed the door on the Crusades when else have political pundits engaged in discussion as to whether 'history had ended,' albeit in the US, the globe's only remaining hegemonic state and celebrating its own socio-political ideology? Hopeful discourses of this kind suggest we believe the probabilities of 'risk society' to be skewed in our favour, evidently to be solved by technology and science. The negative discourse on 'risk' is that we will be destroyed by that very same technology and science (cf. Wildavsky and Dake 1990; Beck 1992). In both cases science and technology appears as something separate from ourselves – evoking empiricism's positive display of 'nature', and negative representation of 'society' – a notion towards which I am strongly opposed.

10 This collage, or 'bricollage', of excesses is based on my reading of Jameson (1985, 1991) and Baudrillard (1988), which may be poignantly compared with Baumann (1993) and Thompson (1995).

11 Strathern notes that in spite of such theoretical tides, the use of the notions of 'race' and 'gender' (among those I would call quasi-radical, 'cosmopolitan' academics, especially in the US, such as, for instance, Bhabba (1990, 1994)) appear to have remained sacrosanct, or subject to different styles of reinterpretation than might potentially problematise them, also, as categories (Strathern 1988; 1996: 520). This points us toward a key problem of the explicit (self-) politicisation of academic discourse. If belief in certain concepts is dearer than exposing them to the same analytic procedures to which we address concepts towards which we are more willingly hostile (such as colonialism, racism and sexism), then any potential analytic advance is muted by our own 'dangerous' forms of (analytic) blinkers, blinders and prejudice. As such we might more realistically note that we share process, and thereby humanity, with our ideological 'enemies'. Rorty puts the point across nicely, 'We would rather die than be ethnocentric, but ethnocentrism is precisely the conviction that one would rather die than share certain beliefs' (1991: 203).

12 This becomes perhaps especially evident, it may be noted, as the persons with whom anthropologists have traditionally conducted fieldwork – while obviously subject, like us, to its global effects – often have little or no direct experience of high-technology communications.

13 'Anthropology at home' has of course always been done but, to my thinking, requires observational and analytic capacity of a far higher calibre than that which anthropologists, as people trained, and who have often lived, in unordinary ways, would seem to commonly deploy with considerable skill.

14 I fully acknowledge that the political economy of academia must not be left out of this picture. Lack of funding in anthropology increasingly, and unfortunately, limits training for and access to field sites further afield. In turn, research closer to home requires theoretical justification. Of course, the proper explanation is neither solely resources nor problems with theory or method, but their necessary co-production.

15 I am not suggesting that we should soon expect a series of articles on academic departments written by anthropologists, though there is no reason to think that anthropologists do not often, privately, scrutinise their workplaces with the same tools used at more orthodox sites. (Indeed, anthropologists have probably always done this form of unwritten analysis. As such it would occupy the same kind of intellectual space as the – formerly taboo – public recounting of private matters during fieldwork that have always been privately recounted as 'in-house' 'tales of the field' (Malinowski 1967)).

Rather, my concerns are both theoretical and practical. What happens to the parameters of presumed audience as the 'field' becomes more spatially intimate. For instance, the vernacular of Stewart's West Virginian Appalachian subjects is deployed in an italicised language that is itself only recognisable to persons with some familiarity with the American South (Stewart 1996). As a New Yorker with Texan kin, I find this language use meaningful and aesthetically warming. However, this aspect of her presentation would be as unrecognisable to a Glaswegian as Glaswegian written (or heard) in the vernacular is to me. I would suggest that in the effort to overcome the vicissitudes of 'translation', either literally or as a notion evoking anthropologists' various conversions of field experience, the boundaries within which analyses 'communicate' are being more closely drawn and, therefore, the audience welcomed, and heard, at the table of discussion more strictly limited.

Figures

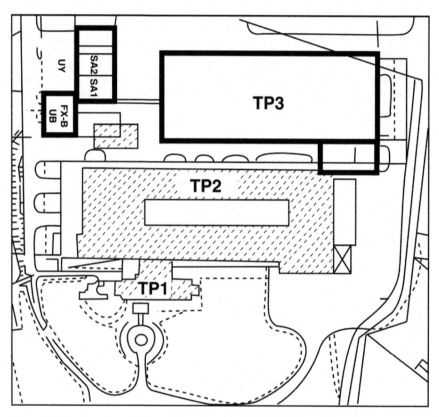

Figure 1 The footprint of YamaMax, showing buildings TP1, TP2 and TP3.

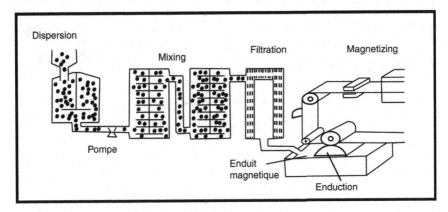

Figure 2 Videotape production process (I).

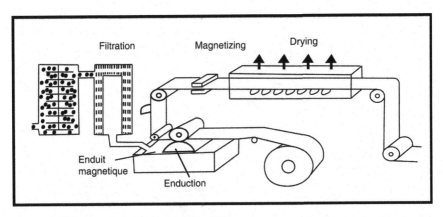

Figure 3 Videotape production process (II).

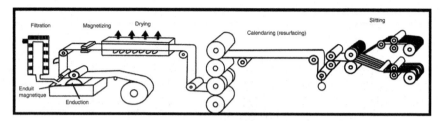

Figure 4 Videotape production process (III).

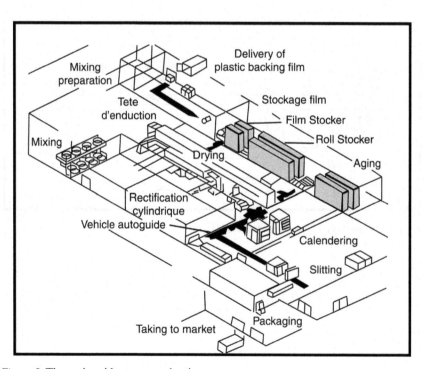

Figure 5 The entire videotape production process.

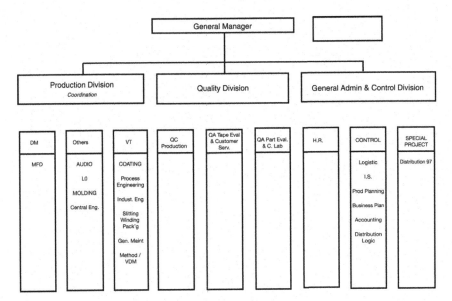

Figure 6 Organisational chart of YamaMax.

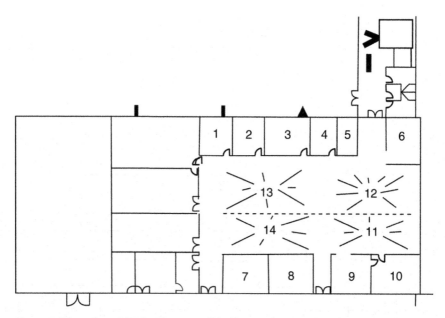

Figure 7 Floorplan of TP3 office space/'the time-and-motion tool box'.

	91		92		93		94		95		96		97	
init	xxxxx	xxxxx												
step2		xx	xxxxx											
step3				xxxxx	xxxxx									
step4					xx	xxxxx	xxxxx							
step5							x	xxxxx	xxx					
step6									xxxxx	xxxxx				
from then										xx	xxxxx	xxxxx	x	

Figure 8 Time chart/'the time-and-motion tool box'.

Bibliography

Abegglen, J. C. and Stalk, Jr., G. (1985) *Kaisha: The Japanese Corporation*, Tokyo: Charles E. Tuttle.

Allison, A. (1994) *Nightwork: Sexuality, Pleasure and Corporate Masculinity in a Tokyo Hostess Club*, Chicago: University of Chicago Press.

Anderson, B. (1983) *Imagined Communities: Reflections on the Origins and Spread of Nationalism*, London: Verso.

Aoki, M. (1988) *Information, Incentives, and Bargaining in the Japanese Economy*, New York: Cambridge University Press.

Appadurai, A. (1986) 'Theory in anthropology: center and periphery', *Comparative Studies in Society and History*, Vol. 28, 356–61.

——(1990) 'Disjuncture and difference in the global cultural economy', in *Global Culture: Nationalism, Globalization and Modernity*, (ed.) M. Featherstone *Theory, Culture, and Society*, Vol. 7, 295–310.

——(1996) *Modernity at Large: Cultural Dimensions of Globalization*, Minneapolis: University of Minnesota Press.

Ardener, E. (ed.) (1971) *Social Anthropology and Language*, London: Tavistock.

Asad, T. (ed.) (1973) *Anthropology and the Colonial Encounter*, Amherst, MA: Humanities Press.

Austin, J. L. (1962) *How to Do Things with Words*, Harvard University William James Lectures (1955), Oxford: Oxford University Press.

Bach, K. and Harnish, R. (1979) *Linguistic Communication and Speech Acts*, Cambridge, MA: MIT Press.

Bakhtin, M. (1981) *The Dialogic Imagination*, (trans.) C. Emerson and M. Hosquist, Austin: University of Texas Press.

—— (1984) *Rabelais and His World*, (trans.) H. Iswolsky, Bloomington: University of Indiana Press.

Bartlett, C. A. (1986) 'Building and managing the transnational: the new organizational challenge', in *Competition in Global Industries*, (ed.) M. E. Porter, Boston: Harvard Business School Press.

Bartlett, C.A. and Ghoshal, S. (1989) *Managing Across Borders: The Transnational Solution*, Boston: Harvard Business School Press.

Bartlett, C. A. and Yoshihara, H. (1988) 'New challenges for Japanese multinationals: is organization adaptation their Achilles heel?', *Human Resource Management*, Vol. 27, No. 1, 19–43.

Bateson, G. and Mead, M. (1942) *Balinese Character, A Photographic Analysis*, New York: New York Academy of Sciences.

Baudrillard, J. (1981) *For a Critique of the Political Economy of the Sign*, (trans.) C. Levin. St Louis: Telos Press.

—— (1988) *The Ecstacy of Communications* (ed.) S. Lotringer, (trans.) B. Schutz and C. Schutz, New York: Semiotext(e).

Bauman, Z. (1987) *Legislators and Interpreters: On Modernity, Postmodernity and Intellectuals*, Cambridge: Polity.

——(1993) *Postmodern Ethics*, Oxford and Cambridge, MA: Blackwell.

Beck, U. (1992) *Risk Society: Towards a New Modernity*, London: Sage.

Ben-Ari, E. (1997) *Japanese Childcare: An Interpretive Study of Culture and Organization*, London, New York: Kegan Paul International.

Bendix, R. (1977 [1960]) *Max Weber: An Intellectual Portrait*, Berkeley: University of California Press.

Benedict, R. (1946) *The Chrysanthemum and the Sword*, New York: Houghton Mifflin.

Berger, P.M. and Luckman, T. (1967) *The Social Construction of Reality*, Harmondsworth: Penguin Press.

Berglund, E. K. (1998) *Knowing Nature, Knowing Science: An Ethnography of Environmental Activism*, Cambridge: White Horse Press.

Bhabha, H.K. (1990) *Nation and Narration*, New York: Routledge.

——(1994) *The Location of Culture*, London: Routledge.

Blau, P.M. (1956) *Bureaucracy in Modern Society*, New York: Random House.

——(1959) 'Social integration, social rank, and processes of interaction', *Human Organization*, Vol. 18, No. 4.

——(1963) *The Dynamics of Bureaucracy*, revised edition. Chicago: University of Chicago Press.

Blau, P. M. and Scott, W. R. (1962) *Formal Organizations: A Comparative Approach*, San Francisco: Chandler Publishing.

Bloch, M.E.F. (1998) *How We Think They Think: Anthropological Approaches to Cognition, Memory and Literacy*, Boulder, CO: Westview Press.

Blom, J. P. and Gumperz, J. J. (1972) 'Social meaning in linguistic structures: codeswitching in Norway', in *Directions in Sociolinguistics*, (eds) J. J. Gumperz and D. Hymes, New York: Holt, Rinehart, and Winston.

Bourdieu P. (1977) *Outline of a Theory of Practice*, Cambridge: Cambridge University Press.

——(1984 [1979]) *Distinction: A Social Critique of the Judgement of Taste*, (trans.) R. Nice. London: Routledge & Kegan Paul.

Botti, H. F. (1995) 'Misunderstandings: a Japanese transplant in Italy strives for lean production', *Organization*, Vol. 2, No. 1, 55–87.

Brannen, M. Y. (1993) 'Your next boss is Japanese: negotiating cultural change at a Western Massachusetts paper plant', unpublished thesis, University of Massachusetts, Amherst.

Brown, R. H. (1989) *Social Science as Civic Discourse: Essays on the Invention, Legitimation and Uses of Social Theory*, Chicago: University of Chicago Press.

Callon, M. (1986) 'Some elements of a sociology of translation: domestication of the scallops and the fishermen of St. Brieuc Bay', in *Power, Action and Belief: A New Sociology of Knowledge?*, (ed.) J. Law, London, Boston and Henley: Routledge & Kegan Paul.

Callon, M. and Latour, B. (1981) 'Unscrewing the big Leviathan: how actors macrostructure reality and how sociologists help them to do so', in *Advances in Social*

Theory and Methodology: Toward an Integration of Micro- and Macro-Sociologies, (eds) K. Knorr-Cetina and A. V. Cicourel, Boston: Routledge & Kegan Paul.

Castells, M. (1996) *The Information Age, vol. I. The Rise of the Network Society*, Oxford: Blackwell.

——(1997) *The Information Age, vol. II. The Power of Identity*, Oxford: Blackwell.

——(1998) *The Information Age, vol. III. End of Millennium*, Oxford: Blackwell.

Chomsky, N. (1957) *Syntactic Structures*, The Hague: Mouton.

——(1964) *Aspects of the Theory of Syntax*, Cambridge, MA: MIT Press.

——(1975) *Logical Structure of Linguistic Theory*, Chicago: University of Chicago Press.

Clark, R. (1979) *The Japanese Company*, New Haven and London: Yale University Press.

Clemons, E. W. (1999) 'Transcending national identity: foreign employees and organizational management in corporate Japan', unpublished thesis, Columbia University.

Clifford, J. (1997) 'Diasporas', in *Routes: Travel and Translation in the Late Twentieth Century*, Cambridge, MA and London: Harvard University Press.

Clifford, J. and Marcus, G. E. (eds) (1986) *Writing Culture: The Poetics and Politics of Ethnography*, Berkeley and Los Angeles: University of California Press.

Cole, R.E. (1971) *Japanese Blue Collar*, Berkeley and Los Angeles: University of California Press.

——(1989) *Strategies for Learning*, Berkeley and Los Angeles: University of California Press.

Cooper, R. (1992) 'Formal organization as representation: remote control, displacement and abbreviation', in *Rethinking Organization: New Directions in Organization Theory and Analysis*, (eds) M. Reed and M. Hughes, London, Newbury Park, New Delhi: Sage Publications.

Condry, I. (2006) *Hip-Hop Japan: Rap and the Paths of Cultural Globalization*, Durham: Duke University Press.

Coulmas, F. (1992) *Language and Economy*, Oxford: Blackwell.

Crozier, M. (1964 [1963]) *The Bureaucratic Phenomenon*, London: Tavistock Publications.

Cullen, S. and Howe, L. (1991) 'People, cases, and stereotypes: a study of staff practice in a DSS benefit office', *Cambridge Anthropology*, Vol. 15, No. 1.

Culler, J. (1982) *On Deconstruction: Theory and Criticism after Structuralism*, Ithaca: Cornell University Press.

Czarniawska, B. (1997) *Narrating the Organization: Dramas of Institutional Identity*, Chicago: University of Chicago Press.

Czarniawska, B. and Hernes, T. (2005) 'Constructing macro actors according to ANT', in *Actor–Network Theory and Organizing*, (eds) B. Czarniawska and T. Hernes, Malmo, Sweden: Liber AB, and Copenhagen Business School Press.

Davidson, M. (1992) *The Consumerist Manifesto: Advertising in Postmodern Times*, London and New York: Routledge.

Deal, T. and Kennedy, A. (1988) *Corporate Cultures*, Harmondsworth: Penguin.

DeNero, H. (1990) 'Creating the "hyphenated" corporation', *McKinsey Quarterly*, Vol. 4, 153–73.

Derrida, J. (1967) *L'écriture et la différence*, Paris: Editions du Seuil.

——(1973 [1967]) 'Différance' in *Speech and Phenomena*, Chicago: Northwestern University Press.

——(1976) *Of Grammatology*, (trans.) G. C. Spivak, Baltimore: Johns Hopkins University Press.

——(1982) *Margins of Philosophy*, (trans.) A. Bass, Chicago: University of Chicago Press.

Diamond, J. (1998 [1997]) *Guns, Germs and Steel: A Short History of Everybody for the Last 13,000 Years*, London: Vintage.

Dore, R.P. (1973) *British Factory, Japanese Factory*, Los Angeles: University of California Press.

——(1987) *Taking Japan Seriously: A Confucian Perspective on Leading Economic Issues*, London: Athlone Press.

Douglas, M. and Isherwood, B. (1979) *The World of Goods: Towards an Anthropology of Consumption*, New York: Basic Books.

Duranti, A. and Goodwin, C. (eds) (1992) *Rethinking Context: Language as an Interactive Phenomenon*, Cambridge: Cambridge University Press.

Escobar, A. (1995) *Encountering Development: The Making and Unmaking of the Third World*, Princeton: Princeton University Press.

Fabian, J. (1983) *Time and the Other: How Anthropology Makes Its Object*, New York: Columbia University Press.

Ferguson, J. (1990) *The Anti-Politics Machine: 'Development', Depoliticization, and Bureaucratic Power in Lesotho*, Cambridge: Cambridge University Press.

Firth, J.R. (1956) 'Linguistic analysis and translation', in *For Roman Jakobson: Essays on the Occasion of His Sixtieth Birthday, 11 October (1956)*, (eds) M. Halle, H.G. Hunt, H. McLean and C.H. Schooneveld, The Hague: Mouton.

Fishman, J.A. (ed.) (1968) *Readings in the Sociology of Language*, The Hague: Mouton.

——(ed.) (1999) *Handbook of Language and Ethnic Identity*, New York, Oxford: Oxford University Press.

Foucault, M. (1975) *Surveiller et Punir: Naïssance de la Prison*, Paris: Gallimard.

——(1980) *Power/Knowledge: Selected Interviews and Other Writings by Michel Foucault, (1972–1977)*, (ed.) C. Gordon, New York: Pantheon.

Freud, S. (1955 [1927]). 'Fetishism', in *The Standard Edition of the Complete Psychological Works of Sigmund Freud*, (trans.) J. Strachey, with A. Freud, A. Strachey and A. Tyson, London: Hogarth Press.

Fruin, M. (1999) *Remade in America: Transplanting and Transforming Japanese Management Systems*, Oxford: Oxford University Press.

Fucini, J. and Fucini, S. (1990) *Working for the Japanese: Inside Mazda's American Auto Plant*, New York: Free Press.

Fukuyama, F. (1992) *The End of History and the Last Man*, London: Hamish Hamilton.

Gamble, C. (1993) *Timewalkers: The Prehistory of Global Colonization*, Phoenix Mill: Alan Sutton Publishing.

Gao, B. (1998) 'Efficiency, culture, and politics: the transformation of Japanese management', in *The Laws of the Markets*, (ed.) M. Callon, Oxford: Blackwell Publishing.

Garfinkel, H. (1967) *Studies in Ethnomethodology*, Englewood Cliffs, NJ: Prentice Hall.

Garrahan, P. and Stewart, P. (1992) *The Nissan Enigma: Flexibility at Work in a Local Economy*, London: Mansell.

Geertz, C. (1973) *The Interpretation of Cultures*, New York: Basic Books.

——(1988) *Works and Lives: The Anthropologist as Author*, Princeton: Princeton University Press.

Gellner, E. (1968) *Words and Things: A Critical Account of Linguistic Philosophy and a Study of Ideology*, Harmondsworth: Penguin.

Gergen, K.J. (1992) 'Organization theory in the postmodern era,' in *Rethinking Organization: New Directions in Organization Theory and Analysis*, (eds) M. Reed and M. Hughes, London, Newbury Park, New Delhi: Sage Publications.

Giddens, A. (1979) *Central Problems in Social theory: Action, Structure and Contradiction in Social Analysis*, London: Macmillan Press.

——(1984) *The Constitution of Society: Outline of the Theory of Structuration*, Cambridge: Polity Press.

Goffman, E. (1961) *Asylums: Essays on the Social Situation of Mental Patients and Other Inmates*, New York: Anchor Books.

Goody, E. (ed.) (1978) *Questions and Politeness: Strategies in Social Interaction*, Cambridge: Cambridge University Press.

Gordon, A. (ed.) (1993) *Postwar Japan as History*, Berkeley: University of California Press.

——(1988a) *The Wages of Affluence: Labor and Management in Postwar Japan*, Cambridge, MA: Harvard University Press.

——(1988b) 'The invention of Japanese–style management', in *Mirror of Modernity: Invented Traditions of Modern Japan*, (ed.) S. Vlastos, Berkeley: University of California Press.

Gramsci, A. (1971) 'Americanism and Fordism' in *Selections from the Prison Notebooks*, (eds and trans.) Q. Hoare and N. Smith, New York: International Publishers.

Granovetter, M. (1981) 'Economic action and social structure', *American Journal of Sociology*, Vol. 91, No. 3, 481–510.

Grice, H.P. (1975) 'Logic and conversation', in *Syntax and Semantics 3: Speech Acts*, (eds) P. Cole and J. Morgan, New York: Academic Press.

——(1978) 'Further notes on logic and conversation', in *Syntax and Semantics 9: Pragmatics*, (ed.) P. Cole. New York: Academic Press.

——(1981) 'Presupposition and conversational implicature', in *Radical Pragmatics*, (ed.) P. Cole, New York: Academic Press.

Grillo, R. (1989) 'Anthropology, language, politics', in *Social Anthropology and the Politics of Language*, (ed.) R. Grillo. London: Routledge.

Grimshaw, P. (1997) 'Outside-in: British people's perceptions of working in Japanese organisations', unpublished dissertation, Oxford Brookes University.

Grint, K. and Woolgar, S. (1997) *The Machine at Work: Technology, Work and Organization*, Cambridge: Polity.

Grosjean, F. (1982) *Life with Two Languages: An Introduction to Bilingualism*, Cambridge, MA: Harvard University Press.

Gumperz, J.J. (1968) 'Speech communities', in *International Encylopedia of Social Sciences*, London: Macmillan.

Gumperz, J.J. and Hymes, D. (eds) (1972) *Directions in Sociolinguistics: The Ethnography of Communication*, New York: Holt, Rinehart and Winston.

Habermas, J. (1971) *Toward a Rational Society*, Cambridge: Polity Press.

——(1985) *The Theory of Communicative Action*, New York: Beacon Press.

Halliday, M.A.K. (1985) *An Introduction to Functional Grammar*, Baltimore: University Park Press.

Hamada, T. (1991) *American Enterprise in Japan*, Albany: State University of New York Press.

—— (1992) 'Under the silk banner: the Japanese company and its overseas managers', in *Japanese Social Organization*, (ed.) T. S. Lebra, Honolulu: University of Hawaii Press.

Hannerz, U. (1969) *Soulside*, New York: Columbia University Press.

——(1979) 'Town and country in southern Zaria: a view from Kadanchan', in *Small Urban Centers in Rural Development in Africa*, (ed.) A. Southall, Madison: African Studies Program, University of Wisconsin.

——(1980) *Exploring the City*, New York: Columbia University Press.

——(1985) 'Structures for strangers: ethnicity and institutions in a colonial Nigerian town', in *City and Society*, (eds) A. Southall, P.J.M. Nas and G. Anari, Leiden: Institute of Cultural and Social Studies.

——(1986) 'Theory in anthropology: small is beautiful? The problem of complex cultures', *Comparative Studies in Society and History*, Vol. 28.

——(1989) 'Culture between center and periphery: toward a macroanthropology,' *Ethnos*, Vol. 54.

——(1996) *Transnational Connections*. London: Routledge.

Haraway, D. (1985) 'A manifesto for cyborgs: science, technology, and socialist feminism in the 1980s', *Socialist Review*, Vol. 80.

——(1989) *Primate Visions: Gender, Race, and Nature in the World of Modern Science*, New York: Routledge.

Hedlund, G. (1986) 'The hypermodern MNC: a heterarchy?,' *Human Resource Management*, Vol. 25, 9–35.

Hendry, J. and Watson, C.W. (eds) (2001) *An Anthropology of Indirect Communication*, London and New York: Routledge.

Hobsbaum, E. and Ranger, T. (eds) (1983) *The Invention of Tradition*, New York: Columbia University Press.

Howell, D.L. (1996) 'Ethnicity and culture in contemporary Japan,' *Journal of Contemporary History*, Vol. 31, No. 1.

Hymes, D. (ed.) (1964) *Language in Culture and Society: A Reader in Linguistics and Anthropology*, New York: Harper & Row.

——(1969) *Reinventing Anthropology*, New York: Random House.

——(ed.) (1971) *Pidginization and Creolization of Languages: Proceedings of a Conference Held at the University of the West Indies, Mona, Jamaica, April, (1968)*, Cambridge: Cambridge University Press.

——(1974) *Foundations in Sociolinguistics: An Ethnographic Approach*, Philadelphia: University of Pennsylvania Press.

Imai, K. (1992) 'Japan's corporate networks', in *The Political Economy of Japan, Volume 3: Cultural and Social Dynamics*, (eds) S. Kumon and H. Rosovsky, Stanford: Stanford University Press.

Inoguchi, T. and Okimoto, D.I. (eds) (1988) *The Political Economy of Japan, Volume 2: The Changing International Context*, Stanford: Stanford University Press.

Ivy, M. (1995) *Discourses of the Vanishing: Modernity, Phantasm, Japan*, Chicago: University of Chicago Press.

Iwabuchi, K. (2002) *Recentering Globalization: Popular Culture and Japanese Transnationalism*, Durham: Duke University Press.

Jameson, F. (1985) 'Postmodernism and consumer society', in *Postmodern Culture*, (ed.) H. Foster, London: Pluto Press.

——(1991) *Postmodernism, or the Cultural Logic of Late Capitalism*, London: Verso.

——(1998) 'Preface', in *The Cultures of Globalization*, (eds) F. Jameson and M. Miyoshi, Durham and London: Duke University Press.

Johnson, C. (1982) *MITI and the Japanese Miracle: The Growth of Industrial Policy, (1925–1975)*, Stanford: Stanford University Press.

Kamata, S. (1982) *Japan in the Passing Lane*, New York: Pantheon.

Katzenstein, P.J. and Shiraishi, T. (1997) *Network Power: Japan and Asia*, Ithaca: Cornell University Press.

Kenney, M. and Florida, R. (1993) *Beyond Mass Production: The Japanese System and Its Transfer to the U.S.*, New York and Oxford: Oxford University Press.

Kinsella, S. (2000) *Adult Manga: Culture and Power in Contemporary Japanese Society*, Richmond: Curzon.

Kleinberg, J. (1994) 'The 'crazy group': emergent culture in a Japanese-American binational work group,' *Research in International Business and International Relations*, Vol. 6, No. 4.

Knorr-Cetina, K. and Cicourel, A.V. (1981) *Advances in Social Theory and Methodology: Toward an Integration of Micro- and Macro-Sociologies*, Boston: Routledge and Kegan Paul.

Kondo, D. (1990) *Crafting Selves: Power, Gender, Discourses of Identity in a Japanese Workplace*, Chicago: University of Chicago Press.

Kuhn, T.S. (1970) *The Structure of Scientific Revolutions*, Chicago: University of Chicago Press.

Kumon, S. and Rosovsky, H. (eds) (1992) *The Political Economy of Japan, Volume 3: Cultural and Social Dynamics*, Stanford: Stanford University Press.

Labov, W. (1972) *Sociolinguistic Patterns*, Philadelphia: University of Pennsylvania Press.

Lasch, C. (1978) *The Culture of Narcissism: American Life in an Age of Diminishing Expectations*, New York: Norton.

Latour, B. (1986) 'The Powers of Association', in *Power, Action and Belief: A New Sociology of Knowledge?*, (ed.) J. Law, London, Boston and Henley: Routledge and Kegan Paul.

——(1987) *Science in Action*, Cambridge, MA: Harvard University Press.

——(1988) *The Pasteurization of France*, Cambridge, MA: Harvard University Press.

——(1991) *Nous n'avons jamais été modernes* [We Have Never Been Modern], Paris: Editions La Decouverte.

—— (1996) *Aramis, or the Love of Technology*, Cambridge, MA: Harvard University Press.

—— (1999) *Pandora's Hope: Essays on the Reality of Science Studies*, Cambridge, MA: Harvard University Press.

—— (1999) 'On recalling ANT', in *Actor Network Theory and After*, (eds) J. Law and J. Hassard, Oxford: Blackwell.

—— (2005) *Reassembling the Social: An Introduction to Actor-Network-Theory*, Oxford and New York: Oxford University Press.

Latour, B. and Woolgar, S. (1979) *Laboratory Life: The Social Construction of Scientific Facts*, Beverly Hills and London: Sage.

Law, J. (ed.) (1986) *Power, Action and Belief: A New Sociology of Knowledge?*, London, Boston and Henley: Routledge and Kegan Paul.

—— (1994) *Organizing Modernity*, Oxford and Cambridge, MA: Blackwell.

Leach, E.R. (1977 [1954]). *Political Systems of Highland Burma: A Study of Kachin Social Structure*, London and Atlantic Highlands, NJ: Athlone Press.

——(1984) 'Notes on the mythology of Cambridge anthropology,' *Cambridge Anthropology*, Vol. 9, No. 1.

Lee, N. and Hassard, J. (1999) 'Organization unbound: actor-network theory, research strategy and institutional flexibility,' *Organization* Vol. 4, No. 391–404.

Lefebvre, H. (1991 [1974]) *The Production of Space*, Oxford: Blackwell.

Lejeune, P. (1989) *On Autobiography*, Minneaopolis: University of Minnesota Press.

Lie, J. (2001) *Multiethnic Japan*, Cambridge: Harvard University Press.

Lifson, T.B. (1992) 'The managerial integration of Japanese business in America', in *The Political Economy of Japan, Volume 3: Cultural and Social Dynamics*, (eds) S. Kumon and H. Rosovsky, Stanford: Stanford University Press.

Malinowski, B. (1922) *Argonauts of the Western Pacific*, London: G. Routledge and Sons.

——(1935) *The Language of Magic and Gardening (Coral Gardens and their Magic), Volume 2*, London: Allen and Unwin.

——(1967) *A Diary in the Strict Sense of the Term*, New York: Harcourt, Brace and World

Marcus, G.E. (1986) 'Contemporary problems of ethnography in the modern world system', in *Writing Culture: The Poetics and Politics of Ethnography*, (eds) J. Clifford and G.E. Marcus, Berkeley, Los Angeles and London: University of California Press.

——(1995) 'Ethnography in/of the world system: the emergence of multi-sited ethnography', *Annual Review of Anthropology*, Vol. 24, 95–117.

Marcus, G.E. and. Fischer, M.M.J (eds) (1986) *Anthropology as Cultural Critique: An Experimental Moment in the Human Sciences*, Chicago: University of Chicago Press.

Matanle, P.C.D. (2003) *Japanese Capitalism and Modernity in a Global Era: Refabricating Lifetime Employment Relations*, London: RoutledgeCurzon.

Matsunaga, L. (2000) *The Changing Face of Japanese Retail: Working in a Chain Store*, London: Routledge.

Mayo, E. (1933) *The Human Problems of an Industrial Civilization*, New York: Macmillan.

——(1949) *The Social Problems of an Industrial Civilization*, London: Routledge and Kegan Paul.

McConnell, D.L. (2000) *Importing Diversity: Inside Japan's JET Program*, Berkeley: University of California Press.

McDonald, M. (1989) 'The exploitation of language mis-match: towards an ethnography of customs and manners', in *Social Anthropology and the Politics of Language*, (ed.) R. Grillo, London: Routledge.

Middleton, D. and Brown, S.D. (2005) 'Net-working on a neonatal intensive care unit: the baby as virtual object', in *Actor-Network Theory and Organizing*, (eds) B. Czarniawska and T. Hernes, Malmo, Sweden: Liber AB, and Copenhagen Business School Press.

Miller, D. (1987) *Material Culture and Mass Consumption*, Oxford and Cambridge, MA: Basil Blackwell.

Miller, L. (2006) *Beauty Up: Exploring Contemporary Japanese Body Aesthetics*, Berkeley: University of California Press.

Milroy, L. and Margrain, S. (1980) 'Vernacular language loyalty and social network,' *Language in Society*, Vol. 9, No. 1, 1–26.

Miyazaki, H. (In press) *Arbitraging Japan: The Economy of Hope in the Tokyo Financial Markets*, Berkeley: University of California Press.

Moeran, B. (1996) *A Japanese Advertising Agency: An Anthropology of Media and Markets*, Richmond: Curzon Press.

Moerman, M. (1988) *Talking Culture: Ethnography and Conversation Analysis*, Philadelphia: University of Pennsylvania Press.

Morgan, D.H.J. (1985) *The Family, Politics and Social Theory*, London: Routledge and Kegan Paul.

Morris-Suzuki, T. (1996) 'A descent into the past: the frontier in the construction of Japanese identity', in *Multicultural Japan: Palaeolithic to Postmodern*, (eds) D. Denoon, M. Hudson, G. McCormack and T. Morris-Suzuki, Cambridge: Cambridge University Press.

——(1998) 'Becoming Japanese: imperial expansion and identity crises in the early twentieth century', in *Japan's Competing Modernities: Issues in Culture and Democracy (1900–1930)*, (ed.) S. A. Minichiello, Honolulu: University of Hawai'i Press.

Morrow, P. and Hensel, C. (1992) 'Hidden dissension: minority-majority relationships and the use of contested terminology,' *Arctic Anthropology*, Vol. 29, No. 1, 38–53.

Mosse, D. (2005) *Cultivating development: an ethnography of aid policy and practice.* London: Pluto Press.

——(2006) 'Anti-social anthropology? objection, objectivity, and the ethnography of public policy and professional communities', *Journal of the Royal Anthropological Institute*, Vol. 12, 935–56.

Nader, L. (1974 [1969]) 'Up the anthropologist—perspectives gained from studying up', in *Reinventing Anthropology*, (ed.) D. Hymes, New York: Random House.

Narayan, K. (1993) 'How native is a 'native' anthropologist?', *American Anthropologist*, Vol. 95, 671–86.

Nonoka, I. (1988) 'Toward middle-up-down management: accelerating information creation,' *Sloan Management Review*, Vol. 29, No. 3, 9–18.

Okumura, A. (1989) 'Guro-barize-shon to nihonteki keiei no shinka' in *Guro-baru Kiko to Kaigai Shinshutsu Butai: Takokuseki Kigyo to Kodusai Soshiki*, (eds) A. Okumura and M. Kato, Tokyo: Tokyo Daiichi Hoki Shuppan KK.

Oliver, N. and Wilkinson, B. (1992) *The Japanization of British Industry*, Oxford: Blackwell.

Ong, A. (1987) *Spirits of Resistance and Capitalist Discipline: Factory Women in Malaysia*, Albany: State University of New York Press.

Orlikowski, W.J. (1992) 'The duality of technology: rethinking the concept of technology in organizations', *Organization Science*, Vol. 3, 398–426.

Ouchi, W.G. (1981) *Theory Z*, Reading, MA: Addison-Wesley.

Ouchi, W.G. and Wilkins, A.L. (1985) 'Organizational culture,' *Annual Review of Sociology*, Vol. 11, 457–83.

Papastergiadis, N. (1995) 'Restless hybrids', *Third Text*, Vol. 32, 9–18.

Pascale, R. and Athos, A. (1982) *The Art of Japanese Management*, Harmondsworth: Penguin.

Peters, T. and Waterman, R. (1982) *In Search of Excellence*, New York: Harper and Row.

Pettigrew, A. (1979) 'On studying organizational cultures', *Administrative Science Quarterly*, Vol. 24, 570–81.

Poggi, G. (1993) *Money and the Modern Mind: George Simmel's Philosophy of Money*, Berkeley: University of California Press.

Powell, W.W. and DiMaggio, P.J. (eds) (1991) *The New Institutionalism in Organizational Analysis*, Chicago: University of Chicago Press.

Prahalad, C.K. and Doz, Y. (1987) *The Multinational Mission: Balancing Local Demands and Global Vision*, New York: Free Press.

Prahalad. C.K. and Hamel, G. (1990) 'The core competence of the corporation,' *Harvard Business Review*, Vol. 68, No. 3, 79–91.

Pratt, M.L. (1986) 'Fieldwork in common places', in *Writing Culture: The Poetics and Politics of Ethnography*, (eds) J. Clifford and G.E. Marcus, Berkeley, Los Angeles, London: University of California Press.

Pride, J.B and Holmes, J. (eds) (1972) *Sociolinguistics: Selected Readings*, Harmondsworth: Penguin.

Rabinow, P. (1977) *Reflections on Fieldwork in Morocco*, Berkeley: University of California Press.

Rabinow, P. and Sullivan, W.M. (eds) (1987 [1979]). *Interpretive Social Science: A Second Look*, Berkeley: University of California Press.

Reed, J. (2005) 'Corporate colors, corporate cultures: narratives of selfhood and otherness among Japanese businesspeople and black professionals in Tokyo offices', unpublished thesis, University of Oregon.

Ricoeur, P. (1974) 'Structure, word, event', in *Conflict of Interpretations: Essays in Hermeneutics*, Evanston: Northwestern University Press.

Roberson, J.E. (1998) *Japanese Working Class Lives: An Ethnographic Study of Factory Workers*, London: Routledge.

Roberts, G.S. (1994) *Staying on the Line: Blue-collar Women in Contemporary Japan*, Honolulu: University of Hawaii Press.

Robertson, R. (1992) *Globalization: Social Theory and Global Culture*, London: Sage.

Rohlen, T.P. (1974) *For Harmony and Strength: Japanese White-Collar Organization in Anthropological Perspective*, Berkeley: University of California Press.

Rorty, R. (ed.) (1967) *The Linguistic Turn: Recent Essays in Philosophical Method*, Chicago: University of Chicago Press.

——(1979) *Philosophy and the Mirror of Nature*, Princeton: Princeton University Press.

——(1991) 'Inquiry as recontextualization: an anti-dualist account of interpretation', in *Objectivity, Relativism and Truth: Philosophical Papers, Volume 1*, Cambridge: Cambridge University Press.

Rosenberg, N. and Steinmueller, W.E. (1988) 'Why are Americans such poor imitators?' *American Economic Review*, Vol. 78, No. 2, 229–34.

Roy, D. F. (1952) 'Quota restrictions and goldbricking in a machine shop,' *American Journal of Sociology*, Vol. 57.

——(1954) 'Efficiency and the fix: informal intergroup relations in a piece-work machine shop,' *American Journal of Sociology*, Vol. 60.

——(1959) 'Banana time: job satisfaction and informal interaction,' *Human Organization*, Vol. 18, No. 4.

Sacks, H. (1992) *Lectures on Conversation*, (ed.) G. Jefferson. Oxford: Blackwell.

Sahlins, M. (1976) *Culture and Practical Reason*, Chicago: University of Chicago Press.

Said, E.W. (1978) *Orientalism*, London: Routledge and Kegan Paul.

Sakai, J. (2000) *Japanese Bankers in the City of London: Language, Culture and Identity in the Japanese Diaspora*, London: Routledge.

Sako, M. (1992) *Prices, Quality and Trust: Inter-firm Relations in Britain and Japan*, Cambridge: Cambridge University Press.

Schutz, A. (1965) *Phenomenology of the Social World*, Evanston: Northwestern University Press.

Scott, J.C. (1976) *The Moral Economy of the Peasant: Subsistence and Rebellion in Southeast Asia*, New Haven: Yale University Press.

——(1985) *Weapons of the Weak: Everyday Forms of Peasant Resistance*, New Haven: Yale University Press.

Searle, J. (1969) *Speech Acts: An Essay in the Philosophy of Language*, Cambridge: Cambridge University Press.

Sedgwick, M.W. (1985) 'Ethnocentrism in Japan: the dilemma of the Korean minority in the context of history, law, and social structure.' unpublished manuscript.

——(1996) 'Does Japanese management travel in Asia? Managerial technology transfer at Japanese multinationals in Thailand,' paper presented at the Conference on International Transfer of Management Technology, Asia Pacific Research Center, Stanford University.

——(1999) 'Do Japanese business practices travel well? Managerial technology transfer to Thailand', in *Japanese Multinationals in Asia: Regional Operations in Comparative Perspective*, (ed.) D.J. Encarnation, New York: Oxford University Press.

——(2000a) 'The globalizations of Japanese managers', in *Globalization and Social Change in Contemporary Japan*, (eds) H. Befu, J.S. Eades and T. Gill, Melbourne: TransPacific Press

——(2000b) 'Japanese manufacturing in Thailand: an anthropology in search of 'efficient, standardized production', in *Japanese Influences and Presences in Asia*, (eds) I. Reader and M. Soderberg, Richmond: Curzon.

—— (2001) 'Positioning 'globalization' at overseas subsidiaries of Japanese multinational corporations', in *Globalizing Japan: Ethnography of the Japanese Presence in Asia, Europe and America*, (eds) H. Befu and S. Guichard-Anguis, London: Routledge.

—— (2003) 'Nihon no fuomaru na soshiki ni akeru infuomaru katsudo, [Informal activities in (formal) Japanese organisations],' in *Nihon no soshiki: Syaen bunka to infuomaru katsudo (The Anthropology of Japanese Organisations) [Japanese organisations: Associational culture and informal activities]*, (eds) M. W. Sedgwick and H. Nakamaki, Tokyo: Toho Shupansha.

—— (2007) 'Anthropology of organisations: the thick and the thin,' unpublished manuscript.

Sennett, R. (1977) *The Fall of Public Man*, New York: Knopf.

——(1980) *Authority*, New York: Knopf.

——(1998) *The Corrosion of Character: The Personal Consequences of Work in the New Capitalism*, London: Norton.

Serres, M. (1982) *Hermes: Literature, Science, Philosophy,* Baltimore: Johns Hopkins University Press.

Shapin, S. and Schaffer, S. (1985) *Leviathan and the Air-Pump: Hobbes, Boyle and the Experimental Life*, Princeton: Princeton University Press.

Silverman, D. (1998) *Harvey Sacks: Social Science and Conversation Analysis*, Cambridge: Polity Press.

Simmel, G. (1978 [1907]) *The Philosophy of Money*, (trans.) T. Bottomore and D. Frisby, London: Routledge and Kegan Paul.

Simon, H. (1955) 'A behavioral model of rational choice,' *Quarterly Journal of Economics*, Vol. 69, 99–118.

Smircich, L. (1983a) 'Concepts of culture and organizational analysis', *Administrative Science Quarterly*, Vol. 28, 339–59.

—— (1983b) 'Studying organizations as cultures', in *Beyond Method*, (ed.) G. Morgan, Beverly Hills: Sage.

Sorokin, P. and Merton, R. (1937) 'Social-time: a methodological and functional analysis', *American Journal of Sociology*, Vol. 42, 615–29.

Sperber, D. and Wilson, D. (1986) *Relevance: Communication and Cognition*, Oxford: Basil Blackwell.

Stewart, K. (1996) *A Space on the Side of the Road: Cultural Poetics in an 'Other' America*, Princeton: Princeton University Press.

Stocking, G.W. (1987) *Victorian Anthropology*, New York: Free Press.

——(1992) *The Ethnographer's Magic and Other Essays in the History of Anthropology*, Madison: University of Wisconsin Press.

Strathern, M. (1988) *The Gender of the Gift*, Berkeley and Los Angeles: University of California Press.

——(1991) *Partial Connections*, Savage, MD: Rowman and Littlefield.

——(1992) *After Nature: English Kinship in the Late Twentieth Century*, Cambridge: Cambridge University Press.

——(1995) 'The nice thing about culture is that everyone has it', in *Shifting Contexts: Transformations in Anthropological Knowledge*, (ed.) M. Strathern, London and New York: Routledge.

——(1996) 'Cutting the network,' *Journal of the Royal Anthropological Institute*, Vol. 2, 517–35.

Sumihara, N. (1996) 'Negotiating a third culture: roles of knowledge and 'cross-knowledge': an example of performance appraisal in a Japanese corporation in New York', paper presented at the Conference on International Transfer of Management Technology, Asia Pacific Research Center, Stanford University.

Sykes, J.B. (ed.) (1982) *The Concise Oxford Dictionary*, Oxford: Clarendon Press.

Tachiki, D. (1999) 'The business strategies of Japanese production networks in Asia', in *Japanese Multinationals in Asia: Regional Operations in Comparative Perspective*, (ed.) D.J. Encarnation, Oxford: Oxford University Press.

Taussig, M. (1992) *The Nervous System*, New York: Routledge.

Taylor, C. (1987 [1979]) 'Interpretation and the sciences of man', in *Interpretive Social Science: A Second Look*, (eds) P. Rabinow and W.M. Sullivan, Berkeley: University of California Press.

Thompson, E.P. (1967) 'Time, work discipline, and industrial Capitalism', *Past and Present*, Vol. 38, 56–97.

Thompson, J.B. (1995) 'Self and experience in a mediated world', in *The Media and Modernity*, Cambridge: Polity Press.

Tollefson, J.W. (1993) 'Language policy and power: Yugoslavia, the Phillipines, and Southeast Asian refugees in the United States', *International Journal of the Sociology of Language*, Vol. 103, 73–95.

Trinh, M.T. (1991) *When the Moon Waxes Red: Representation, Gender, and Cultural Politics*, New York: Routledge.

Tsing, A. (1994) *In the Realm of the Diamond Queen*, Princeton: Princeton University Press.

—— (2000) 'The global situation,' *Cultural Anthropology*, Vol. 15, No. 3, 327–60.

Tsurumi, Y. (1968) 'Technology transfer and foreign trade: the case of Japan (1950–66), unpublished thesis, Harvard Business School.

——(1976) *The Japanese Are Coming: A Multinational Interaction of Firms and Politics*, Cambridge, MA: Ballinger Publishing Co.

Tsutsui, W. M. (1998) *Manufacturing Ideology: Scientific Management in Twentieth-Century Japan*, Princeton: Princeton University Press.

Turner, C. (1995) *Japanese Workers in Protest: An Ethnography of Consciousness and Experience*, Berkeley, Los Angeles, London: University of California Press.

Tyler, S. (1986) 'Post-modern ethnography: from document of the occult to occult document', in *Writing Culture: The Poetics and Politics of Ethnography*, (eds) J. Clifford and G.E. Marcus, Berkeley: University of California Press.

Vlastos, S. (ed.) (1998) *Mirror of modernity: invented traditions of modern Japan*, Berkeley: University of California Press.

Vogel, E. (1979) *Japan as Number One*, Cambridge, MA and London: Harvard University Press.

Wadel, C. (1979) 'The hidden work of everyday life', in *Social Anthropology of Work*, (ed.) S. Wallman, ASA Monograph 19, London: Academic Press.

Wagner, R. (1986) *Symbols that Stand for Themselves*, Chicago: University of Chicago Press.

Wallerstein, I. (1979) *The Capitalist World Economy*, Cambridge: Cambridge University Press.

Wardhaugh, R. (1983) *Language and Nationhood: The Canadian Experience*, Vancouver: New Star Books.

Wardle, H. (n.d.) 'Anthropologists and the Creole paradigm', unpublished manuscript.

Watson, T.J. (2000) 'Ethnographic fiction science: making sense of managerial work and organizational research processes with Caroline and Terry,' *Organization*, Vol. 7, No. 3, 489–510.

Weber, M. (1946) *From Max Weber: Essays in Sociology*, (trans.) H.H. Gerth and C. W. Mills, New York: Oxford University Press.

—— (1947) *The Theory of Social and Economic Organization*, (trans.) A.M. Henderson and T. Parsons, New York: Oxford University Press.

Weiner, M. (1997) 'The invention of identity: 'self' and 'other' in pre-war Japan', in *Japan's Minorities: The Illusion of Homogeneity*, (ed.) M. Weiner, London: Routledge.

Werbner, P. (1997) 'Introduction: the dialectics of cultural hybridity', in *Debating Cultural Hybridity: Multi-Cultural Identities and the Politics of Anti-Racism*, (eds) P. Werbner and T. Modood, London and New Jersey: Zed Books.

Werbner, P. and Modood, T. (eds) (1997) *Debating Cultural Hybridity: Multi-Cultural Identities and the Politics of Anti-Racism*, London and New Jersey: Zed Books.

Westney, D.E. (1987) *Imitation and Innovation: The Transfer of Western Organizational Patterns to Meiji Japan*, Cambridge, MA: Harvard University Press.

——(1999) 'Changing perspectives on the organization and management of Japanese multinational corporations', in *Japanese Multinationals Abroad: Individual and Organizational Learning*, (eds) S.L. Beechler and A. Bird, New York: Oxford University Press.

Wildavsky, A. and Dake, K. (1990) 'Theories of risk perception: who fears what and why?', *Daedalus*, Vol. 119, No. 4, 41–61.

Williams, K. (1994) *Cars: Analysis, History, Cases*, Providence: Berghan Books.

Womack, J., Jones, D. and Roos, D. (1990) *The Machine that Changed the World*, New York: Macmillan.

Wong, H.W. (1999) *Japanese Bosses, Chinese Workers: Power and Control in a Hong Kong Megastore*, Richmond: Curzon.

Wynne, B. (1996) 'May the sheep safely graze? a reflexive view on the expert/lay knowledge divide', in *Risk, Environment and Modernity: Towards a New Ecology*, (eds) S. Lash, B. Szerszynski and B. Wynne, London: Sage.

Yamamura, K. and Yasuba, Y. (eds) (1987) *The Political Economy of Japan, Volume 1: The Domestic Transformation*, Stanford: Stanford University Press.

Yeung, H.W. (1998) 'The social-spatial constitution of business organizations: a geographical perspective,' *Organization*, Vol. 5, No. 1, 101–28.

Yoshino. M.Y. (1968) *Japan's Managerial System: Tradition and Innovation*, Cambridge, MA: MIT Press.

——(1976) *Japan's Multinational Enterprises*, Cambridge, MA: Harvard University Press.

Zizek, S. (1991) *For They Know Not What They Do: Enjoyment as a Political Factor*, London: Verso.

Index

Printed in the United States
by Baker & Taylor Publisher Services